Sefer Hasidim
and the Ashkenazic Book
in Medieval Europe

JEWISH CULTURE AND CONTEXTS

Published in association with the
Herbert D. Katz Center for Advanced Judaic Studies
of the University of Pennsylvania

Steven Weitzman, Series Editor

A complete list of books in the series
is available from the publisher.

Sefer Hasidim and the Ashkenazic Book in Medieval Europe

Ivan G. Marcus

PENN

UNIVERSITY OF PENNSYLVANIA PRESS

PHILADELPHIA

Published by
University of Pennsylvania Press
Philadelphia, Pennsylvania 19104-4112
www.upenn.edu/pennpress

Printed in the United States of America on acid-free paper
1 3 5 7 9 10 8 6 4 2

Library of Congress Cataloging-in-Publication Data
Names: Marcus, Ivan G., author.
Title: Sefer hasidim and the Ashkenazic book in medieval Europe /
   Ivan G. Marcus.
Other titles: Jewish culture and contexts.
Description: 1st edition. | Philadelphia : University of Pennsylvania Press,
   [2018] | Series: Jewish culture and contexts | Includes bibliographical
   references and index.
Identifiers: LCCN 2017058051 | ISBN 9780812250091 (hardcover : alk. paper)
Subjects: LCSH: Judah ben Samuel, approximately 1150–1217. Sefer hasidim. |
   Jews—Europe—History—To 1500. | Jews—Europe—Intellectual life.
Classification: LCC BJ1287.J83 S438 2018 | DDC 296.3/6—dc23
LC record available at https://lccn.loc.gov/2017058051

In loving memory of our son,
Magen Dror Marcus, MD (1969–2010)

Ki laqah oto elohim (Gen. 5:24)

Contents

Abbreviations

Abbreviations of manuscript catalogs are found at the beginning of the catalog following Chapter 4. Abbreviations of *Sefer Hasidim* manuscripts follow the general abbreviations below.

b.	ben (son of)
B.	Babylonian Talmud
Bologna	*Sefer Hasidim*, first ed. Bologna, 1538=SHB
d.	date of death
F	microfilm
FJTSB45	former Jewish Theological Seminary Boesky 45
H or héb.	Hebrew
IMHM	Institute for Microfilmed Hebrew Manuscripts. National Library of Israel, Jerusalem
JQR	*Jewish Quarterly Review*
JTS	Jewish Theological Seminary of America, New York
Mich.	Michael MS in Oxford, Bodleian Library
MS(S)	manuscript(s)
Ninety-nine stories	Jerusalem, National Library of Israel Hebrew MS Oct. 3182, published by N. Brüll and by Eli Yassif, *Me'ah Sippurim Haser Ehad*.
NLI	National Library of Israel, Jerusalem
NP	No place of publication
Oct.	Octavo-size manuscript
Opp.	Oppenheim MS in Oxford, Bodleian Library

Or.	Oriental MS in Oxford, Bodleian Library
Parma	*Sefer Hasidim*, Parma, Biblioteca Palatina H 3280=SHP
PH	photograph
PUSHD	Princeton University *Sefer Hasidim* Database
r	recto, or the "a" side of a folio
R.	Rabbi
REJ	*Revue des études juives*
SH	*Sefer Hasidim*
SHB	*Sefer Hasidim*, Bologna, 1538 (not the same as SHM)
SHB I	SHB 153-440
SHB II	SHB 441-587
SHB III	SHB 588-1135
SHK	*Sefer Hasidim*, Krakow, 1581
SHM	*Sefer Hasidim*, ed. Reuven Margoliot (1924, 1956).
SHP	*Sefer Hasidim*, Parma ed. Wistinetzki 1891; Frankfurt am Main, 1924
SHP I	pars. 37-1426 of SHP following Samuel's *Sefer ha-Yir'ah* and some non-Ashkenazic authors like Saadia Gaon
SHP II	pars. 1427-1983 appendices on topics.
ShH	*Sefer ha-Hasidut*
Simon	Simon, Joseph. "Les manuscrits hébreux de la bibliotheque de la ville de Nîmes." REJ 3 (1881): 225–237.
v	verso, or the "b" side of a folio
z"l	*zikhrono li-verakhah* (may his memory be for good [lit., a blessing])
zz"l	*zekher zaddiq li-verakhah* (may the memory of the righteous be for good [lit., a blessing])

Abbreviations of *Sefer Hasidim* Manuscripts

The alphanumeric codes that appear in parentheses after each abbreviation refer to a section of the catalog that follows Chapter 4.

Cambridge Add. 379 (E 1)
Cambridge, Cambridge University Library, Add. 379, f. 1v–74r [IMHM F 16298]

Former JTS Boesky 45 (F 2)
former Jewish Theological Seminary Boesky 45 [IMHM F 75736]
Privately held manuscript formerly owned by Mrs. Seema Boesky on temporary loan to the JTS Library for several years until sold to another private collector, December 21, 2015

Frankfurt or Frankfurt Oct. 94 (A 4)
Frankfurt am Main, Goethe Universität, Universitätsbibliothek Johann Christian Senkenberg (formerly Stadt- und Universitätsbibliothek) Oct. 94, f. 270r–272r (formerly: Merzbacher 56) [IMHM F 25916]

Freiburg or Freiburg 483 (B 1)
Freiburg, Universitätsbibliothek, Heb. MS 483/29, f. 4r–5v [IMHM F 11392]

Hamburg 303 (G 1)
Hamburg Staats- und Universitätsbibliothek, Cod. Heb. 303, f. 24r–25v [IMHM F 26368; Fiche 221]

JTS 2499 (A 2)
New York, Jewish Theological Seminary Library, Microfilm 2499, f. 1r–29r
[IMHM F 28752]

Milan, Ambrosiana X.III sup. (C 2)
Milan, Biblioteca Ambrosiana, X.III sup., f. 166v–201v Cat. Bernheimer 119
[IMHM F 12336]

Moscow 103 (C 3)
Moscow, Russian State Library, Günzburg 103/4, f. 100r–124v [IMHM F
6783]

Nîmes 26 (D 1)
Nîmes, Bibliothèque municipale, 26, f. 154v–174r [IMHM F 4424]

Oxford, Mich. 155 (D 2)
Oxford, Bodleian Library, Mich. 155 Neubauer 1984k, f. 279r–283v [IMHM
F 19146]

Oxford Mich. 569 (B 3)
Oxford, Bodleian Library, Mich. 569, Neubauer 1098, f. 104v [IMHM F 17293]

Oxford, Opp. Add. Fol. 39 (A 8)
Oxford, Bodleian Library, Opp. Add. Fol. 39, Neubauer 865, f. 1r–3r, in margins. [IMHM F 21626]

Oxford, Opp. 614 (A 6)
Oxford, Bodleian Library, Opp. 614, Neubauer 2275/3 f. 30r–31va [IMHM F
20967]

Oxford, Or. 146 (A 7)
Oxford, Bodleian Library, Or. 146, Neubauer 782 f. 69av–70r [IMHM F
20319]

Oxford, Opp. 340 (C 1)
Oxford, Bodleian Library, Opp. 340, Neubauer 875, 3, f. 131r–151r [IMHM F 21834]

Oxford, Add. Fol. 34 (E 2)
Oxford, Bodleian Library, Opp. Add. Fol. 34, Neubauer 641, f. 43v–57r [IMHM F 20557]

Parma (F 1)
Parma, Biblioteca Palatina, H 3280, De Rossi 113 [IMHM F 13957]

Parma H 2486 (A 9)
Parma, Biblioteca Palatina, H 2486, De Rossi 1420/5, f. [45r] [F 13489]

Parma H 3266 (A 10)
Parma, Biblioteca Palatina, H 3266, De Rossi 1131, f. 52r [IMHM F 34168]

Vatican 285 (A 1)
Vatican, Vatican Library, ebr. 285/26, f. 108v–127v [IMHM F 8632] published by Moshe Hershler in *Genuzot* 1

Vatican 285A (A 3)
Vatican, Vatican Library, ebr. 285, f. 150r–152r [IMHM F 8632] [not in Hershler, *Genuzot* 1]

Zurich 51 (A 5)
Zurich, Zentralbibliothek, Heidenheim 51/4, f. 9r–10v (middle) [IMHM F 2613]

Zurich Fragment (B 2)
Zurich, Zentralbibliothek, no shelf number. [IMHM PH 5330] (bottom line/s not included in photograph)

Introduction

My purpose is always to write history.

—Erich Auerbach

For some time, scholars have been studying the history of the book as a way to understand a culture.[1] This book is a reassessment of the classical Hebrew text known since the thirteenth century as *Sefer Hasidim* (The Book of the Pietists), written anonymously but attributed to Rabbi Judah b. Samuel *he-hasid* (the pietist) of Regensburg (d. 1217).[2] It presents a case study of the history of the Ashkenazic Hebrew book that offers a new approach to the medieval Jewish subculture in Germany, northern France, and England, known as Ashkenaz.[3] In exploring *Sefer Hasidim*, unexpected areas of research have emerged about the library of Hebrew books Jews produced in medieval Christian Europe. In comparison with other post-classical Jewish books, the form of Hebrew books from medieval Ashkenaz demonstrates the limits of Jewish acculturation.

In some respects, *Sefer Hasidim* is unusual compared to other books Jews wrote in medieval Ashkenaz. This book has been called a "strange work"[4] and "a book that is different from any other in our literature."[5] It is "strange" but rather than being "different," *Sefer Hasidim* turns out to be similar to other Ashkenazic Hebrew books. In turn, many of the other Hebrew books written in Ashkenaz resemble *Sefer Hasidim* more than has been realized.

Although Moritz Güdemann remarked in 1880 that *Sefer Hasidim* is a book that was little studied, it was widely read.[6] Two dozen manuscripts contain versions of it, and almost sixty printed editions appeared, most of them in the nineteenth century in Eastern Europe.[7] After a long period of scholarly neglect, *Sefer Hasidim* has recently become an important subject of research. In the last thirty-five years alone a flurry of studies have made use of this strange Hebrew book from medieval Germany. In *Piety and Society* (1981), I included a bibliographical essay on works about *Sefer Hasidim* from the eighteenth century down to the late 1970s that discussed some thirty of almost sixty publications on this book listed in the bibliography, nearly all of them written in Hebrew. Since then, over a hundred and fifty more articles and a few books have been published, more than half of them written in languages other than Hebrew.[8]

Unlike most Jewish books written in northern France or Germany in the late twelfth and early thirteenth centuries, *Sefer Hasidim* is not a commentary on another book, nor is it primarily devoted to Jewish law or the liturgy. It contains thousands of interpretations of biblical verses, but it is not a new biblical commentary nor is it an anthology of earlier ones. A book of religious instruction, it contains hundreds of stories that mirror situations in everyday medieval social living unparalleled in Hebrew literature or in most contemporary Christian sources, but it is not an anthology of Hebrew stories.

Sefer Hasidim as an Inverted Pyramid

To date, scholars have addressed different religious and social questions and selectively quoted from *Sefer Hasidim* or anthologized it. They have written about its ascetic ideals and penitential practices; its egalitarian views about society; the production of the medieval codex as a physical object; women in business and family life; and Jewish-Christian relations, among many other topics. In each case, scholars selected passages from some versions of *Sefer Hasidim* for evidence about the subject that interested them as historians or folklorists or students of *halakhah* (Jewish law). The working assumption behind these studies is that *Sefer Hasidim* is an important source about the everyday life of the Jewish world of thirteenth-century Germany. And it is.

But it is not the contents alone that make *Sefer Hasidim* important. Although *Sefer Hasidim* and other medieval Hebrew books have long been studied critically over the last two centuries for their contents—the message—and in the last few decades for their properties as physical objects—the medium—only recently have they also been examined for their literary form—*the medium of the message*.[9] By this I refer not to the shapes of the letters (paleography) or to the properties of the material on which a text is written (codicology) or to the design of the page (*mise-en-page*), but to how units of text were composed and put together.[10]

Few studies have been devoted to the form of the text of *Sefer Hasidim* that survived in several manuscripts since the thirteenth century. Early on, scholars observed that *Sefer Hasidim* exists in two editions or versions. One was published in Bologna in 1538 (SHB), based on a manuscript that no longer exists. It consists of 1,176 paragraphs that are defectively numbered so that it concludes with paragraph 1,178 (see Catalog). A version of this text was reissued some sixty more times in the ensuing years, down to 1924 and 1957, when Reuven Margoliot published his two annotated editions, based on Bologna, still in print (SHM 1 and SHM 2).

A much longer version appeared in Berlin in 1891 based on an undated Ashkenazic Hebrew manuscript from around 1300, now located in the Biblioteca Palatina in Parma, Italy (SHP). It, too, is based on a manuscript that is now lost. It was annotated by Jehuda Wistinetzki and reissued with a new scholarly introduction by Jacob Freimann in 1924 in Frankfurt am Main. It consists of 1,999 paragraphs but because of errors in the numbering it ends with number 1,983.[11] These are sometimes referred to in the scholarly literature as Bologna or Parma, or as the short or the long text, since Parma is about twice as long as Bologna.

Charts of the paragraph numbers from the Parma manuscript to parallel passages in the familiar Bologna edition appeared in Wistinetzki's edition of Parma in 1891. Freimann produced a reverse table of paragraph numbers in his "mavo" (introduction) in 1924 so that readers of Bologna could find parallels, when they existed, in the longer new edition of MS Parma.[12] Scholars now could find parallel passages that existed in both directions.

But no one asked why *Sefer Hasidim* was written in such a way that tables of parallel passages were needed in the first place. They were needed because the parallel paragraphs are *not in the same sequence* in the two versions.[13]

Generally, we assume that an author composed a book and that it is preserved in one or more manuscripts. Scholars examine the manuscripts, divide them into families, based on copying errors, create a stemma or map of resemblances among them, and ultimately try to reconstruct an author's original version or lost urtext. This model of a book may be compared to a pyramid with the author's unique original version at the top and various manuscript witnesses of it at the broad base. This is true of most Western classical books, of the Latin and Arabic traditions in the Middle Ages, and of the Hebrew or Judeo-Arabic books Jews produced in the Muslim world.[14]

It is not true, however, of *Sefer Hasidim* or, it turns out, of many Hebrew books that Jews wrote in early Ashkenazic Europe. Authors there composed books in small-paragraph units and then combined them into different editions in the form of an *inverted pyramid*. At the broad top are the multiple acts of an author's composition preserved as single paragraphs that make up the particular work. The author (or sometimes a student or relative) combined these short units of text into different parallel editions of *Sefer Hasidim* and of some other Ashkenazic Hebrew books. We can think of these parallel editions as the narrower bottom of the inverted pyramid. *Sefer Hasidim* never was written as the author's single, original composed work that others copied.

A good way to think of *Sefer Hasidim* and many Hebrew books produced in medieval Ashkenaz is as an "open text" or "open book." Umberto Eco introduced the concept of "open text" in 1962 and meant by it the multiple readings that a reader brings to a work or the way some modern artists require the reader or performer to complete a work left semi-finished.[15] Israel Ta-Shma used the term "open book" in 1993, without reference to Eco, to mean an author like Maimonides who writes a version of his *Commentary on the Mishneh* and then revises it himself, as demonstrated by surviving drafts from the Cairo Geniza, for example.[16] Others did it as well, even in Ashkenaz.[17] Had the passages in both editions of *Sefer Hasidim* been arranged in the same sequence, even with additions or deletions, this might point to an original book that an author revised, the kind of composition that Israel Ta-Shma referred to as an "open book."

The meaning I am giving to "open book" in the case of *Sefer Hasidim* and of many other Ashkenaic books refers to an author:

- composing a work in short text units that he sometimes rewrites;
- combining them disjunctively (without linear coherence); and
- producing more than one *parallel* edition, as opposed to composing one edition that the author or someone else revises one or more times. The term "open book" here refers to writing parallel editions of a book so that there never was only one original edition from which the others are derived.[18]

A good example from classical literature of an open book created in parallel editions is discussed in David Konstan's study of the Latin *Romance of Alexander.* He refers to it as "a special kind of text, which I shall call an open text."[19] That term refers to "the way in which a certain kind of literary work is produced."[20] For example, the Greek *Life of Aesop* "is composed in segmented fashion" and "the textual history of the *Alexander Romance* confirms the impression that the text presents of its segmentary composition, which may accrue or lose elements without damage to its structure."[21]

The implications about this episodic form of composition and variability in the transmission of these texts means that there never was an urtext: "In the case of what I am calling open texts, such as the *Alexander Romance,* the *History of Apollonius King of Tyre,* or the *Life of Aesop,* however, the effort to retrieve an original form is not only futile but detrimental. For such a procedure would generate a text less authentic than any of the diverse recensions transmitted by the manuscript tradition—a work that in fact no one had ever read or written."[22] He concludes that "an editor's responsibility is to present one or more of the existing versions as independent texts. . . . The mistake, however, is to suppose that the various existing versions are false or inferior forms. . . . Open texts, then, are by nature multiple";[23] "they are authentic instantiations of a work that is not subject to limitation or closure by way of appeal to an original." The *Alexander Romance* "is an agglutinative work, remarkably susceptible to additions, subtractions, and transpositions of passages and episodes."[24] The same can be said about *Sefer Hasidim* and about many of the best-known Hebrew texts produced in medieval Germany and northern France in the twelfth through the fifteenth centuries.

The overwhelming evidence of the manuscripts of *Sefer Hasidim* and of many other Ashenazic books does not support the possibility that an author wrote a single composition once and revised it one or more times. Unlike the type of open book that Ta-Shma discusses, *Sefer Hasidim* is made up of small, independently written passages that the author arranged in different sequences in more than one parallel edition. These editions are *all* original versions of the same book and are "open" in the sense of being written in parallel editions. There was no single original book and so no single edition is the "real" *Sefer Hasidim*. All of them are.

Until now, scholars have analyzed *Sefer Hasidim* according to the standard model of a book by assuming that even though it was written anonymously, the manuscripts and printed versions of *Sefer Hasidim* were remnants of an author's single original version (urtext) that was now lost. But the form of the two printed editions of *Sefer Hasidim* points to it as an open book in the sense of being written in multiple parallel editions. And it turns out that many other Hebrew books that authors wrote in medieval northern France and Germany resemble the book form of *Sefer Hasidim* in several significant respects.

In Muslim lands, Jews wrote Hebrew or Judeo-Arabic books mainly in continuous, lengthy, multi-page passages divided into chapters or other relatively long parts. Sometimes they wrote one version of a book and revised it. In Ashkenaz, on the other hand, Jewish writers tended to compose Hebrew works as independent paragraph passages, assembled them disjunctively, often without literary continuity, and combined them into large units of text. Often they produced parallel editions of the same book.

In the former type of book, if a passage is omitted, a semantic gap is created that interrupts the flow of the composition, and one realizes that something is wrong. In the latter type, like *Sefer Hasidim*, and some other

Hebrew books produced in medieval Ashkenaz, it is often possible to remove a passage without the reader sensing that something is missing. The passages are disjunctive; they are independent text units, not parts of a continuing exposition.

One scholar recently compared the short, disjunctive style of such Hebrew book composition to Lego, the colored plastic bricks manufactured by the Danish toy company whose CEO recently said about his product that it "acts as if it was glued and yet you can easily take it apart."[25] That is an apt way of looking at the modular or disjunctively constructed Hebrew compositions many medieval Ashkenazic authors produced.

Authorial composition of texts in short, disjunctive paragraphs should also be distinguished from the contribution of activist scribes. Although scribes contributed to the appearance on the page of these disjunctive texts, they did not create them. True, in the transmission of ancient rabbinic texts or of the early mystical *heikhalot* (Palace) manuscripts, for example, learned scribes in Ashkenaz, unlike rote copyists, did not hesitate to modify or even add their own comments into the text they were copying. This scribal activism implies a collective or collaborative view of authorship.[26]

Nor are we dealing with editors compiling anthologies or miscellanies by cutting and pasting works that already existed but of a form of authorial *composition* in discrete, relatively short textual units.[27] The authors themselves produced the types of books that *Sefer Hasidim* resembles and they did so in segmented paragraphs that they combined into parallel editions.

Selective Inward Acculturation and Persistence

Why were these compositions written in Lego-like segments, more open-ended and fluid compared to the familiar single-authored "book" that we find more in Jewish Muslim culture than in Ashkenaz? Jewish culture in medieval Ashkenaz was an extension and development of ancient rabbinic culture that itself had resisted allowing the influence of Greco-Roman civilization to reshape it into the latter's literary forms and genres. *Sefer Hasidim* and many other Ashkenazic Hebrew books are not written in the same form as was ancient rabbinic culture, but they are one of its extensions and developments. Like ancient rabbinic culture, the form of Ashkenazic Hebrew books exhibits *selective inward acculturation*. Rabbinic authors in Roman Palestine knew Greek in many cases but selectively appropriated only the Greco-Roman lexicon, not the literature, in their cultural world. They also did not write some books in the widespread classical Greco-Roman form of a single-authored work.

Even the ancient rabbis' introduction of thousands of Greek words and terms into the works they wrote in Hebrew or Aramaic was done selectively: when it came to writing liturgy, they insisted on using a pure Hebrew vocabulary, despite all the Greek they were comfortable using in their studies of Scripture or in legal compilations.[28] However, in inscriptions such as those on surviving tombstones, Greek and Latin with a minimal use of Hebrew was common in late antiquity and in early medieval Italy and northern France.

But from the eighth century, things changed, and European Jewish funerary inscriptions were written only in Hebrew.[29] The rabbis in northern Europe refused to read, let alone write, Roman letters and instead developed their indigenous traditions in Hebrew, even when they were open to adapting and internalizing Christian cultural forms and themes.[30]

The Ashkenazic Hebrew book is also part of Jewish cultural persistence and self-definition in medieval Christian Europe, an aspect of Jewish self-fashioning that has not been studied as a defining feature of medieval Jewish culture. It is not enough to note that some aspects of Christian culture were adapted in Jewish circles.[31] We also need to ask why others were not. Had Jews been willing to read Christian authors in Latin, we would know it. They would have cited Latin authors or at least alluded to them. And unlike the ancient rabbis, but like their Christian contemporaries, medieval Ashkenazic rabbis would have written Hebrew books that look like Latin books. They did not.

The *form* of many Ashkenazic books, then, is an important part of the new Jewish cultural studies that emphasize the openness of Jewish writers to their Christian surroundings and their appropriation or adaptation into Jewish culture. In the case of text composition, as opposed to physical book production, Jews developed a world of their own, resisting how Latin or vernacular books were composed, even when they shared codicological features and even paleographical pen strokes in Hebrew influenced by Gothic verticality typical of contemporary Latin book hands. The medium was shared but the "medium of the message," the way the text itself was *composed*, remained Jewish.[32]

It is beyond the scope of this study to explore when Ashkenazic Jews began to write books in the Geonic-Sephardic style of a work divided into chapters that progress from start to finish. Is this change linked to the well-known influence in Central or Eastern European Jewish circles of the Sephardic Hebrew book or of the book written in Latin or vernacular Western languages that Jews now began to read? If so, we need to ask when northern European Jews began to read Roman letters and add works written in those languages to the exclusive Hebrew library and language that had been their reading and writing medium for hundreds of years—but this needs to be worked out.[33]

For now, there is no comprehensive study of the form of Ashkenazic book composition. By raising these questions in the process of studying *Sefer Hasidim* in depth, I hope that others will research this important topic and also explore further the cultural filter through which medieval Jews took over some features of Christian Europe or just experienced them in common, whereas they ignored others. These issues suggest how the study of the forms in which Hebrew books were composed can shed light on comparative cultural issues in European Jewish history.

The Ashkenazic Book in Medieval Europe

What, then, is an Ashkenazic "book" in medieval Europe? The present study sets out to raise this question for future research by focusing on the case study of *Sefer Hasidim*, one of the most enigmatically written exemplars of segmented book writing in medieval German lands and northern France. The chapters that follow present new conclusions about *Sefer Hasidim* that have implications for understanding some of the other segmented Hebrew books Jews wrote in medieval Europe.

Chapter 1 discusses *Sefer Hasidim* as an "open text" in the specific sense of *a work written in small, disjunctive units, arranged differently in several parallel editions that cannot be reduced to an author's single original composition*. *Sefer Hasidim* is preserved in over twenty manuscripts. The fourteen manuscript and early print editions of *Sefer Hasidim* (see Chapter 1) are each made up of unique sequences of short text passages that need to be studied together as *Sefer Hasidim*. There is no evidence that *Sefer Hasidim* can be described as a single original authored text, with a defined structure, that the author or others revised one or more times, as Ta-Shma argued about Maimonides' and a few other Jewish authors' works and that Yisrael Peles refers to as a work of "multiple editions" (*merubeh 'arikhot*), which the author himself composed and reedited more than once.[34]

Chapter 2 looks at different aspects of rewriting in German Pietist (*hasidei ashkenaz*) culture in the circle of the principal pietist authors. The composition of *Sefer Hasidim* traditions is placed in the broader context of the other works that R. Judah b. Samuel *he-hasid* (d. 1217) and his student R. Eleazar b. Judah of Worms (d. ca. 1230) wrote as overlapping or fluid compositions. Their works are a series of rewritings of short paragraph-length texts. A different kind of rewriting resulted in the so-called "French *Sefer Hasidim*," the first 152 paragraphs of the first edition, Bologna, 1538. Despite its unique features, that text is but one of several rewritings of *Sefer Hasidim* traditions.

Biographical and hagiographical sources about the traditional author of *Sefer Hasidim*, R. Judah *he-hasid*, are discussed with a close look at genre and historical methodology in Chapter 3. From comments his students and his son, R. Moses Zaltman, made about him and from local Hebrew and Yiddish story cycles, including sources that resemble some of the traditions in *Sefer Hasidim* that are mainly about anonymous pietists, we can try to sketch out what we know about R. Judah *he-hasid* and other pietist Jews who formed around him a small circle of students and family members, not a movement.

Moreover, these pietists lived in one or more of four German towns in the twelfth and thirteenth centuries: Speyer, Regensburg, Worms, and Mainz. This chapter looks into this "tale of four cities" in an attempt to illuminate better the traditions preserved about one or more of the pietist authors: Judah's father R. Samuel ben Qalonimos the Elder of Speyer; Judah himself, who grew up in Speyer but spent the last two decades of his life in the medieval boom town of Regensburg on the Danube, today in the German State of Bavaria; Judah's cousin, R. Eleazar of Worms, who studied with his father in Mainz, and with others including R. Judah *he-hasid* in Speyer and Regensburg, and then moved on to be a leading rabbinical figure in Worms.

In some ways, Speyer displaced Mainz, the earliest of the Rhineland towns, weakened by anti-Jewish riots there in 1096. The pietists flourished first in Speyer, most of whose Jews survived 1096, but it was to Regensburg, another town of Jewish survivors, that Judah emigrated. Worms, like Mainz, also suffered in 1096, but it remained a center of Jewish legal scholarship where Eleazar combined German pietism with Jewish law, as Judah did to some extent in Regensburg.[35] An examination of how the Rhineland towns of Mainz, Worms, and especially Speyer are related to Regensburg, the West to the East, offers a way to map changes in the cultural geography of this group of Jewish thinkers.

Chapter 4 places the peculiar form of Ashkenazic Hebrew book writing into another historical context by briefly comparing it to earlier Jewish book production as well as to classical Greco-Roman, medieval Muslim and Christian book writing. In surveying the structures of several major Hebrew works written in medieval Ashkenaz it becomes clear that many of them are similar in their segmented paragraph text units and multiple parallel editions to the way *Sefer Hasidim* was written. A few are examples of Ta-Shma's "open book" composition of an early edition that the author himself revised into a later edition of the same book.

The book concludes with two new research tools. The first is an annotated catalog of the manuscripts and printed editions of *Sefer Hasidim*. From the printing history of *Sefer Hasidim*, it is clear that it was popular especially where East European Hasidism expanded during the nineteenth century. In contrast to the many editions of *Sefer Hasidim* that appeared in areas of Hasidic populations, only one modern edition was published in Lithuania (Vilna, 1819, in Yiddish), the base of anti-Hasidic activity. The twenty manuscripts and sixty editions of *Sefer Hasidim* suggest that the book had a significant impact on Jewish cultural history. The abundant passages from the book found in early modern Hebrew books and the relationship of the stories in *Sefer Hasidim* to modern Hebrew literature, for example, have barely been explored.[36]

The multi-tiered Select Bibliography is divided into several sections of primary sources, followed by secondary sources on *Sefer Hasidim* and German pietism. It is clear that over the last thirty-five years, the study of *Sefer Hasidim* has become a central subject of scholarly research. It is my hope that this book will offer a new comprehensive treatment from which to move forward.

Chapter 1

Sefer Hasidim as an Open Book

Undistinguished and even awkward in style, often
resembling a mass of casual jottings rather than a coherent
literary composition, it is yet undoubtedly one of the most
important and remarkable products of Jewish literature.
                                            —Gershom Scholem

When Gershom Scholem described *Sefer Hasidim* as "often resembling a mass
of casual jottings rather than a coherent literary composition," he was onto
something.[1] Not finding in the book a coherently written argument about a
single subject divided into chapters, Scholem saw the segmented way the
book is compiled as a defect. But there is another way of reading *Sefer Hasidim* and many other books written in medieval Ashkenaz, and that is to
see them as embodying a unique approach to book composition. Scholars
who work on individual rabbinic authors and their texts usually focus on
the contents of the work, not on the way the text is structured.

The present chapter discusses *Sefer Hasidim* as a case study about ideas
of composition and authorship also found in several other Hebrew texts from
medieval Ashkenazic culture briefly surveyed in Chapter 4. These books are
"open" in the sense that they were composed in small text units that the
authors themselves sometimes combined into *more than one parallel edition*.
The result is that there never was one original author's composition (urtext)

for many of these books. The surviving manuscripts consist of combinations of parallel and unique short passages that are often arranged in different sequences. *Sefer Hasidim* is an unusually well documented case of this kind of Hebrew open book written in early Ashkenaz.

Sefer Hasidim as Many Parallel Editions

Sefer Hasidim manuscripts consist of a series of short passages, defined by indentation, and sometimes numbered in some of the longer combinations. Very few of the many manuscripts of *Sefer Hasidim* have original paragraph numbers. The two longest manuscripts, Parma and former JTS Boesky 45 (see below), as well as most of the others, do not.[2] Only a small number of late, short manuscripts refer to individual passages by indicating their paragraph number.[3] Although printing in some sense created a book called *Sefer Hasidim*, as it created a book called the *Zohar*,[4] new manuscripts continued to be written based on earlier ones, and some scribes copied down new selections of short passages from *Sefer Hasidim* traditions.

Although Leopold Zunz already knew in 1845 about SHP as well as SHB, and Moritz Güdemann took both editions into account in his discussion of *Sefer Hasidim* in 1880, rabbis and scholars took a while to compare the differently numbered parallel paragraphs found in the two published editions.[5] For most of the twentieth century, scholars assumed that the manuscripts other than SHP must be short sections of it or of SHB and therefore of little interest.

A potential departure from this binary way of looking at *Sefer Hasidim* as SHB and SHP came from an awareness that there was a rewriting of *Sefer Hasidim* that Zunz already recognized from a manuscript, dated 1299, owned by David Oppenheim, now in Oxford, Bodleian Library Opp. 340 (Neubauer 875), where the text is called "Sefer ha-Hasidut." This text became the first 152 paragraphs of SHB (see Chapter 2).[6]

Despite its existence, the binary model of *Sefer Hasidim* as SHB and SHP has prevailed since the late nineteenth century. The dominant assumption has been that these two versions somehow represent different configurations of a lost original single composition that the author composed (urtext).

Nevertheless, a model that assumes that one original composition of *Sefer Hasidim* ever existed is untenable. This is not only because the sequence of the paragraphs in the two printed editions is so completely different but also because most of the twenty or so other manuscripts of different sizes of *Sefer Hasidim* are not textual witnesses to or fragments of either *Sefer Hasidim* Bologna or Parma, as we would expect if there had been an original single edition.[7]

This could have become clearer in 1985, when Rabbi Moshe Hershler published one of the other manuscripts: Vatican 285. Actually, he published the longer of two separate collections of *Sefer Hasidim* passages in that manuscript. Hershler's annotations showed that the part of the Vatican manuscript that he published consisted of single paragraphs that he numbered, some topically unrelated to each other and without parallels in either SHB or SHP. Vatican 285 is not closely related to either SHB or SHP but is a separate edition.

The appearance in the 1980s of former JTS Boesky 45, still in private hands, did not lead to new textual studies, since this manuscript resembled the sequence of SHP and reinforced it as *Sefer Hasidim*. Then in 2006, three other short manuscripts of *Sefer Hasidim* were published and two others mentioned but not transcribed. The editor numbered in brackets the unnumbered paragraphs of each text. The three short manuscripts were different in many respects from the two printed editions, and this demonstrated that *Sefer ha-Hasidut* and Hershler's Vatican 285 text were not the only manuscripts of *Sefer Hasidim* traditions that were different in form, as well as substance, from both SHB and SHP.[8]

The existence of such manuscripts, and several more not yet discussed in the scholarly literature, proves that *Sefer Hasidim* began not as a single original composition, but as many single paragraphs that the author and others combined differently into several editions of varying lengths. SHB and SHP were but two published versions of several different editions. It was an accident that they and not the others were published first. The more *Sefer Hasidim* manuscripts were published, the more obvious it became that neither SHB nor SHP could be the "real" *Sefer Hasidim* in any objective sense because they were outnumbered by several other editions from some twenty manuscripts (see Catalog and below).

The most ambitious set of publications of *Sefer Hasidim* traditions appeared online in 2007 as the Princeton University *Sefer Hasidim* Database (PUSHD), an invaluable research tool. For the first time, scholars could digitally search and compare sixteen versions of *Sefer Hasidim*. In 2015 the editor added three more: Moscow 103, Frankfurt am Main 94, and the Zurich Fragment. A few others remain to be added.[9] These manuscripts confirmed further that *Sefer Hasidim* traditions were preserved in many short and some long editions made up of parallel and unique short passages arranged in different sequences and not as a single original composition that corresponded to either SHB or SHP, for example, or to some lost manuscript that the others resembled in structure.

But PUSHD also inadvertently reinforced the binary Bologna-versus-Parma character of *Sefer Hasidim* traditions in the editor's analysis of the manuscripts, "The Recensions of *Sefer Hasidim*." Despite wanting to transcribe all the manuscripts as equal, parallel editions of *Sefer Hasidim*, PUSHD divided the manuscripts into two groups. It then classified and described all of the manuscripts as they were supposedly related to either or both of the two printed editions (SHB or SHP). The editors of PUSHD apparently did this because most of the manuscripts have at least some parallel passages that are shared with the familiar Bologna edition or Parma manuscript or with both of them. The editorial decision to input SHB and SHP first because of their size or familiarity was one thing. To compare all the other manuscripts to one or both of them *separately* results in privileging those two editions as somehow being more *Sefer Hasidim* than all the other manuscripts, including former JTS Boesky 45, for example. This was an unintended but unfortunate consequence of how the database was structured. In the description section, the editors also refer to SHP and SHB as the "principal" versions of *Sefer Hasidim*, a misleading claim if truly parallel editions were intended.

Size alone does not make Bologna and Parma the "principal" manuscripts of *Sefer Hasidim* any more than a specific content justifies referring to SHP as "the comprehensive statement of German Pietism recorded in the Parma manuscript."[10] That formulation would exclude from German Hasidism not only the majority of *Sefer Hasidim* manuscripts but also the other pietistic works of R. Samuel *he-hasid*, of R. Judah *he-hasid*, and those of R. Eleazar of Worms as well.

Most of the *Sefer Hasidim* manuscripts contain some paragraph passages that are not found in either SHB or SHP, and each edition or small set of editions is independent of SHB and SHP even when one or more blocks of passages appear in more than one of them. The editions differ with respect to the order of the paragraphs as well as the contents. Since neither SHB nor SHP was the author's original composition or derived from a lost original composition, all of the manuscripts need to be treated independently. *This also means that each paragraph of any manuscript needs to be compared to all of its parallels.*

With the exception of the Parma manuscript that was published in facsimile, we do not have much-needed published facsimiles of the other manuscripts.[11] Without them, scholars must rely on transcriptions that are of varying degrees of accuracy. PUSHD notes that it does not correct letters it transcribes even when it is obvious that they are scribal errors; the other short published texts have several errors of transcription.

Single Paragraphs as the Initial Unit of Composition

A clue to *Sefer Hasidim*'s origins in short paragraph units is suggested by the fifteenth-century moralistic work from medieval Germany called either *Sefer Hasidim Qatan* or *Sefer ha-Maskil* by R. Moses b. Eleazar ha-Kohen. The author admonishes his reader not to use a codex as a place to store "scraps of your written ideas" (*pitqei ketavekha ve-'inyanekha*).[12] That may be a good way of thinking about the beginnings of *Sefer Hasidim* and other Ashkenazic Hebrew books. Authors wrote down short paragraphs on scraps of parchment and then copied the paragraph units on pages or gatherings of parchment pages.

The process of rabbinic authors and students keeping notebooks (*yalqutim*) of passages that they wanted to recall or recopy, commonplace books, suggests how Judah might have composed, rather than collected, short passages of *Sefer Hasidim*, and how students wrote down what they heard from him directly, as we learn from his student, R. Isaac b. Moses of Vienna, and from Judah's son, R. Moses Zaltman, or from what they read. The fact that most of the short manuscripts or parts of longer ones are referred to as *liqqutim* or *yalqutim* may but need not mean "miscellany" in the sense of an anthology taken from one or more authors' writings. It may also refer to scholars and students writing down passages or notes for future reference, regardless of their source.[13] Many of the short manuscripts are introduced by the title "liqqutim."[14] The so-called *liqqutim* of *Sefer Hasidim* are not taken from the longer manuscripts of *Sefer Hasidim* but are independent gatherings taken from many hundreds of single paragraphs, some of which also appear, with variants, as parallels in other editions. Any paragraph may contain a better reading than its parallels in other editions, regardless of the date of the manuscript in which it is preserved.

Another sign that editions of *Sefer Hasidim* were composed in small units of text is found in a report by Judah *he-hasid*'s son, R. Moses Zaltman, who preserved his father's comments on the Humash (Pentateuch) that they studied together. In one passage, R. Moses Zaltman reports that just before his father died in 1217 he "wrote two pages of *Sefer Hasidim*" (*katav bet dappim mi-sefer hasidim*).[15] Groupings of up to a dozen paragraphs, enough text to occupy two pages, are common in parallels between SHP and former JTS Boesky 45; Cambridge Add. 379 and Oxford Add. Fol. 34 (Neubauer 641); and SHB, the editions with the most topically arranged passages.

For the idea of a bi-folio as the meaning of "bet dappim," compare in *Sefer Hasidim*: "If a person comes across a bi-folio (*shenei dappim*), on one page of which there is writing and one that is blank, and he needs the blank page, he should not cut it off."[16]

The process of how some of the longer editions of *Sefer Hasidim* were written from small text units is suggested in a passage in *Sefer Hasidim* that describes how the Talmud was put together:

> If a man has to sell books, he should sell books of Oral Torah
> rather than books of Written Torah. For books of Oral Torah are

like wool and flax that people work and weave. That is why
(a tractate of Talmud) is called a *masekhta*, a term taken from
weaving, as in "into the web" (*'im ha-masekhet*) (Judges 16:13–14),
as is written about Samson. Laws (*halakhot*) (are combined) into
chapters (*li-feraqim*), and one gathers together everything pertain-
ing to a subject and that is called a tractate (*masekhta*).[17]

This passage appears only in SHP 667 and SHB 932 but not in former
JTS Boesky 45, 290, even though parallels to SHP 666 and to SHP 668, the
passages immediately before and after SHP 667, are found in it. This pattern is another sign that individual paragraphs migrated from one edition to
another. The passage refers to the building up of the Talmud text from
smaller to larger units. By analogy, *Sefer Hasidim* is made up of the author's
single paragraphs or groupings of them, many of which he then further combined into topical booklets (*mahbarot*). This is the case in Parma and former
JTS Boesky 45; Cambridge Add. 379 and Oxford Add. Fol. 34 (Neubauer 641);
and eventually in SHB.

Paragraphs are indicated by indentations, sometimes with an enlarged
initial word or letter, and at times also numbered. In the longer manuscripts
we see the product of different combinations of topical booklets. These topical editions, such as the first part of Parma (SHP I) and the first edition in
ed. Bologna (SHB I=par. 153 ff.), both of which consist of fourteen topical
blocks, are arranged in the same topical order, but the individual parallel
paragraphs contained in notebooks on the same topic are arranged in *different* sequences. Editions of *Sefer Hasidim* made up of topical notebooks may
each be each thought of as a book (*sefer*) (see below).[18]

At the beginning of ed. Bologna there is a reference to a book made up of
different topical booklets: "And the author of this book (*sefer*) who composed/
compiled in a booklet (*be-mahberet*) discussions on pietism, humility, and the
fear of God" (*ba'al zeh ha-sefer asher hibber divrei ha-hasidut, ve-ha-'anavah, ve-
ha-yir'ah kol ehad ve-ehad be-mahberet*).[19] Writing short passages and then
copying them into topical booklets and then combining those into a book is
what characterizes SHB, SHP, and the other three manuscripts mentioned
earlier.

The passage just quoted is found at the beginning of *Sefer ha-Hasidut*, the separate work that eventually became the beginning of SHB (see Chapter 2). A reference to a topical notebook, like those found in some *Sefer Hasidim* editions, is found in R. Eleazar of Worms's *Sefer ha-Roqeah*. After discussing several customs connected with the dead, R. Eleazar of Worms says that they are "from R. Judah hasid's notebook" (*mi-mahberet r. yehudah hasid*), and this suggests that Judah himself wrote a topical *mahbe-ret* on the subject of the dead, one of the fourteen topics arranged as a book in SHP and former JTS Boesky 45, in Cambridge Add. 379 and Oxford Add. Fol. 34 (Neubauer 641), and three different times in SHB.[20] Elsewhere, "sefer" is also found as a large unit of text. For example, SHP 721 has a title in the middle of the section on books: "I found this in another book" (*zeh mazati be-sefer aher*), and the last part of SHB begins "This is copied from another Sefer Hasidim" (*zeh hu'ataq mi-sefer hasidim aher*).

The independence of the single paragraph as the unit of composition, regardless of how such short units were combined in different editions, is also seen in how stories are placed one after the other on related themes but without any literary connection. Rearrange the order or remove one and nothing would be missed. Consider the following three *exempla* from a section in SHP on prayer (391–585) and note how disjunctive they are despite their overlapping themes. These are three of four paragraphs that appear in the same sequence in both SHP and former JTS Boesky 45 and SHB with significant variations between each parallel paragraph:

> SHP 463, former JTS Boesky 45, 196, and SHB 781
> It once happened that people were protesting (in the synagogue when the Torah was being read), and the protester would not allow the Torah scroll to be returned to its place in the ark. It was a fast day, and someone said, "Say the Prayer [i.e., *Shemoneh 'esreh*] seated or else the proper time for praying the afternoon service will pass. But do not walk out on the Torah scroll, (as it is said), 'And they that forsake the Lord shall be consumed' (Isa. 1:28)."
> But he made a mistake (when he was reciting the Prayer), which

proves that if he had so desired he could have prayed the Prayer standing. And (the verse) "And they that forsake the Lord shall be consumed" (Isa. 1:28) applies only to when the Torah is actually being read. A man should not leave the synagogue until the entire Prayer is completed, unless he must relieve himself or throw up.

SHP 464, former JTS Boesky 45, 196, and SHB 782

A story about an old woman who used to come early to pray (in the synagogue) and (who did other) good deeds. After she died, she appeared in a dream to the good men. They said to her, "What (is it like) in that world?" She said to them, "They are judging me [SHB: hitting me] harshly. When the other righteous men and women are happy and at peace, they chase me away." (They said, "What did you do wrong?") She said, "When I was alive, I used to leave the synagogue during the Qedushah prayer. I did not wait until (everyone else) left the synagogue."

SHP 465, former JTS Boesky 45, 196, SHB 783

There once was a woman who went out of the synagogue before the community finished praying. She sent her maid to her husband to bring her the house key. When (her husband) left the synagogue, he asked his wife, "Why was it necessary for you to have the keys (then)"?

She said, ("I needed them) because gentile women were coming to exchange some pawns that are needed in the house of frivolity" [SHB: prayer] [i. e., church vessels].

Her husband said to her, "You have sinned because you left the synagogue (during the service). Besides, you sent for the keys in order to give the pawns to (the Christian women) who would then go to their house of frivolity [SHB: prayer], [i.e., church]. Look how you have replaced the holy (synagogue) with an abomination" [SHB: impure, i.e., church]!

No effort was made to connect these paragraphs. They function as separate texts that are related thematically to women and/or prayer, like three research notes that are put into the same file for future reference.

Linguistic Independence of Single Paragraphs

Although it is sometimes assumed that the language of SHB tends to be smoother and reworked compared to the language of parallel passages in SHP, linguistic evidence actually supports the independence of individual paragraphs, wherever they may be found, as being more or less awkward or reworked. Moreover, the linguistic independence of individual paragraphs applies to all parallels in the twelve editions of *Sefer Hasidim*, not just to SHP compared to SHB. A single paragraph in any edition can have an earlier linguistic form than any of the other parallels of that passage found anywhere else. This is another reason why all parallel passages need to be compared.

Simha Kogut demonstrated this in his detailed comparative study of the language of SHP and SHB (actually SHM 2).[21] His linguistic analysis of a sample of parallel passages in both printed editions showed that a single passage found in either one could be linguistically earlier than the parallel passage in the other. The textual quality of individual parallels varies, showing omissions by scribes based on similar phrase endings (*homoioteleuta*) in both directions, and there are variant readings due to scribal errors when any two or more text parallels are compared.[22]

Kogut's findings support the approach taken here that *Sefer Hasidim* was composed in single or small groups of paragraph units that the author at first and then others combined differently in various short and long editions. Because paragraphs were combined more than once, we see variance in the sequencing of parallel passages in the different editions.

It is also sometimes claimed that Parma is closer to Mittelhochdeutsch and is therefore earlier than SHB. But it is not the case that the convoluted Hebrew found in many *Sefer Hasidim* passages, in SHB as well as SHP and in other manuscripts, derive from contemporary medieval German syntax. There were no written prose models of medieval German available even to hear, only poetry, and everyday spoken medieval German or proto-Yiddish that Jews could hear and speak would not be convoluted but relatively clear and linear. The complicated Hebrew syntax of *Sefer Hasidim* is due to Judah's attempt to create a new form of narrative Hebrew from earlier Hebrew models, not from contemporary German patterns. Any parallel paragraph in any edition of *Sefer Hasidim* can be more or less awkward than its parallel elsewhere.[23]

Single Paragraphs of *Sefer Hasidim* Circulate in Other Texts

Examples of Scholem's and Dan's impression that most of *Sefer Hasidim* is made up of relatively disjunctive passages are short quotations from *Sefer Hasidim* found in Judah's other writings and in the works by other authors. In such cases, single paragraphs stand out as independently produced texts. For example, Dan cited *Sefer Hasidim* passages found in different texts as in Oxford Opp. 540 (Neubauer 1567) and Oxford Opp. 111 (Neubauer 1566). They are traditions that were not only composed but also transmitted singly. A story in *Sefer Hasidim* also appears in the thirteenth-century Hebrew story cycle of ninety-nine stories, and there are other such brief *Sefer Hasidim* parallels in other Hebrew compositions.[24]

From these single passages, Dan inferred that when they are not found in our *Sefer Hasidim* (*ha-sefer she-be-yadeinu*), meaning mainly in Parma, they derive from the lost "original sefer hasidim" (*sefer hasidim ha-meqori*).[25] But such paragraph texts are not traces of "the original *Sefer Hasidim*" because there is no evidence that one original *Sefer Hasidim* ever existed, and the paradigm that assumes Judah himself wrote only one edition of his short passages needs to be set aside. The paradigm I am proposing instead is of an inverted pyramid. It assumes that Judah first wrote thousands of individual paragraph traditions. He combined these into some of the dozen or so editions preserved in over twenty manuscripts. Some editions are made up of topical notebooks, but others contain short passages with no obvious similarities. The origins of how *Sefer Hasidim* came into existence should be sought not in the long edited texts but in the short paragraph units that

circulated and that the author, and then others, combined into the dozen or
so parallel editions of *Sefer Hasidim* that survived. The rest of this chapter
illustrates how individual paragraphs circulated throughout the corpus of *Sefer Hasidim* manuscripts and in the first edition.

Single Paragraph Parallels in Short Manuscripts of *Sefer Hasidim*

One way to see how single paragraphs circulated as *Sefer Hasidim* is to consider the shorter manuscripts and compare how parallel single paragraphs
vary within blocks of text parallels from manuscript to manuscript. This section of the chapter is not a description of the different manuscripts of *Sefer
Hasidim*. That is found in the Catalog. Rather, I want to illustrate here how
individual paragraphs differ when we compare blocks of parallel texts in different manuscripts. Although the analysis that follows requires paying close
attention to many details, this is the best way to demonstrate how paragraph-
length texts circulated throughout the corpus of *Sefer Hasidim* parallel
editions.

Of the dozen editions of *Sefer Hasidim* (see below), six are found in only
one manuscript each. They are: Frankfurt Oct. 94; Zurich Heidenheim 51;
Oxford Mich. 568 (Neubauer 1098); the Zurich Fragment; Vatican 285 A, and
Freiburg 483. When we look at each of these manuscripts and compare any
parallel passages in other manuscripts, we find the presence or absence of
individual parallel paragraphs. These comparisons demonstrate that single
paragraphs circulated throughout the corpus of *Sefer Hasidim* manuscripts.

For example, in the Frankfurt manuscript, single, unnumbered paragraphs on different topics are mostly found as single paragraph parallels in
other manuscripts. Unnumbered paragraphs are indicated below in square
brackets. Three different paragraphs each claims that it is a shortened
version of a fuller parallel paragraph found elsewhere. For example, in Frankfurt f. 270r, line 11, [1] the text says: "and he elaborated on this further"
(*ve-he'erikh sham yoter*). A parallel passage with such additional sources is
found in parallels in Milan Ambrosiana X.III sup. [18], Oxford Opp. 340
(Neubauer 875) [18], Moscow 103 [18], as well as in Nîmes 26 [18] and SHB 18.

Only Frankfurt par. [1] abbreviates the text, and that paragraph is more derivative than the parallels that contain the fuller version of the passage.

Or, Frankfurt, f. 270v, [14] ends with the phrase "and he expanded further with verses and other proof texts" (*ve-he'erikh yoter bi-fesuqim u-re'ayot*). The version of the same passage but with biblical and other proof texts is found in SHB 1120, its only parallel.

In contrast to these two examples of MS Frankfurt abbreviating a paragraph that has a parallel elsewhere with more sources, Frankfurt, f. 271r, [19] refers at the end to such a parallel but it does not exist: "and he added many talmudic proofs" (*ve-he'erikh harbeh re'ayot min ha-talmud*). But in the parallel to Frankfurt [19], SHB 1065, there are no additional references, and this means that the expanded paragraph to which Frankfurt [19] refers apparently has not survived.

Frankfurt [33–40] and [46] correspond to single parallels in the same sequence but with omissions in Ox. Opp. 614 (Neubauer 2275) and Ox. Or. 146 (Neubauer 782) [1, 2, 5, 7, 9, 15, 17, 18] (for both). An exception to the parallel sequence is Frankfurt [46] that corresponds to Oxford Opp. 614 (Neubauer 2275) [13] and Oxford, Or. 146 (Neubauer 782) [13] and also to SHP 211 and former JTS Boesky 45, 103. There also are single paragraph parallels for each of these paragraphs in SHP and former JTS Boesky 45 but, with one exception, not in SHB and its parallels.[26] Frankfurt [42, 44, 45, 47–49] seem to be unique to this manuscript, but Frankfurt [43] has parallels in SHP 72 and former JTS Boesky 45, 56; in Vatican 285 [30] and JTS 2499 [30]; and in SHB 21–22. This pattern is a good illustration of how single paragraphs circulated. Even when blocks of paragraphs appear in two or more manuscripts, some individual paragraphs do not appear in all of the parallel blocks.

Another illustration of how individual paragraphs circulated from manuscript to manuscript is seen in Zurich Heid. 51. It consists of unnumbered single paragraphs on different topics, some of which have single parallels elsewhere. The first three paragraphs are about women and have single parallels in SHP (and its parallels not listed here) in a topical notebook on women (SHP 1084–1193): Zurich [1]=SHP 1169 and former JTS Boesky 45, 471; Zurich [2]=SHP 1136 and SHB 498; and Zurich [3]=SHP 1154 and SHB 506.

Following this we find single paragraphs about prayer: Zurich [4] is parallel to SHP 574 in a topical notebook on prayer (SHP 391–585); Zurich [PUSHD 5] on *hasidut* is parallel to SHP 1049 in a topical notebook on that subject (975–1065), and so on.[27]

From an annotated published version of Oxford Mich. 568 (Neubauer 1098), we see that most of the single paragraphs are about praying or writing liturgical items connected to prayer. Only [1] and part of [6] and [8] have any parallels. The manuscript is mid-thirteenth century, and in the same codex is a copy of Judah *he-hasid's* "Shir ha-Kavod (Song of Glory)."[28]

The Zurich Fragment consists of two short blocks of topically related paragraphs. The first block, [1–8], is on the dead and has parallels in SHP 331–337, former JTS Boesky 45, 147–148, and also in SHB 733–739, but Zurich Fragment [5] is also found in Vatican 285 [52] and its near twin, JTS 2499 [52].

The second block, Zurich Fragment [9–12], is on prayer and is parallel to SHP 394–397, former JTS Boesky 45, 167–168, and SHB 754–757, but [10] is also found in Vatican 285 [60] and JTS 2499 [60]. Large notebooks on the two topics of the dead and prayer appear in the same order in SHB III, and nearly together in other topical editions in SHP I and SHB I and II. When we compare the parallel blocks, individual paragraphs are found in some manuscripts but not in others.[29]

Vatican 285 A, a separate edition of *Sefer Hasidim*, consists of 37 paragraphs that have single parallels mainly in SHB and not in SHP or former JTS Boesky 45. A significant number of them are from the first 152 paragraphs of SHB, that is, the separate text known as *Sefer ha-Hasidut*. Vatican 285 A is now numbered in PUSHD with paragraph numbers added to the longer text in Vatican 285 from [148–184]. A new numbering just of this text would run from [1–37]. Although some paragraphs may be unique [1–2], and others found as single parallels in SHB, the largest part is a block parallel to SHB 68–113 with several single paragraphs missing from Vatican 285 A.

Another example of parallel blocks of text that differ with respect to single parallel paragraphs is seen in the torn Freiburg manuscript. It consists of three short groups of paragraphs that have blocks of parallels in SHP. Freiburg [966–969] is parallel to those numbered paragraphs in SHP I in a topical block about honoring parents (*kibbud av va-em*) (SHP 929–974); Freiburg [979–986] is parallel to those numbered paragraphs in SHP I in a topical block on pietism (*hasidut*) (SHP 975–1065); and Freiburg [1056–1073] is parallel to those numbered paragraphs in SHP I in a topical block on pietism and ritual slaughter and purity (*hasidut, shehitah ve-taharah*) (SHP 1066–83).

One of the parallel paragraphs found in both Freiburg and SHP is not in the parallel block in SHB. Although Freiburg [966, 967, and 969] are found in SHB 579 and 580, Freiburg [968] is not there. This difference also shows how single paragraph parallels can vary within parallel blocks of text in different manuscripts.[30]

Single Paragraphs in Editions with More Than One Manuscript

The independence of single paragraph units can be further illustrated when we compare *Sefer Hasidim* editions that each contains two manuscripts. Some manuscripts were copied from others, resulting in sets of two manuscripts that resemble each other in much of their sequencing. Editions of *Sefer Hasidim* with two manuscripts each are Parma Heb. MS 3280, De Rossi 1133 (SHP), and former JTS Boesky 45; Cambridge Add. 379 and Oxford Add. Fol. 34 (Neubauer 641); Vatican 285 and JTS 2499; Oxford, Opp. 614 (Neubauer 2275) and Oxford Or. 146 (Neubauer 782); Nîmes 26 and Oxford, Mich. 155 (Neubauer 1984).

Even when the majority of paragraphs in both manuscripts of the same edition are in the same sequence, some individual paragraphs are found in one but not in the other manuscript, testifying again to the independent circulation of individual paragraphs.

For example, the text of former JTS Boesky 45 follows the structure of SHP. Parallel passages are in the same sequence most of the time, but a few paragraphs found in former JTS Boesky 45 are not in SHP, and some *two hundred individual paragraph passages* found in SHP are not in former JTS Boesky 45.

Similarly, Cambridge Add. 379 and Oxford Add. Fol. 34 (Neubauer 641) are structurally similar to each other. Both of these manuscripts consist of three large blocks of text: *Sefer ha-Hasidut*, a version of SHB I and a version of SHP II. Although many passages are present in the same order in both, other passages are missing in one or the other, especially in the second and third blocks of text.

So, too, Vatican 285 is closely related to JTS 2499, but some paragraph parallels are missing in the latter that starts with Vatican 285 [10]. Most of the text has single parallels either in SHP and former JTS Boesky 45 or SHB or all three, but Vatican 285 [123–147] has parallels only in JTS 2499.

Oxford Or. 146 (Neubauer 782) is very close to Oxford Opp. 614 (Neubauer 2275), but individual paragraphs are not always in both manuscripts of each set. These two manuscripts are made up of single paragraphs many of which have parallels in SHP, plus former JTS Boesky 45, or SHB and its parallels. These two Oxford manuscripts consist of two texts joined together here: PUSHD [1–9] and [10–19] that begins with a separate title: "This, too, is from Sefer Hasidim" (*gam zeh mi-sefer hasidim*). If the second text were located in a different manuscript or separated from the first part by other passages, it would be listed as an independent edition. Joined together, it is more like a compound edition, like SHP I and II, rather than as two separate ones.

Many of the paragraphs in the first text, and one in the second, have parallels in Frankfurt 94 as well as in single parallels of SHP and SHB. All these texts, then, are related and there is no closer relationship between these two Oxford texts and SHP than to the others. It is not clear if Oxford, Or. 146 (Neubauer 782) is a copy of Opp. 614 (Neubauer 2275) or the other way around or if both derive from a third manuscript.[31]

In addition to the six editions of *Sefer Hasidim* that exist in single manuscripts and the five found in two manuscripts each, SHB itself constitutes a compound text that contains three topical editions that I referred to as SHB I, SHB II, and SHB III, making a total of fourteen editions of *Sefer Hasidim*.[32] Thus, although we have over twenty manuscripts, there are only fourteen editions. None of these editions can be reduced to the author's original single composition. All of them are parallel versions of *Sefer Hasidim*. A parallel paragraph in any one of them can contain better readings than the parallels found in the other editions, regardless of the date of the manuscript. Late manuscripts can contain better readings of a parallel paragraph than early manuscripts.

Some of the editions of *Sefer Hasidim* probably go back to R. Judah *he-hasid* himself, who wrote, copied, and recombined many paragraphs in different ways in multiple parallel topical notebooks and combined them into parallel editions. A few of his students or his son may have copied down other editions. Throughout, it is the single paragraph and small groups of them that need to be examined for establishing the best text of any passage, not any one edition in which a paragraph appears, regardless of when a manuscript was copied.

The conclusion that follows from the structural variance in single manuscript editions, in the sets of *Sefer Hasidim* manuscripts, and from the structure of SHB is that the fourteen editions are not derived from a single original composition. Rather, all of them ultimately drew on a reservoir of thousands of short passages. R. Judah *he-hasid* composed *Sefer Hasidim* in individual paragraph units that he and later others combined and recombined into blocks of different sizes. Some were written down in units of two or more paragraphs from the beginning. In some cases, notebooks of a hundred or more, including "duplicates" that may be his rewritings of single paragraphs, were produced. None was written as a single integrated composition or book. *Hasidei ashkenaz* quoted Saadia but they did not imitate him when it came to book composition.

From a consideration of the manuscripts and patterns of parallels and unique passages, one should consider all manuscripts of *Sefer Hasidim* and SHB to be different combinations of single-paragraph compositions. Assigning greater weight to any of these editions is a consequence of a tradition in nineteenth- and twentieth-century scholarship that thought of *Sefer Hasidim* as a conventional book. In fact, it is an Ashkenazic open text, in the sense defined here of parallel editions from the beginning, and it needs to be understood as multiple in form, as an inverted pyramid, not as an author's single original composition that he revised, Israel Ta-Shma's meaning of "open book."

It is likely that R. Judah *he-hasid* was the author of most of these single paragraphs and also of the sequences of fourteen topics that form different editions in Cambridge Add. 379 and Oxford Add. Fol. 34 (Neubauer 641); in SHP and former JTS Boesky 45; and in SHB that itself contains three sets of topically arranged booklets of related paragraphs. Once Judah was gone, students or his son may have selected single paragraphs from the many that Judah had written and assembled them into various combinations of "liqqu-tim," without most of the social vision that he had advocated. Regardless of the subjects in any manuscript, all of them are *Sefer Hasidim*, a series of writings and rewritings of Judah's short texts. In addition, Judah and his student R. Eleazar b. Judah of Worms wrote and rewrote different overlapping compositions, and it is to those forms of open texts that we now turn.

Chapter 2

Rewriting Jewish Pietist Traditions

Once published, S[efer] H[asidim]—without distinction
between what Soloveitchik termed S[efer] H[asidim] I and
the rest of the book—stood as an independent work of
medieval rabbinic scholarship that carried the halo of
German Jewish piety with it into the sixteenth century and
beyond.

—Edward Fram

Sefer Hasidim was always a work in progress, an open text of a special kind,
rather than a single fixed book. Over time, some fourteen different editions
came into being, some topical, others made up of unrelated paragraph units;
some of over a thousand paragraphs, others but a few passages strung
together.

Besides *Sefer Hasidim*, Judah also produced different but related texts
such as his *Zava'ah* (Commands) and *Sefer ha-Kavod* (Book on the Divine
Glory). R. Eleazar of Worms, for his part, wrote many private penitentials
and different but overlapping halakhic works, large compositions about theological matters, different commentaries on the prayer book, and dozens of
piyyutim (see below and the bibliography). Because each author's own compositions overlap, other writers can cite passages that appear in more than one
work by referring to different titles. A comparison of the texts attributed to

each author indicates not a set of unique, original, and distinct compositions but a fluid range of overlapping and multiple expressions of different though related texts all composed of small text units. After considering how Judah and Eleazar each wrote overlapping or fluid texts, I look at how one French Jewish author rewrote *Sefer Hasidim*.

Overlapping or Fluid Texts

Textual overlap or fluidity has long been noted about ancient rabbinic works and about *heikhalot* texts that unknown editors produced. Short sections of related texts circulated, and editors combined them in different works.[1] In many Ashkenazic books, an additional kind of fluidity exists: one rabbinic author might *write* more than one related text in short paragraph units on the same subject. This pattern of composition is different from an author revising a single work. Saadia Gaon recycled some of his earlier writings in later ones, and Maimonides revised parts of his *Commentary on the Mishneh*, as we know from drafts of early versions found in the Cairo Geniza. That is different from the fluidity we find in R. Judah *he-hasid*'s *Sefer Hasidim* and his other pietistic writings or in some of R. Eleazar of Worms's compositions.[2]

When an author writes multiple parallel versions of a single composition or names them differently or gives the same title to a single work and to a collection of related works, we need to rethink what we mean by a text. We would normally be inclined to try to sort out what appears to us as bibliographical confusion by assigning a unique title and author to each work, but we should not project our ideas of bibliography, derived from familiar single-authored unique compositions, back into medieval Ashkenaz where ideas about an author and a text were often more fluid.

Among examples of textual fluidity in R. Judah *he-hasid*'s writings is *Sefer ha-Kavod*, a composition he may have written more than once and that overlaps in some ways with *Sefer Hasidim*.[3] Jacob Freimann showed that manuscripts of *Sefer 'Arugat ha-Bosem*, written by R. Judah *he-hasid*'s student R. Abraham b. 'Azriel, contain quotations from a *Sefer ha-Kavod* attributed to R. Judah *he-hasid*.[4] Two Oxford manuscripts that contain a work called *Sefer ha-Kavod* and a truncated second discussion also about the Divine Glory (*kavod*) do not contain the passages quoted from "that work" in *Sefer 'Arugat ha-Bosem*. The two Oxford manuscripts do, however, contain passages attributed to R. Judah *he-hasid*'s *Sefer ha-Kavod* that are found in R. Moses Taqu's *Ketav Tamim*, a work that polemicized with Judah's writings.[5]

Joseph Dan presents as a dilemma having to decide either that one of the two medieval authors is wrong in attributing his quotations to Judah's *Sefer ha-Kavod* or that Judah wrote two versions of *Sefer ha-Kavod*. He considers which possibility is "more reasonable" (*sevirah yoter*). Although he thinks choosing between the two possibilities is "somewhat arbitrary" (*yesh bah middah shel sheriratiyut*), he decides in favor of Moses Taqu's reliability, with the result that the Oxford manuscripts containing the quotations R. Moses Taqu attributes to *Sefer ha-Kavod* is in fact *Sefer ha-Kavod*. However, in light of Ashkenazic book culture's fluidity, Dan's second hypothesis, that Judah wrote more than one *Sefer ha-Kavod*, is very probable.[6] R. Abraham b. 'Azriel had one version of *Sefer ha-Kavod*, possibly lost, and R. Moses Taqu had a different one, that which was found in the Oxford manuscripts.[7] There was no author's single original text of *Sefer ha-Kavod* any more than there was one of *Sefer Hasidim*.[8]

The multiple character of Hebrew book composition in medieval Europe also explains some apparent anomalies in the sources such as a reference to "Sefer Hasidim" in a paragraph in *Sefer Hasidim*.[9] The author did not think of a title as belonging uniquely to only one edition of related passages that he strung together more than once.[10]

Aside from *Sefer Hasidim* and *Sefer ha-Kavod* each consisting of more than one edition, the two works themselves seem to overlap. We see this from quotations of *Sefer ha-Kavod* found in *Sefer Hasidim*. Sometimes the author of *Sefer Hasidim* refers the reader to *Sefer ha-Kavod* for a longer treatment of something he mentions briefly in *Sefer Hasidim*. This would mean that a version of *Sefer ha-Kavod* already existed before that part of *Sefer Hasidim* was written. But in other passages in *Sefer Hasidim*, Judah indicates that more *will* be written in *Sefer ha-Kavod*. Here it seems that at least parts of *Sefer Hasidim* are earlier than a version of *Sefer ha-Kavod*.[11]

That such an overlapping relationship between Judah's different writings exists is reflected in a comment R. Eleazar of Worms makes in his legal code *Sefer ha-Roqeah*. He says that he has taken passages on the topic of caring for the dead "from the notebook of R. Judah *hasid*," but then he continues, "and you will find proof of his words in *Sefer ha-Kavod*" (*mi-mahberet r. yehudah hasid u-ve-sefer ha-kavod timza re'ayah li-devarav*).[12] These comments suggest that Judah was writing passages in one "book" with the other "book" in mind; or, we might even think of them as two forms of his short pietist writings that he incorporated into differently named works, some as paragraphs of *Sefer Hasidim* and the other as paragraphs of *Sefer ha-Kavod*. The evidence suggests that he wrote some passages more than once and put them into separate works that had different titles.

A third text attributed to R. Judah *he-hasid* can overlap with *Sefer Hasidim* or with *Sefer ha-Kavod*. R. Judah *he-hasid*'s list of *Commands* (*Zava'ah*) is preserved in scores of manuscripts in different combinations of up to seventy short paragraphs.[13] The title is often mistranslated as an ethical "will," but the term refers to a series of discrete religious demands. The text was very popular. In the first edition is an introduction that says Judah was writing his rules for three different audiences: his family, other Jews, and the whole world. The "will" includes: "If there are two weddings the same week, one will become poor or go into exile and die. As to gentiles, they should not make two knights (*shenei parashim*) on the same day, but don't tell them or they will be careful to avoid doing it"![14]

Sometimes the *Zava'ah* was copied into codices that also contain parts of *Sefer Hasidim*.[15] The two texts were often cited interchangeably, especially paragraphs of the *Zava'ah* as "Sefer Hasidim."[16] For example, in MS New York, JTS Mic. 5252 f. 93r: "I found in writing (something) copied from *Sefer ha-Hasidim* from the *Commands* of Rabbeinu Juda *he-hasid*, may his memory be for a blessing, and they are seventy commands" (*mazati katuv ve-hu mu'ataq mi-sefer ha-hasidim mi-zava'avot* (?) *rabbeinu yehuda* [*alef* at end] *he-hasid . . . ve-hem shiv'im zivuyyim*)."[17] Both texts have the same attributed author. Both are written in numbered paragraphs and command pietistic behavior. And both were often copied in the same manuscript codex or printed together.

There is also overlap between *Sefer ha-Kavod* and Judah's *Zava'ah*. R. Jacob b. Moses Ha-Levi Mölln (Maharil) refers to seeing *Sefer ha-Kavod*, and that it included Rabbi Judah's *Zava'ah*.[18] Consider again the passage on mourning customs that is found in R. Eleazar of Worms's *Sefer ha-Roqeah* (par. 316, end) that begins: "Copied from *Sefer ha-Kavod* written by the great man, R. Judah *Hasid* m[ay] the m[emory] of the r[ighteous man] (be for a blessing)" (*ne'etaq mi-sefer ha-kavod she-yasad he-ish ha-gadol r. yehudah hasid zz"l*). The text quoted is a very close version of the first nine paragraphs of Judah he-hasid's *Zava'ah* even though it refers to the text as "Sefer ha-Kavod."[19]

Apart from the compositions that R. Judah *he-hasid* wrote more than once, he also wrote multiple versions of short texts on the Divine Unity (*shirei ha-yihud*), and he wrote more than one commentary on the prayer book.[20] Other parallel passages are to be found in other compositions that Judah wrote, such as his writings about nature, *Zekher 'asah le-nifleotav*.[21]

R. Eleazar of Worms's Fluid Writings

R. Eleazar of Worms also produced more than one edition of some of his many different writings. He wrote several short penitential texts about how to atone for one's sins, not just one that he revised. This act of recomposing resulted in related penitential texts with different names such as two versions called *Hilekhot Teshuvah*, and others called *Moreh Hata'im, Yoreh Hata'im*, and *'Isqei Teshuvot*. They all contain overlapping parallel passages in different sequences as well as unique ones. One composition cannot be reduced to the others as the product of the author's revision of an original text or of scribal errors. The textual evidence argues for Eleazar of Worms's composing each of them.[22]

Overlap also exists in Eleazar's halakhic writings. He composed a specific halakhic work that he called "*Sefer ha-Roqeah*,"[23] but that title can also refer to a different halakhic text whose modern editor named it "*Ma'aseh Roqeah*" (the Work of Roqeah), but medieval authors cited that text simply as "Roqeah." Eleazar wrote a third legal text that is also sometimes referred to as "Roqeah."[24] Thus, when medieval authors refer to "*Sefer ha-Roqeah*" or

"*Roqeah*" and the quoted passage is not in "our" *Sefer ha-Roqeah,* it is not because these authors had passages from a larger *Sefer ha-Roqeah* in the author's original unique composition that did not survive, but because the title was applied to related, overlapping, but different texts that the same author composed from hundreds of short text units that he wrote.[25]

In the case of R. Eleazar of Worms, the title "roqeah" also denotes the author's name, "Eleazar," since he explains in the introduction to his *Sefer ha-Roqeah* that he called the book "Roqeah" after his name "Eleazar," a numerical equivalent. Each Hebrew word adds up to 308. By doing this, Eleazar in effect equated his name as author with the title or titles of his books. As a result, several books written by the same author could be called by his name-title, regardless of what other titles they might have.

Eleazar's speculative writings that include *Sefer ha-Shem* (Book of the [Divine] Name), on God's mystical names, or his *Peirush 'al Sefer Yezirah* (Commentary on the Book of Creation), have those titles, but they are also part of a larger work that Eleazar called *Sodei Razayya* (Hidden Mysteries). The title "Sode Razayya," in turn, can refer to a specific work by that name, but it also can refer to the collection of five related works including *Sefer ha-Shem* and the *Peirush 'al Sefer Yezirah.*

Like R. Judah *he-hasid,* Eleazar also wrote different versions of a commentary on the standard prayer book that includes many Psalms, and he also wrote a commentary on the Book of Psalms. Passages from each "work" were copied into the other. He also wrote over fifty *piyyutim.*[26]

Adapting the Works of Others in Ashkenaz and the French *Sefer Hasidim*

Continuous adaptation was a characteristic feature of Jewish subcultures in medieval Europe, and a northern French Jewish rewriting of *Sefer Hasidim* can be viewed as part of a broad process of Jewish cultural migration and adaptation. From time to time, a feature of one subculture was brought to another that absorbed and modified it. For example, Ashkenaz imported Iberian quantitative Hebrew poetic meter, and writers such as R. Jacob b. Meir, known as Rabbeinu Tam (d. 1171), adapted it.[27] Later, R. Meir b. Barukh (Maharam) of Rothenberg (d. 1293) used it when he wrote his lament on the burning of the Talmud in Paris in 1242 and combined it with the genre Judah Halevi had used in his "Odes to Zion" (*Shirei Ziyyon*).[28] A prose example is the early modern Iberian story cycle in Solomon Ibn Verga's *Shevet Yehudah* (*The Scepter of Judah*) that was transformed into a Yiddish version with an Ashkenazic point of view.[29]

In addition to Ashkenazic authors adapting Iberian Jewish cultural features, some French Ashkenazic texts show the influence of German Hebrew works. An example of such a text is *Huqqei ha-Torah* (Rules of the Torah) that describes a Jewish study community or yeshivah-like boarding school. Jewish males are described as studying there during the week and older ones go home to their wives for the Sabbath. The provenance of the text has been proposed in southern France or further north as in the Evreux brothers' community in Normandy or in Paris.[30]

Regardless of its social context, some of the ideas found in the text remind us of *Sefer Hasidim* and some recommended patterns of study found in it. It may be an example of German pietist influence on a French Jewish thinker, even if there was no implementation of its recommended practices, a conclusion that may also be drawn about the utopian and sectarian world of *Sefer Hasidim* itself. Although the social program envisioned in *Sefer Hasidim* did not get implemented as a utopian society, the regimen of fasting, atonement, and related practices it advocated did became widespread as part and parcel of East European "common Judaism"[31] or of East European Jewish "piety."

Despite the influence of *hasidei ashkenaz* modes of atonement, not everyone agreed with this approach, as we see in the northern French adaptation of *Sefer Hasidim* traditions. This text appears as the first part of the printed edition, preceding Samuel's *Sefer ha-Yir'ah* that begins with paragraph SHB 153. It is not found in SHP (or its adaptation in former JTS Boesky 45). This text circulated in three manuscripts as an independent composition. In Oxford, Bodleian Library, Opp. 340 (Neubauer 875), dated 1299, it is called "Sefer ha-Hasidut (ShH)." It is also found in Milan, Biblioteca Ambrosiana, X.iii sup. and in Moscow, Russian State Library, Günzburg 103.[32]

Sefer ha-Hasidut also became the first 152 numbered paragraphs of Cambridge Add. 379 and the shorter related manuscript Oxford Add. Fol. 34 (Neubauer 641). Two other manuscripts, Nîmes 26 and Oxford Mich. 155 (Neubauer 1984), are fragments of either that text or of it combined with a version of SHB I and SHP II. Since one cannot determine if Nîmes 26 and Oxford Mich. 155 (Neubauer 1984) contained more than ShH or ShH alone, neither can be counted as a manuscript just of ShH.

This particular text is unusual because it is very stable. Unlike the pairs of manuscripts of *Sefer Hasidim* discussed in Chapter 1 that have most parallel paragraphs in the same sequence but have different single paragraphs missing, the several witnesses of *Sefer ha-Hasidut* tend to agree with each other. Only the Oxford text is defective, apparently because a page or two was lost, and the text is missing for pars. 102 (middle)-117.[33] In all of the other full versions, these paragraphs as well as all of the other parallels are found. This difference suggests that the French *Sefer Hasidim* was composed once and copied, not written more than once, as was the case with many German Pietist and other Ashkenazic Hebrew works. It circulated by itself or was combined with other blocks of text, but either way its 152 paragraphs circulated without much variation and this makes it unusual.

Following Haim Yosef David Azulai and Leopold Zunz, Jacob Reifmann, Solomon Wertheimer, and Jacob Freimann studied *Sefer ha-Hasidut* and observed that the first part of SHB contains unattributed Maimonidean passages on piety and repentance and lacks the ascetic penances found in the published *Sefer Hasidim* and in R. Eleazar of Worms's penitential compositions.[34]

In addition to the presence of passages from Maimonides, all the *le'azim* (vernacular expressions) found in this text are French.[35] From Hebrew transliterations of medieval French words and phrases, the Hebrew text seems to come from an area to the west of Paris, between eastern Normandy and the Ile de la Cité.[36] In the rest of SHB or SHP the vernacular terms are mostly in German, although a few French words also appear there as they continue to do in German-Jewish compositions in German Ashkenaz.[37] For this reason, it is sometimes called the "French Sefer Hasidim."

Other than the passages from Maimonides and the dominance of French *le'azim* in this text, little else sets *Sefer ha-Hasidut* apart from the printed versions of *Sefer Hasidim* or from the majority of manuscripts of *Sefer Hasidim,* and its importance should not be exaggerated. For example, references to "the will of the Creator" (*rezon ha-borei*), one of several formulations of an underlying concept of an enlarged hidden divine will, not "the most distinctive element of Sefer Hasidim,"[38] are not frequently found in any of the manuscripts of *Sefer Hasidim*. In all of SHB and SHP, for example, it and similar phrases appear or are elaborated but a few times, so it is not significant if the phrase is not found often in *Sefer ha-Hasidut* either.[39] Similarly, although exegesis by use of numerology is very common in R. Eleazar of Worms's esoteric writings, it is not the case that *gematria* are "ubiquitous in Sefer Hasidim" in the printed *Sefer Hasidim* editions or in the manuscripts, and *Sefer ha-Hasidut* is no different.[40]

The absence of religious stories (*ma'asim*) in *Sefer ha-Hasidut,*[41] also true of many of the shorter manuscripts of *Sefer Hasidim,* correlates with the absence of a program of social criticism in those texts. The majority of manuscripts of *Sefer Hasidim,* like *Sefer ha-Hasidut,* focus on the individual's relationship to God and not on society. For that reason, they do not contain stories that illustrate social relationships. There are also hardly any stories in Samuel's *Sefer ha-Yir'ah* at the beginning of SHP, or in SHB 153–162, and there are none in Eleazar's *Hilekhot Hasidut*. Both Samuel and Eleazar obviously are German pietist authors but their pietistic writings do not contain either social criticism or stories, both of which are found in only some of Judah's writings.

One difference between the longest editions of *Sefer Hasidim* and *Sefer ha-Hasidut* suggests a historical context for each that has not been considered. Although SHP, and the closely related former JTS Boesky 45, and SHB do not seem to refer to the rabbinic idea of ancestral merit (*zekhut avot*), that is, an appeal to biblical and other ancient figures' merit to mitigate later generations' deserved punishment, they do refer to the merit of the pietists' own families going back three or four generations.[42] This theme correlates with their awareness of family traditions that they sometimes refer to as "minhag avoteinu," but *Sefer ha-Hasidut* does not have any awareness of time.[43] Instead, its focus is on the individual pietist's sins and merits alone as the basis of one's reward or punishment.

This difference points to a possible historical link between the martyrs and Jews who survived as forced converts in 1096, the anti-Jewish riots in the Rhineland that accompanied the First Crusade, and R. Judah *he-hasid*'s vision of an ideal society. In Germany, the trauma of the anti-Jewish riots in 1096 was real, and there are other signs that the memory of 1096, including survivor guilt but not contemporary persecution, underlies *Sefer Hasidim*'s world. When someone rewrote *Sefer Hasidim* in northern France, a region that did not experience or remember the converts and martyrs of 1096, it is understandable that he would not invoke the ancestral merit of four genera-tions earlier, that is, of the martyrs of 1096. The Jews of northern France also did not need the same penitential system for the same reasons, assum-ing for the moment that conversion guilt was a factor in generating some of the need for ascetic penances. In point of fact, the penitentials focus much more on sins of pride, anxieties over women, money, and violence carried out between Jews than with apostasy.[44] In stark contrast to these social con-cerns but like *Huqqei ha-Torah*, *Sefer ha-Hasidut* floats in social space. That text does not contain the imagined utopian pietist society that one finds every-where in the longest manuscripts of R. Judah *he-hasid*'s *Sefer Hasidim*.

The most significant difference between *Sefer ha-Hasidut* and some of the manuscripts of *Sefer Hasidim* and other German pietist writings is the absence of penances and the theory of *teshuvat ha-mishqal* (suffering propor-tional to pleasure) and reliance instead on Maimonidean repentance, follow-ing Saadia's approach already quoted in SHP.[45] Such repentance requires a change of will, avoidance of sin, and confession of sins, but not public or even private acts of atonement or penances as the three German pietist au-thors stipulate. The innovation of *Sefer ha-Hasidut* was not in adding to as-cetic penances a different form of atonement based on Maimonides, but in *replacing* the former by the latter. However, since the ascetic penitentials, even in confessing one's sins to another Jew, as in *Sefer Hasidim*, were practiced by some in later Judaism (see below), one could argue that the author of *Sefer ha-Hasidut* failed to neutralize the influence of *hasidei ashkenaz* penitential atonement with the Maimonidean substitute. Regarding penitential practice, at least, it is misleading to claim that "SH I [*Sefer ha-Hasidut*] had a diffusion far greater than that of Sefer Hasidim itself."[46] Unless one insists on arbitrarily defining *Sefer Hasidim* as being only the long manuscripts that contain Judah's social critique, there are some twenty manuscripts of *Sefer Hasidim* in fourteen editions; of *Sefer ha-Hasidut*, there are but three manuscripts that circulated with that text alone.

Penitential Practice in Later Ashkenaz Reconsidered

Athough Judah *he-hasid*'s sectarian vision did not take hold in medieval German towns, *Sefer Hasidim*'s model of confession to another Jew continued in Ashkenaz for centuries after the death of Judah *he-hasid* in 1217. Several Ashkenazic Jews either confessed sins in person to another Jew or wrote to a rabbi to request penances, and this practice continued well into early modern times. Although R. Eleazar of Worms justified writing his several private penitential manuals on the grounds that some Jews were too embarrassed to confess their sins to another Jew and receive penances, confession to a sage or to a rabbi continued in medieval Ashkenaz side by side with the use of R. Eleazar of Worms's private penitential manuals. Thus, German pietist modes of atonement were influential not only through Eleazar's penitential handbooks, but also from the inspiration of confession to a sage as described originally in *Sefer Hasidim*.[47]

The idea of confession to a sage (*hakham*) is found in a fourteenth-century text written by R. Moses b. Eleazar ha-Kohen, who refers to "a story about a man who committed many sins his whole life . . . and went to a sage" (*ma'aseh be-adam ehad she-'asah 'aveirot harbeh kol yamav . . . ba ezel hakham ehad*).[48] This story pictures a Jew confessing his sins to a "sage" and receiving a penance from him to atone for all of his sins, just as we find scores of times in *Sefer Hasidim* itself.[49]

Encouraging confession to an important Jew is a theme in a penitential sermon that has been recently published. The unknown German pietist author places great emphasis on the value of the sinner embarrassing himself by confessing his sins to an important person, the very issue that R. Eleazar of Worms mentions as a problem for some.[50] In addition to the anonymously composed sermon that advocates sage-like confession, R. Eleazar of Worms himself composed a series of rhymed Hebrew penances that complement the prose private penitentials that he wrote.[51] Apparently there was a lively disagreement about confession of sins to another Jew since we find new works encouraging it as well as Eleazar's penitentials that are written to replace it.

There are several indications that the pro-confession camp won some followers. For example, in a collection of German Jewish traditions written down in Italy, we find a description of a penance administered for a violation of the Sabbath.[52] In an oft-cited case, a Jewish father writes to R. Meir b. Barukh (Maharam) of Rothenburg (d. 1293). He was afraid that "the enemies" (ha-oyevim) would kill his family and so he killed his family himself. But before he could take his own life, he was rescued, and he asks R. Meir of Rothenburg if he sinned and requires a penance or if he did the right thing.[53] R. Meir's response is that no penance is needed since administering one now would imply that Jews who had acted the same way in the past had sinned.[54]

The same R. Meir of Rothenburg tells a Jew who publically insulted a respected member of the Jewish community to do penance by fasting, self-flagellation, and giving charity.[55] Two rabbis, R. Jonah and R. Shemaryah, ask one R. Isaac b. Mordecai, a contemporary of R. Meir of Rothenburg, about revealing crimes that Jews had confessed to him. The questioner mentions Christian confession to monks and their vows of secrecy.[56]

The late thirteenth-century, anonymously written French Hebrew work, *Sefer ha-Neyar,* refers to a woman's confession to a R. Haim Barukh. She angered her husband and the rabbi imposed on her a fast of three days.[57] In the fifteenth century, R. Joseph b. Moses Hahn, a student of R. Israel Isserlein, lists cases of confession and penances in his "Laws of Atonement" (*Hilekhot Teshuvah*).[58] From around the same time, the niece of R. Jacob b. Moses ha-Levi Mölln (Maharil) forgot to light Friday candles and she is given a penance.[59]

Given the cases of Jewish confession to another Jew, Eleazar's introductions to his written handbooks should no longer be interpreted as a sign that confession to a sage or rabbi disappeared and was replaced by written peni-

tentials. Rather, Eleazar added them for those Jews who resisted such confession, while others were doing this very thing.[60] It is also important to
realize that hagiographical stories in Hebrew and Yiddish that portray Jews'
and Christians' confessions to Judah *he-hasid* and asking him for penances
show that he was remembered for his role as dispensing penances. None of
the hagiographical stories in Hebrew or Yiddish about Samuel or Judah picture a Jew using a written penitential. Some Jews continued to follow Judah
he-hasid's form of penitence long after he was gone.[61]

Sefer Hasidim, Sefer ha-Hasidut, and the Historical Impact of German Pietism

We should note that Ashkenazic book culture was strong enough to with-
stand Maimonides' presence there from the thirteenth century on. Although
Sefer ha-Hasidut and then *Sefer Mizvot Gadol* and *Sefer Mizvot Qatan* took
on Maimonidean content, Ashkenazic book culture did not emulate the Sephardic book form that Maimonides' works embodied. Ashkenazic authors
who incorporated Maimonides into their works continued to write segmented,
Lego-like compositions. They did not imitate the form of Maimonides' *Sefer
ha-Madda'*.[62]

Although the harsh and restrictive social utopia Judah envisioned in *Sefer Hasidim* was not enacted, the penitential system and many pietistic customs and practices did persist into modern times. The three manuscripts of
Sefer ha-Hasidut did nothing to prevent the success of the penitential regime
that outlasted the harsh social criticism of Judah's utopian program. The
substitution of Maimonides' view of repentance in *Sefer ha-Hasidut* instead
of penances of atonement failed to change anything. Even confession to another Jew, as portrayed in *Sefer Hasidim*, persisted here and there, as we
have seen. *Sefer Hasidim* was printed and quoted robustly dozens of times,
so much so that the impact of the book could be the subject of a separate
study.[63]

Far from being a radical rewriting of *Sefer Hasidim*, *Sefer ha-Hasidut* was
so similar to the rest of German Hasidism that scholars as well as readers of

the printed editions could not tell them apart. In 1976, one scholar did not distinguish between SHB 1–152 and the rest of SHB or SHP and referred to the first twenty paragraphs of SHB—that is, *Sefer ha-Hasidut*—as "something that is akin to a presentation of the principles of the movement [1–20]."[64] How could one expect earlier readers to have thought otherwise?

The German Ashkenazic editions of *Sefer Hasidim*, especially the topical arrangements that we find in several long manuscripts and three times in SHB, go back to R. Judah *he-hasid* himself. Although the social context of his work has been debated over the years, a historical investigation of sources about his life offers a new way to settle the question about the historical setting of the German pietists.

Chapter 3

Judah *he-Hasid*'s Life and Legends

And I heard from the mouth of R. J[udah] *he-hasid* zz"l . . .
—R. Isaac b. Moses of Vienna

To understand the historical context of *Sefer Hasidim* and the other German pietist writers of open texts, we need to look more closely at Judah *he-hasid*. But how does one construct a biographical profile of a Jewish religious figure who insisted on writing everything anonymously? Fortunately for us, his son and students ignored his advice and often identified him as the source of different teachings that they learned directly from him. By looking carefully at these attributed teachings and comparing them to some of Judah's anonymously written stories in his *Sefer Hasidim,* we can glimpse Judah himself. We can try to understand what he considered important and above all how his life story took a dramatic turn when he mysteriously left his family home in the Rhineland town of Speyer and moved to the emerging eastern town on the Danube of Regensburg some two hundred miles away.

What we know about the life and times of R. Judah b. Samuel *he-hasid* comes from several different types of sources: students' reports of what they heard Judah teach them, the anonymously written *Sefer Hasidim* that is attributed to him, a case of the rabbinic court (*beit din*) in Regensburg included in *Sefer Hasidim,* and cycles of near contemporary Hebrew and later Yiddish hagiographical stories told and written about him.[1] Although previous studies have discussed some of these texts, we need to assess each type to see what it can and cannot tell us. Then we can view them together and see how they contribute to a biographical picture of his life and its memory.[2] The sources express differing perspectives, but as we fit together pieces of the mosaic a picture emerges of Judah *he-hasid* and his world.

Firsthand Student Traditions

A good place to start is with R. Isaac b. Moses of Vienna (d. 1250), a student of French and German legal scholars who was also one of Judah's students in Regensburg.[3] He gives us firsthand evidence about what Judah *he-hasid* taught him in person. Although we will soon take up other sources that are either geographically of uncertain origin or that are especially associated with him in either Speyer or Regensburg, it is important to start with this student's testimony because it contains credible evidence that Judah taught students orally. This suggests in turn that some of the stories that Judah wrote down in *Sefer Hasidim* about a *hakham* (sage) and his students may have started as Judah *he-hasid*'s own oral teachings to his students or at least were inspired by his own oral teaching culture.

Although in some *exempla* in *Sefer Hasidim* students play a relatively passive role, almost like a Greek chorus, observing and commenting on how the *hakham* solves a religious problem, in some of the stories about Samuel and Judah found in MS Jerusalem Oct. 3182 (the Ninety-nine stories) students play a more active role than their teachers, suggesting that students' memories about their teachers might account for some of these narratives.[4]

Sometimes we can almost overhear students and teacher exchanging ideas. In one such case, Isaac tells us: "My teacher R. Judah *hasid zz"l* used to say (*hayah omer*) . . . and other students asked him (*ve-sha'alu mimenu*) . . . and he answered (*ve-heishiv*)."[5]

Some of Judah's reported teachings involve signs of tension and discord in the synagogue, the setting for much of German pietist teaching.[6] For example, R. Isaac says: "The great *hasid* my teacher Rabbi Judah *he-hasid zz"l* said to me (*amar li*) that a cantor should be beloved by the (whole) congregation," implying that the opposite was often the case.[7] Other traditions focus on how a *hasid* was supposed to pray slowly and the social tensions that pietist praying might cause in a synagogue. Protracted praying was known as a characteristic of *hasidei ashkenaz*. The first reference we have to the term "hasidei ashkenaz" is from R. Jacob b. Asher's *Arba'ah Turim* that refers to their peculiarly lengthy praying customs. This is reported in the name of Jacob's brother, R. Yehiel b. Asher, who seems to have detailed familiarity with the praying practices of *hasidei ashkenaz*.[8]

We have two versions of three stories, from R. Isaac b. Moses: one set from his *Sefer Or Zarua'* and another, with some variants, from his marginal gloss in the Parma manuscript of *Sefer Hasidim*, par. 427. In *Sefer Or Zarua'*, the text says: "And I heard from the mouth of R. J[udah] he-*hasid* zz"l: 'There once was a great rabbi whom many respected who would get angry in the synagogue when people recited the (morning) blessings at great length. He wanted to pray quickly and get back to his studies, and he was punished in the other world because of this.'"[9]

In *hasidei ashkenaz* sources, the synagogue is often the central institution in traditions about Judah *he-hasid*, not the academy, though *Sefer Hasidim* pictures the model of pietism, the *hakham*, frequently engaged in teaching students. We do not know who the "great rabbi" (*rav gadol u-muvhaq*) was. It is framed anonymously, like the hundreds of *ma'asim* (exemplary stories) in *Sefer Hasidim*. R. Isaac's firsthand report suggests, though, that at least some of the stories in *Sefer Hasidim* might have started as Judah's teachings to one or more of his students, and this raises doubts that the stories were meant, as we tend to assume, for a popular audience. R. Isaac became one of the most learned and distinguished legal authorities of thirteenth-century Austria.

R. Isaac adds a second report of a lesson that he learned from Judah indirectly: "And I also heard (*ve-gam shama'ti*) in the name of our master Judah *hasid* zz"l who said: 'For example, in the winter when it is very cold one should go to the house of those who are not warmly dressed and not shorten praise of the Holy One, blessed be He, because of them.'" Who are "them"? Presumably people who rush the *hasidim* out of the synagogue.

R. Isaac b. Moses then relates a third and much longer story that he
claims in the version in the SHP gloss that he heard directly from Judah
he-hasid, but he reports it in the third person: "And our master Judah *hasid*
said that he knew a certain Jew from Worms. . . ."[10] In *Sefer Or Zarua*, R.
Isaac quotes Judah telling the story himself, in the first person: "And I knew
a Jew from Worms whom they called R. Bunim. He was an old man who
buried the dead."

At this point in both versions of the third story, R. Isaac adds a phrase
that insists that what follows is entirely true: "and I heard this for certain"
(*ve-shamaʿti el nakhon ve-el ha-emet*). The story then continues:

> Once he got to the synagogue early and saw a man sitting in front
> of the synagogue wearing a wreath of herbs called "zipfel," and in
> Polish "kvitni vitzitz," and he was afraid that the figure was a
> demon (*sheid*).[11] He called to him and said, "Are you not So and
> So who died recently and whom I just buried?" "Yes," he said. And
> he asked him, "How are you doing in the other world?" And he
> replied, "Actually, I am very well off." And he asked him, "On
> account of what merit? You were rather ordinary." And he replied,
> "On account of one merit: I used to recite the blessings in the
> synagogue with a pleasant voice. That merit alone brought me to
> Paradise (*gan ʿeiden*) and they honor me (there")."

The story concludes with the spirit (*sheid*) offering proof that he is indeed
the one R. Bunim had recently buried: "'Here is a sign that it is I who is
speaking to you: just look at the sleeve on my torn cloak; you tore it when
you put me into the shroud.' And he asked him, 'What is that on your head?'
and he replied, 'They are herbs of Paradise (*gan ʿeiden*) that I placed on my
head to remove the stench from the (lower) world (from which I reek).'"

Following these three tales, R. Isaac b. Moses adds some words of his
own: "I, the author, wrote down these *maʿasim* so that someone who fears
Heaven will to be mindful of them and recite the praises of the Holy One,
blessed be He, with a pleasant voice and with sincere intention (*be-qol naʿim
u-ve-khavanah*) and merit Paradise."

So far, R. Isaac as a pietist seems to be recommending the praying style of *hasidei ashkenaz* who were known for their drawn-out recitation of the early morning daily blessings, even though he does not refer to their habit of counting letters or use the term for slowly praying *be-meshekh* (in a drawn-out manner). Then R. Isaac, in his role as a legal expert or halakhist, continues:

But on Sabbaths and festivals you must pray in such a way that people can leave the synagogue by the fifth hour and begin to eat during the fifth hour because it is forbidden to fast on the Sabbath up to the sixth hour, as is stated in [Talmud] Yerushalmi, Chapter "Seder Ta'aniyot ha-Eilu" [Ta'anit 3:13, 67a] and in [Talmud] Yerushalmi, Chapter "Qonam Yayin" [Nedarim 8:1, 40d]: R. Aha, R. Abahu in the name of R. Yosa ben Hanina (taught): It is forbidden to fast up to the sixth hour on the Sabbath.

There are other indications of tension in the synagogues where lengthy *hasid* praying irritated people and came close to violating Jewish law or even crossed the line. Thus, in *Sefer Tashbez* that R. Samson b. Zadoq compiled in the fourteenth century, we learn about Judah *he-hasid*'s contemporary, R. Baruch b. Samuel of Mainz (d. 1221):

In a book that our master Barukh of Mainz wrote, he sent to our master Judah *hasid* and asked how he conducted himself on Pesah, Shavuot, and on (the Sabbath morning following) weddings, when the reading of the Shema can be delayed beyond the third hour (of the morning) and thereby violate the rule that (the Shema) must be recited by then. The (correct) time to recite it had passed. How did he become exempt from saying it on time?

Rabbi Judah *he-hasid* replied to him that (one can avoid the problem of reciting the Shema too late) by concentrating on the Shema when he says it during the morning blessings.[12]

Sefer Tashbez reports a second tradition attributed to Judah as his way to resolve the problem of not reciting the Shema beyond its proper time of day:
"A tradition from Rabbeinu Judah *hasid zz"l*: When someone leaves his house
in the morning to go (to the synagogue) to pray, he should (immediately)
recite the verse: "Hear O Israel, the Lord our God, the Lord is one" (Deut.
6:4), that is, the first line of the Shema.[13]

These reports indicate that some halakhic authorities were upset about
German pietists praying too slowly and as a result delaying the recitation of
the morning Shema or fasting too long on certain festivals or on a Sabbath
celebrating a recent wedding when extra liturgical poems (*piyyutim*) are recited. Powerful Jews who did not follow *hasid* prayer practices were also un-
happy being slowed down by pietist practices when they prayed in the same
synagogue as the *hasidim*.

From Judah's replies to this criticism, it is clear that he was as concerned
about following the halakhic norms as in following his pietist prayer practices. He offered different remedies to fulfill his obligation to recite the morning Shema on time. According to these sources, *hasidut* could be seen as an
added religious practice that can be potentially transgressive unless remedies are adopted. This combination challenges the usual assumption that
German *hasidut* is either ultra-pious or anti-halakhic. In these sources it can
be both.[14]

The stories R. Isaac b. Moses tells us that Judah taught can be compared to an anonymous story in *Sefer Hasidim*. It is not necessary to com-
press the two sources into one "event," but it is important to see how similar
assumptions underlie both stories. This suggests that Judah may have taught
at least some of the stories in *Sefer Hasidim* to his students before he wrote
them down:

> In a town there were two synagogues. When a sage would come
> to town sometimes he would go to one synagogue and at other
> times he would go to the other. Eventually he prayed only in the
> small one.
>
> People asked him, "Why did you stop going to the big one? It
> has many important people in it (*rabbim ve-nikhbadim bah*)." He

said to them, "In the big synagogue, they rush through the blessings and Psalms (*razim ha-berakhot ve-ha-tehillot*) and frequently prevent the prayers from being said at the right time. That does not happen in the small synagogue. There they say the blessings and prayers of praise slowly (*be-meshekh*), and I earn reward for the sake of the Holy One. When I say the prayers slowly (*moshekh*), I count on my fingers how many *alef*'s [A's], how many *bet*'s [B's], how many of each and every letter there are in that particular Psalm. Afterwards, when I go home, I supply reasons why it is so."[15]

The story starts out assuming that a *hasid* might pray in the large synagogue, and be counted among the many prominent members of the community (*rabbim ve-nikhbadim bah*). To avoid conflict, he should go to a smaller synagogue, perhaps in the house of someone who is housebound because he did not have warm clothing, mentioned in one of Judah's stories that R. Isaac b. Moses reported. It does not follow that there actually were two synagogues in any town where *hasidim* or Judah lived. The story in *Sefer Hasidim* is about "a town" (*be-'ir ahat*) that has two synagogues, not necessarily a real town like Speyer or Regensburg, and the detail might be just a rhetorical device for making a point. It is more realistic to imagine, as in Judah's story told to R. Isaac b. Moses, that a disgruntled *hasid* leaves the synagogue and goes to someone's house to pray.

The urban setting of the stories R. Isaac b. Moses or other contemporaries report or of those in *Sefer Hasidim* is usually not specified, and it is hard to know if they are from Speyer or Regensburg. Regardless of their provenance, the sources that are not in *Sefer Hasidim* sometimes are similar to the anonymously written *exempla* included in that book. The point is not to reduce one to the other but to see how by comparing them we see new contexts that otherwise would not be visible.

Among Judah's other teachings that have been preserved outside of *Sefer Hasidim* and that have no geographical setting that can be identified are some that are much more demanding than praying slowly in the synagogue. For example, R. Isaac b. Joseph of Corbeil's (d. 1280) popular code

Sefer Mizvot Qatan reports that Judah insisted that students who go to a wedding and are in danger of being attacked on the road may not use divine Names to protect themselves, even if it puts their lives at risk:

> Rabbi Judah *he-hasid* once warned his students not to go to a wedding because of the danger of robbers along the way. The students went anyway and relied on their ability to (magically) invoke the (divine) Name (to protect themselves). They used it and saved themselves. When they returned, he told them, "You have lost (your place in) the world to come unless you go back to that road without invoking the (divine) Name and expose yourselves to being killed." They went back and were all killed.[16]

That can be compared to the following passage in *Sefer Hasidim:*

> A person who embarks on a journey should not say, "I will adjure (the names of) angels to protect me" but should instead pray to the Holy One, blessed be He. Several prophets were killed but they did not adjure the Holy Name. Rather, they stood in prayer saying, "If He does not hear our prayers, we are not worthy of being saved." They relied only on prayer.[17]

The sources agree that using divine Names is forbidden. However, the story in *Sefer Mizvot Qatan* is focused more on atoning for the sin of doing it the first time and not on advocating prayer instead to keep one safe, as in the *Sefer Hasidim* account. They agree that avoiding the use of divine Names, is more important than risking death.

Another sign that pietist values were more important than life is seen in a responsum attributed to Judah *he-hasid* in which he approves death by suicide as atonement for other severe sins:

> Question: Should someone kill himself over his sins or is he violating the verse, "[But for your own life-blood] I will require a reckoning" (Genesis 9:5)?[18]

Answer: It is appropriate for someone to kill himself because of
his sins for we find that when R. Eliezer b. Dordaya killed himself
a divine voice said: You are blessed . . . [Babylonian Talmud
Avodah Zarah 17a] and also in *Midrash Bereishit Rabbah* (sec. 65:18)
the nephew of R. Yossi b. Yo'ezer (Yaqim Ish Zerurot) killed
himself using several means simultaneously and it was deemed a
religious act.[19]

A principled disregard for human life at the expense of pietist values is
also reflected in a passage preserved in one of the short manuscripts of *Sefer
Hasidim*, not included in the longest redactions of SHP and former JTS
Boesky or SHB. It certainly sounds like *Sefer Hasidim*:

If someone whose son who is slow and lacks intelligence prays for
mercy that (the son) live or (if he prays) that a wicked man who
makes others sin or does evil should live, people should not
answer (*lo ya'anu*) "amen" because it is better that he die than
live.[20]

Although it is not possible to know if this refers to anyone related to
Judah *he-hasid*, there is reason to think that Judah's own son, Moses Zaltman, was incapable of understanding his father's esoteric traditions and that
is why his father taught him only biblical interpretations that he thought
that his son could handle. Even then, he could misunderstand his father's
meaning.[21] Altogether, then, a number of independent sources attributed to
or about Judah *he-hasid* shed light on him as a source of pietist teachings
consistent with passages written anonymously in *Sefer Hasidim*.

Regensburg Traditions about Judah *he-Hasid*

But there is much more. Although the independent sources, as well as almost all the paragraphs in *Sefer Hasidim,* cannot be linked to either Speyer
or Regensburg, other sources can be correlated to one or the other town.

When we pay attention to these, a pattern emerges of R. Judah *he-hasid* as especially identified with Regensburg, and this increases the probability that many if not most of the anonymously framed stories in *Sefer Hasidim* were written there. Moreover, some local traditions emphasize that although R. Judah *he-hasid* began his career in Speyer, he was forced to leave his home and migrate to Regensburg under mysterious circumstances.

One Regensburg tradition remembers that Judah was one of the founders of the synagogue there, "the house of our glory, the Holy of Holies, that was founded in holiness and purity by the great rabbi, the hasid, R. Judah, with other righteous ones, may he rest in paradise."[22]

In addition, *Sefer Hasidim* preserves a question that an agitated but otherwise unknown Ephraim b. Meir posed to the Regensburg rabbinic court (*gedolei regensburg*) made up of R. Barukh b. Isaac, R. Abraham b. Moses, and "*he-hasid*, the rabbi, R. Judah (*he-hasid, ha-rav, r. yehudah*)."[23] The case involves twelve powerful and wealthy Jews in Regensburg who want to monopolize the synagogue honor of rolling up the Torah scroll in the synagogue on the Sabbath after it has been read. They want to take away the honor from other Jews, like Ephraim, who contributed less to the poor fund than what the twelve Jews propose to give. Ephraim b. Meir notes that they do not deserve the honor since "some of them do not know even a single verse of Torah." R. Judah *he-hasid* and the others answer that these wealthy Jews should be allowed to do it in order to increase the support of the poor even if they do so by unscrupulous means. Otherwise, the poor would suffer. The issue here is both *halakhah* (Jewish law) and *hasidut* (pietism), and his answer is based on talmudic principles and on *hasidut*.[24]

The presence of Judah *he-hasid* sitting on a court with rabbis who are not *hasidim* seems to contradict the apparently isolationist teachings of German pietism in *Sefer Hasidim*. If he sat on a court, how could Judah describe pietists in *Sefer Hasidim* as being rewarded for suffering abuse from communal officials? But we should remember that the sectarian vision described in some *Sefer Hasidim* manuscripts and in most of SHB does not advocate a withdrawn monastic-community within or near the rest of the Jewish community. It teaches that individual pietists who lack influence should avoid associating with other Jews or with Christians so that their pietism is not compromised. In the present source, Judah is part of the local *beit din* and enjoys influence and authority. The outcome of the case shows that he and two other rabbis agreed, based on shared legal assumptions as well on Judah's pietist values.[25]

The social dynamic in *Sefer Hasidim* presupposes a fluid situation of some pietists having power some of the time and others lacking it. The Regensburg court case is an example of Judah *he-hasid* having some power. For this reason, we do not have any basis for seeing a conflict here between Judah's being part of the local court and his views about pietism expressed through the *exempla* that are found in some *Sefer Hasidim* manuscripts.[26]

Other sources also connect Judah to Regensburg and other new Jewish communities in Eastern Europe. R. Isaac b. Moses' *Sefer Or Zarua'* preserves a letter sent by R. Eliezer b. Isaac of Bohemia or Prague objecting to R. Judah *he-hasid*'s letter to communities in the East that they should not pay *hazzanim* (synagogue cantors) from community charity funds collected on holidays since being a *hazzan* is a matter of holiness. In reply, R. Eliezer b. Isaac rebukes Judah by telling him that he will end up preventing the Jews of the new communities in the East from having synagogues.[27]

Several passages in *Sefer Hasidim* refer back to a great persecution, meaning the anti-Jewish riots of 1096, and are especially focused on the mass conversion of some Jews then, a situation that corresponds to the mass conversion in the Danube of the Jews of Regensburg.[28]

R. Judah *he-hasid* is also directly connected to the travel account (*sibbuv*) of R. Petahiah of Regensburg. One version claims that Judah copied out the text and that Judah *he-hasid* wanted to reveal the date that the Messiah would arrive but was prevented from doing so.[29] This motif also appears in a deathbed story about Judah in the story cycles in Hebrew and Yiddish.[30]

We also have comments by Judah *he-hasid*'s son, R. Moses Zaltman, and his student, R. Eleazar b. Judah of Worms, about Judah's sudden illness and death in 1217. In a comment on Genesis 12:2, Judah mentions his father's premonition about dying that year:

"And you shall be a blessing" (Gen. 12:2):

On that Saturday night in 1217, 3 Adar, my father was writing on
Psalms, on the one that begins, "A prayer of Moses, the man of
God" (*Tefillah le-moshe ish ha-elohim*) (Ps. 90), and he focused on the
verse, "For in Your sight a thousand years are like yesterday that has
passed, like a watch of the night" (*ba-lailah*) (Ps. 90:4). A sign (that
he was about to die) is that *ba-lailah* is numerically 77 in the abbrevi-
ated notation for the year 1217 [(4)240 + (9)77 = 1217], (the year) when
he died [lit., went to his eternal home]. Shortly thereafter, just
before daybreak, he wrote down two pages of *Sefer Hasidim*.[31]

Elsewhere in the Bible commentary, R. Moses Zaltman tells us about his
father's rapid decline a week later:

[On 9 Adar] in 1217, when Parshat Zakhor ["Remember," the
Sabbath before Purim] occurred (the week of the Torah reading)
that begins "Ve-atah tezaveh" ["And you shall further instruct"]
(Ex. 27:20–30:10), my father became ill from the disease from
which he was to succumb, and I asked him on the Sabbath about
the haftarah.[32]

In a continuation of the comment on Genesis 12:2, R. Moses Zaltman
describes his father's last day:

And (subsequently) he also wrote as follows . . . "One should
intend and act so that others benefit from his actions, as is written,
'And you shall be a blessing'" (Gen. 12:2). He completed it with the
word "blessing" and went to the synagogue. After they said the
Qedushah (prayer), he left, lay down, and passed away on 13 Adar.[33]

Independently, R. Eleazar of Worms recorded: "Now, on the 13 of Adar 1217
we lost the righteous man, pillar of the universe."[34]

Aside from giving us solid testimony that Judah *he-hasid* wrote *Sefer Hasidim*, despite Judah's own insistence on authorial anonymity, the son's report also means that Judah wrote at least parts of *Sefer Hasidim* in Regensburg. The son not knowing about or consciously ignoring his father's wish for anonymity is all the more poignant in light of Judah's reason for anonymity. He states that anonymity prevents a writer's children from boasting about their fathers' accomplishments, something that would diminish their reward in the next world.[35] His student, R. Eleazar of Worms, also did not follow his teacher's admonition to write anonymously, as Eleazar put his name on everything he wrote.

A Hebrew and Yiddish hagiographical story about Judah's burial, both associated with Regensburg topography, can be compared to an unusual story from *Sefer Hasidim*. Although most of the stories in that book refer to anonymous pietists and sages, there are a few about named pietists. For example, we read about a "Rabbeinu Mordecai" who assaulted another Jew and then broke his own arm as penance.[36] There also is a story about R. Isaac *he-hasid* that is echoed in two versions of a similar story about R. Judah *he-hasid* himself, one in the Hebrew MS of the Ninety-nine stories and another in the Yiddish *Mayseh Bukh*. The Hebrew version in the Jerusalem manuscript of the Ninety-nine stories, no. 94, runs as follows:

> An incident took place in the days of Rabbi Judah *hasid*. When they would take the dead to the cemetery, they carried them out through a town gate, and over that gate was hung a bell. Each time they went to the cemetery, the gatekeeper would ring the bell. When Rabbi Judah *hasid* came down with the illness from which he was to die, he said: "If I am worthy of going to the World to Come, know that this gate will collapse." And when they carried Rabbi Judah *hasid* to the cemetery and the gatekeeper ran to ring the bell, the gate and the bell collapsed on the Christian (*ha-goy*) who died.
>
> And all the Christians (*goyim*) said, "Now we know that he was truly a holy man during his lifetime and in his death."

And they said, "Blessed is the one who chose the words of the Sages: 'The righteous are greater in their death than during their lifetime [B. Hullin 7b].'"[37]

This story plays off R. Judah and the Christian gatekeeper, but it leaves open the question of how he was ever able to get to the cemetery and be buried. It also does not tell us where it took place. From the *Mayseh Bukh* told in the first person, we get a pietist teaching and story about Judah that illustrates his location, though it leaves open how his body got to the cemetery.

"I will give you a sign whereby you will know that I shall have a share in the world to come. The sign is this. When you carry my body to the gate over which that wicked man is living, he will begin to toll the bell as usual. Directly the gate will fall down and you will not be able to carry me out that way. When that happens you will know that I shall enter paradise."

When the pious man died and they proceeded to carry the body through the gate, the wicked porter became aware of it and began tolling the bell. Immediately the gate fell in, killing the gatekeeper, and they could not carry the body through.

If you do not believe this story go to Regensburg and you will see for yourself, and will hear why the gate cannot be rebuilt. It has been rebuilt many times, but no sooner was it erected than it fell down again and would not stand.[38]

This story adds a local Regensburg legend about the town gate that does not stay built and makes it likely that the earlier Hebrew version also takes place in Regensburg. However, neither version solves the problem of how Judah was buried in the cemetery if the gate was blocked. In *Sefer Hasidim,* we have the following story about a named pietist, R. Isaac. It provides the missing part of the story about Judah and suggests that those stories are expansions of the independent story about R. Isaac in *Sefer Hasidim.*

It once happened that a Sage whose name was Rabbi Isaac *hasid*
would avoid going into a house of idolatry [i.e., a church]. When
he died, he was being taken out to go to the cemetery. There was
idolatry over the town gate, and despite the driver's efforts, the
horses ran away, and took the hearse out (of the town) *through a*
break in the town wall that had collapsed a short time before his death.
There were trenches around the city, but he went through them,
and they continued in a straight path (to the cemetery). It was
because he had been scrupulous while alive not to enter a place
of idolatry that the Holy One, blessed be He, brought about
the miracle of the wall falling in prior to his death so that after he
died the horses could bring him (to the cemetery) through the
break in the wall.[39]

What is missing in the Hebrew and Yiddish stories about Judah *he-hasid*
is supplied here about R. Isaac: a break in the town wall occurred earlier on
account of his piety of not going into a church. This story is different from
either version about Judah, but there are points in common that make them
related. All three claim that there is something symbolizing Christianity over
the town gate: a bell or a hostile Christian or idolatry. Comparison strength-
ens the probability that the story in *Sefer Hasidim* takes place in Regensburg. But the story about R. Isaac, that there was a breach in the wall that
enabled his body to get to the cemetery when the gate collapsed, is presup-
posed but unstated in the two stories about Judah. Otherwise how did Judah's
hearse get to the cemetery when the gate was blocked?

The unusual situation of a named *hasid* in *Sefer Hasidim* raises some possibilities about the relationship between this story in *Sefer Hasidim* and the
cycle of hagiographical stories about Judah. We do not know anything about
this Isaac other than this story in which he is the protagonist. It suggests
that we should not jump to the conclusion that the anonymously framed
stories in *Sefer Hasidim* are about Judah; some might be about other real per-
sons. But in this case, it also opens up the possibility that Judah's great
fame and religious reputation moved his followers to appropriate elements

of a specific story that originated with someone else and used them to praise him.[40]

The Speyer Traditions about Judah *he-hasid*

Since most of our hagiographical and other sources place Judah in Regensburg, it is of special significance that one tradition places him in Speyer and another explains why he left Speyer for Regensburg. In Speyer, Judah criticizes a rich Jew who insists on shaving his beard despite the *hasid*'s admonition that he not do this. This story does not appear in the Jerusalem manuscript of the Ninety-nine stories but in a different Hebrew source and also as a story added on at the end of the Yiddish story cycle of Regensburg traditions about Judah in the *Mayseh Bukh*. The local setting and provenance of a text is an important clue as to its historical significance.[41]

In the fourteenth-century German Ashkenazic *Sefer ha-Gan*, R. Isaac b. Eliezer introduces the story attributed to Judah *he-hasid*'s son, "Zaltman":

> When I studied in Speyer with Rabbi Yedidya, z"l, I found in his house of study (a manuscript) written in the hand of R. Zaltman (son of Judah *he-hasid*) and this is it: "My father, my teacher, *he-hasid*, said to me that it once happened during his lifetime that a rich man in Speyer used to cut off his beard with scissors (*misperayim*) and my father, my teacher, protested to him, but the man ignored him. The rich man said, 'I am a fastidious person (*istenes*), and I cannot stand having a beard.' My father, my teacher, said to him, 'Know that your end will be bitter. After you die, spirits that look like cows are trampling [read: *dorsim*] the edge of your beard. . . . Know that this is so because [in the verse], "You shall not round off the side-growth (*Pe'at*) on your head (*Rosheikhem*), or (*Ve-lo*) destroy (*Tashhitu*) (the side-growth of your beard) (Lev. 19:27)," the first letters spell **Pa-R-O-T** (cows).'
>
> "When the rich man died, all the important people in Speyer sat (watching over the body) at his home, and my father, my

teacher, was there. And he wrote out a (divine) Name, and threw it on the dead rich man who then stood up. All (the important people) sitting there bolted out of the house.

"The rich man started to pull out his hair. My father, my teacher, said to him, 'What is wrong with you?' He said to him, 'Oy, I should have listened to you.' My father, my teacher, said to him, 'Tell me what has happened to your soul?' He said to him: 'When my soul left me, a spirit resembling a large cow appeared and brought a large pail full of tar, sulfur, and salt and took my soul and it was not able to escape from there. The (divine) Attribute of Justice took the pail with my soul from that spirit and brought it before the Creator of Souls. A heavenly voice said to me, "Did you study Torah? Mishnah?" I replied, "I have." Immediately he commanded that a Pentateuch be produced and he said [to me,] "Read in it." I opened the book and I immediately found written the verse, "Do not destroy the side-growth of your beard" (*ve-lo tashkhit et pe'at zeqankha*) (Lev. 19:27), and I did not know what to reply. I then heard a voice decreeing, "Place this person's soul on the lowest step." Just as they were bringing (my) soul to the lowest step, a heavenly voice said, "Wait a moment. Judah [*he-hasid*?] my son is more righteous than this one, and now, (Judah), ask for mercy that [his] soul should not go down to Sheol.'" Until here.[42]

This report, like R. Moses Zaltman's written account of his father's Humash teachings, or those of R. Judah's student, R. Isaac b. Moses in his *Sefer Or Zarua'*, also claims to be based on direct oral testimony. Unlike most of the other firsthand reports that take place in Regensburg, this one is located in Speyer, a rarity for stories about Judah.

According to the Hebrew account in *Sefer ha-Gan*, when the rich man dies the prominent people of Speyer gather in the man's house and Judah *he-hasid* is counted among them. As a descendant of the founding Qalonimos family of Mainz from Italy, it is not surprising that Judah would be among the elite of Speyer. This theme echoes the source cited earlier about a *hasid* praying in the same large synagogue with other prominent men in town: "They said to him, 'Why did you stop going to the big one? It has many important people in it (*rabbim ve-nikhbadim bah*).'"[43]

A different version of this Speyer encounter is found in the Yiddish *Mayseh Bukh* (Basle, 1602), the only story there about Judah *he-hasid* that is situated in Speyer and not in Regensburg. In the Yiddish *Mayseh Bukh* version, the prominent men gather, and Judah then arrives to perform a magical act. In *Sefer ha-Gan*, Judah is both prominent and a sharp critic of his peers. Over time, the two figures become more antagonistic, Judah versus the prominent men of Speyer.

The theme of a rich and powerful Jew close to Christian power in medieval Ashkenaz needs to be explored more.[44] For some context about important court Jews and grooming, consider a passage in the thirteenth-century compilation *Sefer ha-Asufot*. We see a report that R. Eliezer b. Joel ha-Levi, known by the acronym Raviah (d. ca. 1235), permitted courtiers (*hittir li-venei hatzer*) to shave their beards after sitting shiva because "they cannot go to the court of the King unkempt."[45]

R. Simcha of Speyer tells us that his uncle, R. Qalonimos b. Meir of Speyer, was close to royal power and was among the retinue of the Emperor Frederick I Barbarosa (d. 1190) (*qarov la-malkhut hayah mi-benei pelatin shel ha-melekh*).[46] There also is a story in the Ninety-nine stories about a Rabbeinu Qalonimos the Younger who was an important courtier (*hazran me'od*), perhaps a reflection of R. Qalonimos b. Meir of Speyer.[47] Effective family influence with the Emperor may explain why R. Eleazar of Worms was eager to record in his prayer commentary different anti-Jewish accusations that sometimes did not result in violence because Jews could intervene with the authorities and not just pray for relief. In one such incident, Christians accused Jews of killing a Christian woman found in a well where the Jews lived. It did not lead to violence because "God disposed the ruler to be merciful."[48]

Although we know about Jewish courtiers in Ashkenaz, we do not know if pietist Jews or others used their influence at the Christian court to get their way in the synagogue. For example, a protagonist in one story in *Sefer Hasidim* says: "I have access to the king and princes and you had better listen to what I am telling you." It is rhetoric but it may be more than rhetoric.

The passage concludes: "The Holy One, blessed be He, did not want to prolong (his life) because he used to terrorize the God-fearing. To enrage them he rushed through (morning) prayers of praise in the synagogue and prevented the righteous from (observing) the commandments, chased out of the synagogue whom he pleased, gave aid and comfort to sinners but turned his back on those who fear the Lord."[49]

Perhaps the sources, in and outside of *Sefer Hasidim*, are suggesting that there was a rivalry between Jews who were not *hasidim* and *hasidim* for access to Christian power to support their different agendas. A passage in *Sefer Hasidim* points in that direction:

> A story about a pietist who asked the King that every Jew who took an oath in the Name of God should have to pay twelve pence. His intention was to prevent Jews from taking false oaths. For in the same land people would swear falsely without making a monetary claim (that justifies taking a certain kind of oath).
>
> He asked and the King gave him authority so that any Jew who swore truthfully without a connection to a monetary claim or falsely should be fined a *dinar* to prevent them from swearing in vain.
>
> People of the land bribed the King to send the pietist into exile. The local (Jews) put him under the ban until he went away. He took his relatives and friends and emigrated to another land. All of those who put him under the ban as well as their children were punished: some were killed, some were burned alive just because he intended to do the right thing.[50]

We have hints that a *hasid* may have to leave the scene of a conflict when critics ignores him, even though *Sefer Hasidim* generally recommends that a *hasid* experience abuse as an opportunity to earn reward by not minding. There is difference between a *hasid* who is abused for his different practices and thereby earns rewards and a *hakham* who tries to improve a "wicked" or non-pietist community (*resha'im*) and is ignored and resisted: "If he protested the wicked's behavior and it does no good, if he can, he should go away (*yitraheq*) and separate from the wicked, as it says, "Turn away from it. Pass it by" (Proverbs 4:15).[51]

How far? To another synagogue, if there is one, or to a private house? Or should he leave town? It is not clear. The theme of the *hasid* withdrawing from places where he is not able to practice freely or where other Jews ignore or abuse him is commonplace in *Sefer Hasidim* and echoes in the other sources as well.

From Speyer to Regensburg

Judah did not stay in Speyer but at some point migrated to Regensburg, where he helped found the synagogue, taught students, sat on the *beit din*, taught his son a Humash commentary, and continued to write *Sefer Hasidim* and other works until he died there in 1217.

The story of Judah's move to Regensburg is not found in the Hebrew hagiographical cycles about him in the Ninety-nine stories in Jerusalem MS 3182 or in Yiddish in the *Mayseh Bukh* among collections that preserve local Regensburg Jewish collective memory. Rather, it is preserved in the genealogical lists about the rabbis of early Ashkenaz as recorded in the Rhineland traditions written down by the sixteenth-century Polish rabbinic authority R. Solomon b. Yechiel Luria, known by the acronym MaHarRShaL (Moreinu ha-Rav Rabbeinu Shlomo Luria; d. 1574). One of his *Responsa* (Lublin, 1574), no. 29, includes genealogical traditions about Ashkenazic rabbinical families that he says are based on written records. One of these traditions is an attempt to explain why Judah *he-hasid* left Speyer:

> I also found . . . Rabbeinu Qalonimos the Elder (*ha-zaqen*) who fathered Rabbeinu Shmuel hasid, qadosh, ve-navi, who fathered Rabbeinu Avraham of Speyer and Rabbeinu Yehudah he-hasid from Speyer, who [i.e., Judah and his family] were exiled (*hoglu*) from the land of their birth to the city of Regensburg because of the incident that his (Judah's) wife touched his (Judah's) book chest (*teivato*) about which he (Judah) had warned her, "Do not

come near the book chest when you are not ritually clean." But she forgot all about it and touched it and there were holy secrets written down in book gatherings (*quntresim*) in that book chest.[52]

What are we to make of this Rhineland story? There is no evidence that those who left Speyer for Regensburg was Samuel or his older son Abraham, both of whom are associated only with Speyer, but only Judah and his family left. Regardless of the reason offered for Judah's exile, namely, his wife's action, the existence of the story itself suggests a problem: Judah's leaving Speyer bothered people there. Regensburg Jews kept alive many traditions about Judah, but they would not likely remember that their famous resident got there because he or his wife had sinned and was exiled to their town as a punishment.[53]

Scholars have been divided over this story's historical meaning or even if it has any. Most have dismissed it or explained it away, such as: "It is doubtful whether anyone less than a certified aristocrat could have risked propounding in Ashkenaz the strange and novel demands of the *rezon ha-Bore* and not be run out of town, not to speak of his winning a hearing."[54] But the two stories about Judah in Speyer suggest exactly that: being ignored (the rich Jew in Speyer) and being run out of town (*Responsum* 29).[55]

Unlike Samuel, who is pictured in traditions as one who moves around, Judah advocated not moving from where one lives.[56] One responsum attributed to Judah forbade Jews making pilgrimage to the Land of Israel on the grounds that they will not observe religious obligations while on the road.[57] The three hundred rabbis who migrated to Palestine in 1211 were all French, not German, a sign of Judah's influence beyond his narrow circle of pietists in Germany.[58]

Why, then, does he leave the Qalonimos homeland for Regensburg? Precisely because Judah made it known that one should not travel but stay at home, the fact that he migrated to Regensburg needed an explanation. The Speyer story about Judah and the rich Jew who did not listen to him about shaving depicts Judah as a failure to influence a local influential Jew. A critic of Jewish courtiers' religious compromises or of the rich who interact with the Christian power structure, Judah seems to have had to leave Speyer, driven out. Constant emphasis on resisting those who shame you suggests he knew what he was talking about: he suffered ridicule and eventually was pushed out of town to Regensburg and someone blamed his wife. An earlier story from Italy, from where the Qalonimide family traced their family origins, has a different but related tale about a Jewish woman who is ritually impure, but the differences in the stories are significant. In the *Chronicle of Ahima'az* we read:

> And it happened one day on the eve of the Sabbath, . . . the one
> who had to light the candle was not there, to light [it] before the
> *Book of the Chariot.* A woman stood there, and she, the cursed
> woman, was menstruating—may she be removed from the book
> of life, and may she be wiped out from the world to come—she lit
> the candle before the Torah, and the wrath of God was upon the
> family, and many died in that plague, only few survived out of the
> many they were. And there was there an understanding Jew, who
> realized and understood the event that had happened. He took the
> book and placed it in a vessel of lead, to sink it in the depths of
> the sea; . . . and the plague came to an end.[59]

The motif of a Jewish woman coming into contact with a sacred object while menstrually impure is common to both stories, but the striking difference is that in *Ahima'az* the consequences are the collective suffering of the whole family in a plague. In the Judah *he-hasid* story, he alone must leave Speyer, thereby somehow atoning for his wife's sinful action. The story is part of Judah *he-hasid*'s narrative, not the family or community, and it is derived from Rhineland, not Regensburg, traditions.

Compared to other Speyer stories that picture Judah's father, Samuel, wandering in penitential exile, Judah should have returned to Speyer after expiating his sin of not preventing his wife from touching his holy writings. But he never comes back. Being exiled to Regensburg was his punishment. Clearly this is not a Regensburg point of view. Speyer had nothing bad to say about Judah himself and placed the blame on his wife. Regardless of related story motifs elsewhere, the story of Judah's leaving Speyer needs to be taken seriously.[60]

R. Ephraim of Regensburg and Judah *he-hasid*

Judah's relationship to his two towns, Speyer and Regensburg, is suggested by the career of another rabbinic figure that could not get along in Speyer and ended up in Regensburg. R. Ephraim b. Isaac of Regensburg (d. after 1175) was a student of Jacob b. Meir (Rabbeinu Tam) (d. 1171). In Speyer, the former student argued with just about everyone, and local friction forced him to leave Speyer and move eventually to Regensburg.[61] Judah apparently did not make his move until 1195, and he served on the *beit din* there as had R. Ephraim earlier. Even so, several stories connect Judah to Ephraim, and they all show Judah as a pietist having an advantage over Ephraim the legal scholar and student of Jacob Tam, the great French Tosafist.

For example, in the Ninety-nine stories, Judah *he-hasid* overhears R. Ephraim making a mistake teaching his (Judah's) son, Moses Zaltman, a point of *halakhah*. Judah tells his son that he had overheard the lesson but tells him not to correct his teacher in front of the other students.[62]

This account reminds one of the talmudic story about émigré Babylonian Hillel who replaces the Benei Beteira in Jerusalem, and the story in Abraham Ibn Daud's *Sefer ha-Qabbalah* of the supersession in the *beit midrash* by Rabbi Moses b. Hanokh over the local rabbi in Cordoba.[63] It is a story about the "transfer of study" (*translatio studii*), from one Jewish authority to another, here from Ephraim the Tosafist halakhist to Judah the Pietist and halakhist. These competitive encounters resemble the legend that shows Samuel, Judah's father, to advantage over R. Jacob Tam himself and pietism as more important than French Tosafist erudition without *hasidut*.[64]

Judah's criticism about R. Ephraim also reflects a sense that R. Judah *he-hasid* not only bests R. Ephraim, Rabbeinu Tam's student, in *hasidut* but even in *halakhah*. This raises the ante compared to the Samuel *he-hasid*'s

encounter with Rabbeinu Tam where pietism comes out ahead of Jewish
law. It also argues that based on Judah's authority, Regensburg in the East is
religiously more important than the centers of northern France and the
Rhineland in the West.

R. Isaac b. Moses' *Sefer Or Zarua'* preserves a report critical of R.
Ephraim of Regensburg that R. Judah *he-hasid* tells, one not found in the
Hebrew hagiographical Ninety-nine stories in the Jerusalem manuscript
Oct. 3182 or in the *Mayseh Bukh*. R. Isaac claims:

> I heard about it for a certainty (*ve-khen shama'ti 'al ha-emet*) that
> Rabbeinu Ephraim bar Isaac *zz"l* of Regensburg once ruled that
> (the *balbuta* fish) was kosher. That night he dreamed that he was
> served a bowl filled with all kinds of unkosher creatures and he
> got angry with the one (serving him). The latter said, "Why are
> you angry with me? You are the one who ruled that it was kosher!"
> (R. Ephraim) also got angry at the angelic agent (*ba'al ha-halom*)
> who told this to him (in the dream). When he woke up, he
> remembered that he had ruled the *balbuta* permissible that day.
> He got out of bed and smashed all of the pots and dishes that
> they had used to eat (the *balbuta*).[65]

In the hagiography cycle in the *Mayseh Bukh* stories, too, R. Ephraim
gets into trouble with the head of the town of Regensburg, who leaves him
the key to his treasury in the ruler's absence. During the night, thieves break
into the treasury and steal many valuables. R. Ephraim runs to R. Judah
he-hasid to get help finding them, and Judah succeeds in enabling R. Ephraim
to discover where the thieves hid the loot and then R. Ephraim discloses it
to the ruler to his advantage.[66]

In these sources, Judah does not just serve where R. Ephraim once did
in the local *beit din* in Regensburg, but he also triumphs over him by cor-
recting his mistake when Ephraim teaches Judah's son, and helps Ephraim
with the Christian authorities when he gets into trouble for negligence. These
stories suggest that there was a competition in local memory between the

two Regensburg emigrés, and people valued Judah over Ephraim, the *hasid* and halakhist over the Tosafist rabbi.

They also show that local Regensburg memory identified Judah with Ephraim. Ephraim had to leave Speyer because he got into conflict with the local *beit din* there. The traditions that associate Judah with Ephraim imply that Judah, too, had to leave Speyer possibly for a similar reason. The story of Judah's wife and his mystical books is an attempt to explain or cover up how that happened.

In the Jerusalem manuscript of the Ninety-nine stories and again in the Yiddish *Mayseh Bukh* we find a story about a young and future Rabbi "Eliezer" [Eleazar of Worms], still in Mainz, who must choose between obeying his father and seeking out Judah *he-hasid* in Regensburg. Behind Eleazar's story is his father, R. Judah b. Qalonimos b. Moses of Mainz, who himself had been Judah's student, apparently in Speyer,[67] where he was also a student of another Speyer scholar, R. Shemarya b. Mordecai.[68]

Eleazar, in turn, studied in Mainz with his own father and in Speyer with R. Judah b. Qalonimos b. Meir of Speyer, author of *Sefer Tannaim ve-Amoraim*, son of the court banker. Given the intense family and study networks that connected Eleazar to Judah in their Rhineland homeland, the following story should be viewed as a challenge from Regensburg to the Rhineland as an important center of Jewish culture.

The story is about a R. Eliezer [Eleazar] and his father in Mainz.[69] It constructs a polarity between Eleazar's father, as a halakhist, and Judah *he-hasid* of Regensburg as the source of Eleazar's mystical learning.[70] This version of his mystical education conforms to the chain of tradition also found in *Responsum* 29 of R. Solomon Luria in which the story about Judah's migration to Regensburg is found.[71]

In our story, Eliezer disobeys his father, crosses the Danube, and visits his relative, Judah *he-hasid* in Regensburg. He eventually learns Judah's secret traditions and magically joins his father the same day in Mainz in time for the Passover Seder. As a gesture of peace, Judah gives Eliezer a special *mazzah* he has baked himself to bring to his relative, Eliezer's father in Mainz. This gift of a special *mazzah* baked by the teacher of mystical secrets has special significance in both versions of the Mainz-Regensburg story. It looks like a gesture of reconciliation but may also represent a claim to superior religiosity derived from Judah *he-hasid* since it seems to contain magical properties that enable Eliezer to get home the same day and not have to travel on the holiday. Punctiliousness about carefully baking Passover *maz- zah* is an index of religious zeal. The *mazzah* also symbolizes the greater religious value of Judah *he-hasid*'s mystical and magical abilities over the more traditional legal traditions of Mainz, the first town of Ashkenazic rab- binic activity. The story thus expresses both a generational conflict (Eliezer versus his father), a claim to religious superiority (Judah versus Eliezer's father), and also an East-West rivalry between Jewish centers (Regensburg versus Mainz).

The Yiddish version of the Mainz story departs significantly from the Hebrew one. The main difference is not about Judah's attitude toward Eliezer but of Eliezer to his father. According to the Yiddish version, when Eliezer's father commands his son not to cross the Danube, the writer understood the word *zivvah* to mean a deathbed request or will, after which the father died. The word *zava'ah*, meaning "command," had now taken on the more common meaning of a "will." As a result of this reinterpretation of the term, Eliezer does not ask to return to Mainz to celebrate Passover with his father but with his wife and children who have suddenly appeared. The story introduces a magical cloud to explain how Eliezer made the journey home in time, but the geographical tension between Mainz and Regensburg in this story reinforces other stories that contrast the older Rhineland cen- ters such as Speyer to Regensburg, the successive locations of Judah *he-hasid*'s career.[72]

The Regensburg stories and Judah traditions in Speyer, unlike *Sefer Hasidim*, enable us to map Judah's career based on the geographical locale of specific stories. In *Sefer Hasidim*, thousands of individual teachings are not arranged in a linear or chronological sequence and we cannot say that Judah first wrote some in Speyer and composed others later in Regensburg. They do not line up with the hagiographical stories since *Sefer Hasidim* is not a book in the conventional sense but a segmented collection of short passages that the author or others in his circle put together in different ways.

As in the case of seeking a best version of a paragraph that appears in different parallels, if one wants to see a biographical overtone in any single paragraph in *Sefer Hasidim* one must compare it to text parallels not in the book, if there are any. This is what I have done here. It is important not to reduce any of the independent Judah *he-hasid* sources to similar stories found in *Sefer Hasidim*, but to compare them.

These sources offer only different glimpses of R. Judah *he-hasid*, but there are enough to illuminate the trajectory of his life. We do not see Judah delivering sermons in public, as does R. Eleazar of Worms. Nor do we find him leading a large group of pietist followers. Instead, firsthand reports by well-known students, like R. Isaac b. Moses of Vienna, and Judah's son, R. Moses Zaltman, picture a man who teaches by telling stories to an intelligent rabbinic student or teaches comments on the weekly Humash reading to his son, who tells us that Judah was still writing pages of *Sefer Hasidim* until just before he died.

Though a descendant of the Qalonimide founders of the Rhineland communities, Judah appears in Speyer to be an unpopular social critic, in confrontation with the rich communal *parnasim* (community leaders), as anonymous sages are portrayed in parts of *Sefer Hasidim*.

Then, something changed. Unlike his resorting to magical measure for measure revenge on the rich Jew who shaves against Judah's wishes in Speyer, Judah and rest of the *beit din* in Regensburg decide to allow the rich Jews to monopolize the synagogue honor of rolling up the Torah scroll every Sabbath. In Regensburg, Judah is now part of the rabbinic establishment and teaches and relates stories to important students who go there to study with him.

It is not surprising, then, that Hebrew stories about him in the thirteenth century and in later Yiddish versions picture R. Judah *he-hasid* as a local charismatic savior of Jew and gentile alike.[73] Unlike R. Eleazar of Worms, who preached on Jewish law and custom in Worms, Judah's charisma was transmitted to a few in story form, as we saw above, but also survived in his commands that sometimes differed from the Talmud and yet were followed by many and justified by some rabbinical authorities as late as the nineteenth century.[74]

Judah *he-Hasid*'s Circle, Not Movement

Three Qalonimos family authors are part of the circle of Judah *he-hasid* and his family and students: R. Samuel b. Qalonimos the Elder; R. Judah b. Samuel, *he-hasid*; and R. Eleazar b. Judah of Worms. Others connected to this circle include Judah's son, R. Moses Zaltman; Judah's student, R. Isaac b. Moses, author of *Sefer Or Zarua'*, and R. Abraham b. 'Azriel, author of *Sefer 'Arugat ha-Bosem,* among a few other students. These individuals are the people others referred to as *hasidei ashkenaz.* They are family and close students who combined an appreciation for *hasidut* and charismatic or prophetic authority with halakhic knowledge and authority. Altogether, they were about a half dozen men, not a movement.

Evidence that the social context of *hasidei ashkenaz* is a small circle and not a broad movement is the fact that the hundreds of stories or *exampla* found in some manuscripts of *Sefer Hasidim* did not continue to circulate and become part of the canon of Ashkenazic Hebrew stories either in Hebrew or in Yiddish.[75] The hagiographical saints stories told and written down about Samuel and Judah did circulate, at least regionally in German lands, but the hundreds of *exempla* that Judah apparently told one or more students or just wrote down did not.[76]

Hasidei ashkenaz never were a movement but a small circle around Judah. He produced paragraphs about both social and personal matters and created the notebooks with the stories and concerns about social as well as personal living as a *hasid.* The utopian vision as described in the book was not a social reality, but it does overlap in some ways with his biography as we learn from sources not in *Sefer Hasidim.* When he died, most of the social critique aspect of *Sefer Hasidim* died with him.[77] But because manuscripts with Judah *he-hasid*'s sectarian vision did not get copied later does not mean that *Sefer Hasidim* and related Pietist writings had no influence.

The observation that the social program in the long *Sefer Hasidim* manuscripts, especially Parma and Bologna but also in most of Cambridge Add. 379 and its near twin Oxford Add. Fol. 34, did not get enacted does not mean that customs described in many of the manuscripts did not become part of Ashkenazic Judaism. German Pietism is a much greater complex of ideas and practices than Judah's utopian social vision, and the former cannot be reduced to the latter.

Qalonimide family practices associated with Passover, such as removing sixteen drops of wine from the Seder cup to mark the ten plagues, and the three words before and the three acronyms after them, or their Shavuot custom of teaching a small boy the Hebrew alphabet by having him lick honey from a slate or eating cakes on which the alphabet is written, had such an influence that we still do both today.[78] The remarkably selective influence of *Sefer Hasidim* traditions, related writings of Judah's such as the practices he advocated in his *Zava'ah* (Commands), and Eleazar of Worms's halakhic, penitential, and esoteric writings still needs to be studied more.[79]

On the seven hundredth anniversary of Judah *he-hasid*'s death in 1917, Y. N. Simhoni objected to Moritz Güdemann's interpretation of German Hasidism as a reformist program of German Jewry and noted that the extremist demands of *Sefer Hasidim* were designed for the few. As we pass the eight hundredth anniversary of Judah's death in 2017, we should acknowledge the merit of Simhoni's conclusions. The writing of *Sefer Hasidim* and related German pietistic traditions was the work of a small group of pietists, written at the time for a small circle of followers.

And yet, even after his death, R. Judah *he-hasid*'s charismatic authority and his pietistic writings had a significant impact in shaping later Ashkenazic Judaism. German pietists—R. Samuel *he-hasid*, R. Judah *he-hasid*, and R. Eleazar of Worms—helped form the unique religious culture of Ashkenazic Judaism for centuries until modern Hasidism challenged and eventually redefined it.[80]

One of the distinctive features of Jewish pietist culture was their composing open texts, books written and rewritten in short paragraph units. Like other authors of medieval Ashkenazic books, the German pietists did not write books the way their Iberian Jewish colleagues did or follow the mode

Christian Latin or vernacular authors used in medieval Europe. In presenting their pietist views in open texts, the authors of *Sefer Hasidim* and related works continued to write like their Byzantine Jewish ancestors, even when they allowed Christian themes to color the content of their works in medieval Europe.[81]

Selectively negotiating with their cultural environment, the authors of the Ashkenazic book in medieval Europe distinguished between the "message" and the "medium of the message." They internalized some Christian content, but ignored the form of Christian book composition. When Ashkenazic Jews eventually began to read and write in vernaculars and Latin, not just in Hebrew or Yiddish, they began to modify the culture of the Hebrew book in medieval Europe and entered new territory that deserves to be explored further.

Chapter 4

Ashkenazic Hebrew Book Writing
in Historical Context

> Open texts, then, are by nature multiple.
> —David Konstan

Sefer Hasidim in particular and Ashkenazic Hebrew books in general are different from books Jews and others wrote in antiquity and in Muslim lands. In Western classical antiquity and throughout the Latin and Arabic Middle Ages, single-authored books were the standard form, even though some collective works circulated in multiple and different combinations of short literary text units like the Aesopian corpus or the *Alexander Romance*.[1] In contrast, the single-authored book is unusual in ancient Jewish literature.[2] Post-biblical exceptions include the *Wisdom of Ben-Sira*, from the early second century BCE, apparently the only Hebrew book a Jewish author wrote in antiquity.[3] Quotations from the original Hebrew *Ben-Sira* are found in rabbinic literature, but much of the Hebrew original book was lost to Jewish culture until fragments were discovered in the Cairo Geniza at the end of the nineteenth century. Philo of Alexandria and Josephus Flavius wrote books in Greek in the first century CE, and different Christian communities preserved their texts in Greek and in other languages. Jews, on the other hand, did not preserve them in any language.[4] Philo was not part of Jewish culture again until his work reappeared in Azaria de' Rossi's *Me'or 'Einayim* in the sixteenth century.[5] A Hebrew rewriting of Josephus, *Sefer Yosippon*, was the form in which that historian's writings were known in medieval Jewish Italian and Ashkenazic circles.[6]

Midrash collections as well as the Babylonian and Jerusalem Talmuds present themselves as collective, anonymous works, often dependent on an earlier text, such as on Scripture or a festival cycle, in midrash; on the Mishnah, in the case of the Talmuds; and on the order of the fixed prayers in collections of *piyyutim* (liturgical poetry).[7] The collective and anonymous authorship of classical rabbinic literature is taken for granted and rarely explained, despite some Palestinian Rabbis' familiarity with the Greek language and some Babylonian Sages' awareness of Pahlavi in the Persian Empire.[8]

It is generally agreed that rabbinic authors adopted the convention of a single-authored book well after the Muslim Conquest thanks to the influential career of R. Saadia ben Joseph al-Fayyumi, Gaon of Sura (d. 942), commonly known as Saadia Gaon, who did it for the first time. Rabbis now composed works in their own name with first-person introductions, and these works looked like books written in Greek and Latin, some now translated into Syriac and eventually Arabic. The authored book became typical of Jewish rabbinic book writing in the Muslim East and continued in Qairawan (Tunisia) and especially in Muslim Spain.[9]

Although Jews also wrote rabbinic books in medieval Christian Europe, they did not write texts in the linear form of Muslim-Jewish books or of earlier Greek or Latin works that were divided into chapters with a beginning, middle, and end. The peculiarly disjunctive style of many Ashkenazic texts, divided into numbered paragraphs, frequently arranged in different sequences in the manuscripts, may have begun in Byzantine Palestine and southern Italy and then continued northward into the Rhineland and northern France, following a well-known path of some genres of Ashkenazic cultural transmission.[10]

If so, perhaps the tradition of Ashkenazic segmented books goes back to works such as *Ma'asim li-Venei Erez Yisrael,* about which Jacob Mann, one of the first scholars to work on this text, observed: "For the present we have fourteen pages of this book from four different manuscripts. From what we now have before us, we can see that there is no order or arrangement in this collection of laws and decisions. We have a chaotic mix of *ma'asim* (cases) on different subjects and no effort by the writer or compiler to help the user of this book locate a subject when needed."[11] A similar Jewish text from Byzantine Palestine is the list of contrasting Jewish practices in Palestine and Babylonia, *Ha-Hilluqim she-bein anshei Mizrah u-venei Erez Yisrael*. This compilation is preserved in several manuscripts and printed editions that contain the same and different paragraphs. It was written down by an anonymous author who wrote individual paragraphs, and versions made their way to Europe where some Ashkenazic scholars quoted individual paragraphs that are not found in any of the early versions. This suggests that the paragraphs circulated independently of the compiled texts that have been preserved.[12]

Another such composition is known as the *Beraita de-Nidda,* also from early medieval Palestine. It describes recommended practices for Jewish women ritually purifying themselves after their menstrual period and is also composed of paragraph units lacking a coherent linear structure.[13]

Other possible models for some aspects of the Ashkenazic segmented book include medieval midrash collections that rewrote earlier exegetical midrash traditions and that bear a resemblance to the structural fluidity of Ashkenazic Hebrew texts. Among these are such Palestinian writings as the *Midrash Tanhuma* traditions that are not a stable text but are found in different redactions.[14]

Hebrew texts from southern, Byzantine Italy, like *Megillat Ahima'az* or *Sefer Yosippon,* also represent an intermediate stage between late antique Palestinian segmented texts and medieval Ashkenazic ones. The so-called "Chronicle of Ahima'az," preserved in a single manuscript, is episodic and not strictly chronological. It jumps around from story to story, and some segments could be arranged in a different order without readers knowing that something was missing or rearranged.[15] The Hebrew rewriting of Josephus, *Sefer Yosippon,* also displays some features of a segmented text. A loose chronological structure provides some order to these texts, but they are still composed in short literary units.[16] Parts or all of these texts were known in German-Jewish circles in medieval Europe. It is not that surprising, then, to see the segmented book in Ashkenaz emerge out of this Jewish Byzantine Hebrew textual culture.[17]

The medieval manuscripts of the *heikhalot* corpus, also produced perhaps in Byzantine Palestine or Italy, exhibit many of the same features of
segmented composition with varying sequencing of parallel passages.[18] Here,
however, it is not always easy to separate the original state of these texts from
the possibility that German pietist scribes copied them and made contribu-
tions to the final product. Comparison of the longer manuscripts with the
fragmentary ones from the Cairo Geniza suggests that segmented composition in paragraph units was the early form that was later refashioned into
longer compositions.[19] The pattern of parallels shows that, like *Sefer Hasidim*,
single paragraphs circulated and are found in different manuscripts in different sequences.

Whatever its literary pedigree, the segmented Ashkenazic book was different from most genres of ancient rabbinic legal and homiletical texts, on
the one hand, and from the kind of single-authored book pioneered by Saadia Gaon and followed by later rabbinical authors in the Muslim East and
West, on the other. Jews writing in northern European centers such as the
Rhineland or Regensburg or northern France, and its extension in the
communities of Norman and Angevin England, composed many important
works made up of short, disjunctive paragraphs that scribes indented and
sometimes numbered, not long, coherent compositions with a unified or linear literary structure from beginning to end.

Other Open Texts in Ashkenaz

Scholars have written about individual medieval Ashkenazic rabbinic works
in various genres or biographical studies about the authors' relationship to
teachers and students.[20] Less studied are these texts' formal features of
composition. Most if not all of the most important Hebrew standalone
books, as well as commentaries to other texts from medieval Ashkenaz,
were written in disjunctive paragraph text units that are often interchangeable within any section of the text. Moreover, the sequence of the text often
varies from manuscript to manuscript suggesting that there was no author's
single original composition but multiple editions from the beginning.[21]

Although some Ashkenazic books have an author's introduction and survive in a single manuscript or in more than one that amount to an author revising himself one or more times, as noted below, more research is needed to map the wide range of the forms of Hebrew book production in medieval Europe. This chapter is designed to stimulate the comparative study of the Ashkenazic book.

The following are just a few of the well-known surviving Hebrew books written in medieval Ashkenaz that can be viewed, *to one degree or another*, as "open texts" in the sense of parallel editions made up of hundreds of independently written and disjunctively arranged passages.[22] Many of these texts are cited today by numbered paragraphs, and indices were added at the beginning or the end of the book so that readers could find a particular passage without having to skim through the entire book. Some of the works were divided into seven parts for weekly reading and rereading.[23]

Even texts preserved in a single manuscript illustrate segmented composition in small paragraph units that can be moved around without any change of meaning. One legal collection that is extant in a unique complete manuscript is *Sefer Yerei'im* by the French Tosafist Eliezer b. Samuel of Metz (d. 1175). The Paris manuscript was published only from 1892 to 1902 in Vilna. The author divided the numbered paragraphs into seven sections he called pillars ('*amudim*) because he says he designed the book to be read each week as a review of Jewish laws.[24]

Another unique manuscript, still mostly unpublished, is the anonymous Ashkenazic work *Sefer ha-Asufot*, a collection of laws and comments derived from Ashkenazic rabbinic circles from around 1307. It is made up of 525 paragraphs, now numbered, and collected into large divisions with many interpolations of short texts.[25]

Ashkenazic compilations of a single author are rare before the twelfth century in either northern France or the German Empire. The first such work may be R. Judah b. Meir ha-Kohen's *Sefer ha-Dinim* (Book of Laws), a title that reminds one of *Sefer ha-Ma'asim* from Byzantine Palestine.[26]

Among the earliest rabbinic books from medieval Germany is the legal compendium *Even ha-'Eizer* by the twelfth-century Mainz scholar R. Eliezer bar Nathan (ca. 1090–ca. 1170). It, too, survives in one early complete manuscript and is divided into three sections made up of hundreds of short paragraphs. The first part consists of 385 numbered paragraphs. Most of the sections are interchangeable through par. 121; thereafter, we find comments on talmudic tractates not presented in the usual order.[27]

Some important Hebrew story cycles survive in one manuscript, such as the collection in Parma 2295 (De Rossi 563); "*Sefer ha-Ma'asim*" in Oxford Bod. Or. 135 (Neubauer 1466); New York, JTS 2374, f. 110b–124b "Ma'asim shel Hasidim"; and the Jerusalem, National Library of Israel, Oct. 3182, the manuscript of the Ninety-nine stories.[28] In the latter, there are seventeen stories about the life of Judah *he-hasid*, divided into four blocks, interrupted by other stories, and the ones about Judah are not arranged in order from birth to death.[29]

Other collections of Hebrew story cycles, like later Western vernacular collections such as *The Canterbury Tales,* are preserved in different sequences in more than one manuscript. For example, some of the stories in the unique *Sefer ha-Ma'asim* also appear in manuscripts of the earlier work, *Midrash 'Aseret ha-Dibrot*. In *Sefer ha-Ma'asim*, individual stories found in both collections appear in a different sequence, and many stories in *Midrash 'Aseret ha-Dibrot* are missing in *Sefer ha-Ma'asim*.[30]

When a Hebrew work exists in more than one manuscript, contrary to the expectation that the manuscripts will resemble one another and reflect one original book that an author composed, the manuscripts often seem to be alternative editions of many small textual units arranged in different sequences. From the manuscripts of such books, it is impossible to say that there ever was a single original author's composition.

Collections of responsa are the most common type of Hebrew book made up of numbered paragraphs units. Occasioned by specific situations, responsa originate as individual units of text that get copied down in different orders and at different times. When the author or his brother or son or close student gathered them together, responsa were assembled into collections.[31]

An especially clear example of variations in the arrangement of discrete units in German responsa collections are those of R. Meir b. Barukh of Rothenburg (d. 1293), perhaps the largest Ashkenazic collection of responsa gathered close to the lifetime of the author, apparently by his brother, Abraham. Although scholars have known about the various editions of Meir of Rothenburg's responsa and have referred to specific editions and responsum numbers, the full range of this corpus can now be appreciated in Simcha Emanuel's two-volume work, complete with new material and cross-indices to all the collections.[32] Those indices are necessary because there are parallel versions of many individual responsa located in different sequences in various manuscripts, exactly like the parallel passages in different manuscripts or early printings of *Sefer Hasidim*.

Given that responsa are short occasion pieces, one might expect to find them preserved as segmented texts with interchangeable parts, but this form is also true in Hebrew books that belong to other genres such as legal compilations, religious polemics, customs books (*minhag*), texts on religious guidance (*musar*), or even biblical commentaries and historical chronologies.

An important northern French text that includes responsa and comments on parts of the Talmud is *Sefer ha-Yashar*, written by R. Jacob b. Meir (Rabbeinu Tam) of Ramerupt (d. 1171), Rashi's grandson and master Talmud commentator or Tosafist. It is preserved in two early manuscripts that differ significantly in the sequence of their parallel passages.[33]

An early French collection of Jewish law that shows the same kind of divisions into small passages and differing manuscripts is R. Baruch b. Isaac's *Sefer ha-Terumah*. R. Barukh revised his first edition of the book himself, an example of Israel Ta-Shma's usage of "open book," meaning an author's revising his own book himself.[34]

Another important northern French compendium, *Sefer Mizvot Gadol*, by R. Moses b. Jacob of Coucy (fl. mid-thirteenth century), influenced by Maimonides' listing of the traditional 613 commandments, is preserved in a few thirteenth-century manuscripts that are divided into numbered paragraphs and vary in their sequences. R. Moses rewrote the book twice, producing three versions. One can think of this as another example of Israel Ta-Shma's "open book," in his sense of an author revising his original edition himself. The editor of the book, Yisrael Mordechai Peles, terms such multiple authorial revisions as books of "multiple editions" (*merubeh 'arikhot*).[35]

One French rabbinic legal abbreviation of R. Jacob b. Moses of Coucy's *Sefer Mizvot* is R. Abraham b. Ephraim's *Sefer ha-Simanim (Qizzur Sefer ha-Mizvot*).[36] A second that also derived from it is R. Isaac b. Joseph of Corbeil's (d. 1280) *Sefer Mizvot Qatan*, a short popularizing digest of laws based on French Tosafist innovations, frequently copied thanks to the author's self-promotional circular letter encouraging recipients to copy and distribute the book widely, which survives in over a hundred and fifty manuscripts.[37] The earliest ones, with or without the glosses of Rabbeinu Peretz b. Elijah of Corbeil (d. ca. 1295), are segmented and do not agree with each other in their structure in several respects.[38]

The major text of one of R. Judah *he-hasid's* students, R. Isaac b. Moses of Vienna's *Sefer Or Zarua'*, survives in an Amsterdam manuscript from which the first two volumes were published and a London manuscript that is the basis of the third and fourth volumes. The order of the two manuscripts' short, segmented, and numbered paragraphs in these two manuscripts varies significantly.[39]

A different work written by another of R. Judah *he-hasid's* students is the commentary on *piyyut* cycles, *Sefer 'Arugat ha-Bosem*, by R. Abraham b. 'Azriel. The manuscripts differ in their arrangement of parallel material.[40]

Liturgical compositions that ostensibly follow the life cycle or the annual calendar are also made up of segmented paragraphs not written as a continuous composition. Among these is the northern French *Mahzor Vitry*, whose early manuscripts differ significantly from the first edition, and from each another. Simon Horowitz's edition is based on a thirteenth-century British Library manuscript, with late additions indicated throughout. The numbered paragraphs found in the British Library manuscript and in the earlier Klagsbald and Oxford manuscripts are not in the same order.[41]

Related to the *Mahzor Vitry* and also not in any special order of numbered paragraphs are the so-called "School of Rashi" (*De-vei Rashi*) texts: *Sefer ha-Oreh/ha-Orah*, *Sefer ha-Pardes*, and the *Siddur Rashi*, which is the same as the original, shorter *Mahzor Vitry*.[42]

Among the genres of books that authors wrote in medieval Ashkenaz are polemics against Christianity, such as *Sefer Nizzahon Yashan*, from the late thirteenth or early fourteenth century. The manuscripts and early printed version (1681) have large sections that are arranged in different order from one another, although the text can be arranged more or less according to the books of the Old and New Testament, as David Berger has done. Variations can be seen in the two published editions by Mordechai Breuer and David Berger. Breuer numbers the paragraphs in his edition; Berger puts his paragraph numbers in square brackets. The first edition has no paragraph numbers.[43]

Berger correctly observes that there are important omissions from one manuscript to another and also differences in sequence when passages are present in more than one manuscript. It is precisely this Lego-like character of Ashkenazic book composition that *Nizzahon Yashan* shares with many other Ashkenazic books and with *Sefer Hasidim*. Berger's comment about the form of Ashkenazic polemical writings applies to all of their Hebrew works: "This was a culture . . . not suited to architectonic literary composition."[44] Like *Nizzahon Yashan*, *Sefer Nizzahon* of Yom-Tov Lipmann-Mühlhausen (d. after 1420) is also arranged, more or less in the order of the books of the Hebrew Bible and of the New Testament but is made up of numbered paragraphs.[45]

What is of special significance, however, is that even when comments are produced on parts of a biblical text, they do not always follow the order of the verses. In manuscripts of R. Judah *he-hasid's* commentary on the Pentateuch, the comments are organized by the weekly lections (*parshiyot*) but not by the order of the verses in each section. The editor, Yitzhaq Lange, rearranged them to follow the verses in each lection.[46] The same is true of another set of R. Judah *he-hasid's* comments on the Humash, published from several manuscripts that differ, and in which the glosses on verses within each section are not in order and were put in the order of the verses by the editor.[47]

From German Ashkenaz, we also have separate *minhag* (religious practice) collections. *Sefer Maharil* by R. Jacob b. Moses Ha-Levi Mölln (Maharil) (d. 1427) follows the cycle of the year but is made up of short sections that are interchangeably arranged. Editor Shlomo Spitzer says of the twenty-two manuscripts he examined: "They have in common that none of them resemble one another."[48]

Others custom books soon followed, such as R. Avraham Klausner's
Sefer ha-Minhagim and the work of his student, R. Izak Tyrna's, *Minhagim,*
as well as Joseph Yuspa Hahn's *Yosef Omez,* a collection of Frankfurt am Main
customs from the early seventeenth century, still mostly divided into numbered paragraphs.[49] An important collection of customs and laws from
Ashkenaz was preserved in R. Jacob b. Judah's *Sefer ha-Agur* written in
northern Italy in the fifteenth century.[50]

A subgenre of *minhag* books focuses on the religious behavior of a par-
ticularly influential rabbinic teacher. *Sefer Tashbez* was written by R. Samson b. Zadok, a student of R. Meir b. Barukh of Rothenburg (d. 1293). Written
in the early fourteenth century, it is divided into numbered paragraphs. The
manuscripts do not all contain the same small text units, and their sequential numbering of paragraphs differs from manuscript to manuscript.[51]

R. Joseph b. Moses put together *Leqet Yosher* from his conversations with
students about the life of R. Israel b. Petahyah, known as Israel Isserlein
(1390–1460). The author explains at length the process of his writing and
assembling short texts into a book.[52] The same Israel Isserlein produced
Terumat ha-Deshen, an early manuscript and the first edition of which have
different sequences.[53]

An attempt in Ashkenaz to write narrative history is seen in the Hebrew
chronicles about the 1096 First Crusade riots. In addition to two compositions that survive in a single manuscript each, there are several of the one
text attributed to a well-known German rabbi, R. Eliezer b. Nathan of
Mainz, author of *Even ha-'Eizer.* Despite the framework of a common over-
all structure indicated by dates and places, many parallel episodes are found
in different sequences in the three Hebrew accounts and are formulated differently in parallel passages in several cases.[54]

All of these Ashkenazic Hebrew texts, taken from several genres, resemble to varying degrees the way *Sefer Hasidim* is constructed from small
passages and preserved in differently sequenced manuscripts such that it is
often impossible to posit a single original author's composition. Instead, we
are dealing with small units of composition, sometimes written more than
once, that the authors compiled in different sequences in more than one
edition.

At some point, someone numbered most of the short texts units so that now one cites them by paragraph number. In the thirteenth century, R. Eliezer b. Joel ha-Levi, known by the acronym Ravyah and the grandson of R. Eliezer b. Nathan of Mainz, indicated cross-references in his segmented work, *Avi ha-'Ezri*, by referring himself to the paragraph numbers. Other texts, including manuscripts of *Sefer Hasidim* that were also composed in paragraph units, were numbered hundreds of years later for various reasons.

Numbering discrete paragraphs in some of these works served different purposes. The history of numbering and of adding topical indices of contents to some Ashkenazic books is a subject that has only been studied for a short time and not systematically.[55] Since it was difficult for a reader to know where short passages on related topics could be found in the book, an index might be added at the beginning or the end with a brief mention of the contents of the numbered paragraphs.[56] We have no study as yet about systems of numbering parts of medieval Hebrew books, their indices, and other forms of cross-referencing comparable to those on the medieval Latin book.[57]

Aside from enabling a reader to find related passages, numbering paragraphs and adding indices at the beginning or the end of the book could provide a reader with an anthology of passages for daily meditation or study. Thus in the preface to his *Sefer Nizzahon*, Yom Tov Lippmann Mühlhausen offers the reader seven lists of sequential but non-consecutive paragraph numbers from different parts of the book that he thinks readers should study each day of the week.[58] More needs to be learned about the relationship between numbered, segmented books and reading practices in medieval Ashkenaz.

Other authors divided their books into seven parts for daily study. R. Eliezer of Metz's *Sefer Yerei'im* is divided into seven parts, though he does not refer to daily reading in his short introduction.[59] We do find this expectation, however, in R. Isaac b. Joseph of Corbeil's *Sefer Mizvot Qatan* that he divided into seven 'amudim (pillars). In his introductory letter, he says he expects readers to learn one seventh each day.[60] The fourteenth-century little work known as *Sefer ha-Gan*, attributed to R. Isaac b. Eliezer (d. 1360), is also divided into seven days of paragraph units to be read each day.[61] This feature of some Ashkenazic books as well as studying which texts were copied together in various codices could shed light on different reading practices in medieval Jewish culture and have yet to be explored systematically.

These are but some of the typical segmented Hebrew books from medieval Ashkenaz that scholars have studied for their contents. The authors wrote these books in short paragraphs, eventually numbered and sometimes indexed them. Scholars who continue to study these Hebrew works written in segmented units will determine to what degree other aspects of *Sefer Hasidim* as an open text apply also to the other Hebrew books written in medieval Ashkenaz. My intention here has been to point out these features of several types of Hebrew books written in medieval Ashkenaz and to illustrate in detail the important case study of *Sefer Hasidim* and the German Jewish pietists' related writings that may shed light on the phenomenon as a whole.

A Descriptive Catalog of the Manuscripts and Editions of *Sefer Hasidim*

Every copy of a text is a separate piece of documentary evidence.
—G. Thomas Tanselle, *A Rationale of Textual Criticism*

This catalog provides a guide to the manuscripts and printed editions of *Sefer Hasidim*. The scholarly literature until now has tended to focus on two versions, SHB and SHP, but it is necessary to consider all of the manuscript editions, long and short, when discussing this open book.

I. Catalog of *Sefer Hasidim* Manuscripts
Abbreviations of Manuscript Catalogs

Allony and Loewinger I
Allony, N., and D. S. Loewinger. *Hebrew Manuscripts in the Libraries of Austria and Germany* [List of Photocopies in the Institute, Part I]. Jerusalem: State of Israel Department of Education and Culture, 1957.

Allony and Kupfer II
Allony, N., and E. Kupfer. *Hebrew Manuscripts in the Libraries of Belgium, Denmark, the Netherlands, Spain, and Switzerland* [List of Photocopies in the Institute, Part II]. Jerusalem: State of Israel, Department of Education and Culture, 1964.

Allony and Loewinger III
Allony, N., and D. S. Loewinger. *Hebrew Manuscripts in the Library of the Vatican* [List of Photocopies in the Institute, Part III]. Jerusalem: State of Israel, Department of Education and Culture, 1968.

Assemanus
Assemanus, J. S. *Bibliotecae Apostolicae Vaticanae . . .* Pt. 1. 3 vols. Rome, 1756–59.

Bernheimer
Bernheimer, Carlo. *Codices Hebraici Bybliothecae Ambrosianae.* Florence: L. S. Olschki, 1933.

De Rossi
De Rossi, Giovanni Bernardo. *MSS Codices Hebraici Bibliothecae I. B. de-Rossi.* 3 vols. Parma, 1808.

Landauer, *Katalog*
Landauer, S. *Katalog der hebräischen, arabischen, persischen, und türkischen Handschriften der Kaiserlichen* Universitäts- und Landesbibliothek zu Strassburg. Strasbourg, 1881.

Oxford I
Neubauer, Adolph, ed. *Catalogue of the Hebrew Manuscripts in the Bodleian Library.* Oxford: Clarendon Press, 1886; repr. 1994, vol. 1.

Oxford II
Beit-Arié, Malachi, comp., and R. A. May, ed. *Catalogue of the Hebrew Manuscripts in the Bodleian Library.* Supplement of Addenda and Corrigenda to Vol. 1 (A. Neubauer's catalog). Oxford: Clarendon Press, 1994.

Prijs
Prijs, Joseph. *Die Basler Hebräische Drucke, 1492–1866.* Completed and edited by Bernhard Prijs. Olten und Freiburg im Breisgau: URS Graf-Verlag, 1964.

Reif, *Hebrew Manuscripts*
Reif, Stefan C., ed. *Hebrew Manuscripts at Cambridge University Library*: *A Description and Introduction*. Cambridge: Cambridge University Press, 1997.

Richler, *Catalogue*, Parma
Richler, Benjamin, ed., with Malachi Beit-Arié. *Hebrew Manuscripts in the Biblioteca Palatina in Parma*. Jerusalem: Jewish National and University Library, 2001.

Richler, *Catalogue*, Vatican
Richler, Benjamin, Malachi Beit-Arié, and N. Pasternak, eds. *Hebrew Manuscripts in the Vatican Library*. City of the Vatican: Biblioteca Apostolica Vaticano, 2008.

Roth, C. *Catalogue*
Roth, Cecil, ed. *Catalogue of Manuscripts in the Roth Collection*. Philadelphia: s.n., 1950 (reprint from *Alexander Marx Jubilee Volume*).

Róth, E., and Prijs, *Hebräische Handschriften*
Róth, Ernst, and Leo Prijs, eds. *Hebräische Handschriften* (Verzeichnis Orientalische Handschriften in Deutschland vi, 1-a). Wiesbaden: Franz Steiner Verlag, 1982.

Simon, "Les manuscrits"
Simon, Joseph. "Les manuscrits hébreux de la bibliotheque de la ville de Nîmes." REJ 3 (1881): 225–237.

Steinschneider, Hamburg
Steinschneider, Moritz. *Catalog der hebräischen Handschriften in der Staatsbibliothek zu Hamburg*. 1878. Reprinted Hildesheim: Georg Olms, 1969.

Striedl-Róth, *Verzeichnis*
Hans Streidl-Ernst Róth, eds. *Verzeichnis der orientalischen Handschriften in Deutschland*. VI, 2. *Hebraische Handschriften*, Teil 2. Wiesbaden: Franz Steiner Verlag, 1965.

A. Manuscripts with single parallels, or no parallels elsewhere, often referred to as "liqqutim" (selections) of single paragraphs.

A 1

Vatican, Vatican Library, ebr. 285/20, f. 108v–127v

Title: "liqqutim"

IMHM F 8632

PUSHD

Parchment

Byzantine cursive hand

15th/16th century Italy

Semicolon and space after each paragraph

No paragraph numbers

PUSHD supplies paragraph numbers that differ from those that Moshe Hershler added in square brackets in *Genuzot* 1 (1982), 125–182.

Like A 2 (JTS 2499), Vat. 285 is also written in one column.

Assemanus, Vol. 1, p. 257;

Richler, *Catalogue*, Vatican, 211–215:

"230 ff. (157–159 blank). Paper. 205 × 150 (size of text varies from 155 × 105 to 176 × 117) mm. Quaternions and quinions [Byzantium]; mostly Byzantine semi-cursive scripts" (p. 211); "20. Ff. 108v–127v: [Sefer Hasidim]. A short redaction or adaptation of Judah he-Hasid of Regensburg's *Sefer Hasidim*. Includes over thirty paragraphs not included in either of the printed redactions. Ff. 108v–110r: *ta'am havdalah be-moza'ei shabbat* [Heb. char.] on the significance of the *havdalah* service at the termination of the Sabbath. F. 110r *haruzim le-hisha'rut ha-nefesh ve-ha-guf* [Heb. char.] Verses on the immortality of the soul and body beginning: *ana ha-el el yisrael ha-gadol 'imi hasdekha* [Heb. char.]. F. 109v was left blank by the scribe who acknowledged that he skipped over the text *zeh ha-daf dillagti le-khotvo* [Heb. char]. All these texts were edited from this manuscript by M. Hershler, 'Sefer Hasidim le-Rabbeinu Yehudah he-Hasid: Mahadurah ve-Nusha Hadashah mi-Tokh Ketav-Yad.' *Genuzot* [I] (1984):125–162. Hershler also provided an index of the contents and pointed out the paragraphs that were not included in the other editions" (p. 213).

"The texts on ff. 84–98, 108–138 and 143–150 also in MS NY JTSA 2499 (EMC 820) an incomplete parallel manuscript written in an Italian hand" (p. 215).

A 2

New York, Jewish Theological Seminary Library, Mic. 2499, f. 1r–29r

IMHM F 28752

PUSHD

15th century

No paragraph numbers

This MS is related to Vatican 285 but lacks some passages found there.

Tobias, JTS Library, "Philosophy Polemics MSS":

EMC 820

Paper 84 leaves 25 × 14 cm

"The hand is Ashkenazi German or French school ca. late (13th) 14th [corrected] century. The text is incomplete. The version is somewhat different from the printed. . . . Many stories are recorded in this MS not found in the printed version. There is in all not a very great deal in common with the traditional version."

A 3

Vatican, Vatican Library ebr. 285, f. 150r–152r (=Vatican 285A)

Title: f. 150r: "gam eilu liqqutim mi-sefer hasidim"

IMHM F 8632

In PUSHD it is found as a continuation of A 1, not as a separate manuscript.

Not in Hershler edition of A 1

No paragraph numbers

Indented with two short lines at end of each

Richler, *Catalogue*, Vatican, 214:

"30. Ff. 150r–152r: 'gam eilu liqqutim mi-sefer hasidim' [in Heb.]. Additional extracts from *Sefer Hasidim*."

A 4

Frankfurt am Main, Goethe Universität, Universitätsbibliothek Johann Christian Senkenberg (formerly Stadt- und Universitätsbibliothek) Oct. 94, f. 270r–272r (formerly: Merzbacher 56)

Title: f. 270r: "Liqqutim ne'etaqu mi-sefer hasidim"
IMHM F 25916
PUSHD
Online via NLI Online Catalog under "MSS/Hasidim/liqqutim" or directly
from Frankfurt, Universitätsbibliothek
15th century
Ashkenazi rahut
Indentations
No paragraph numbers
Róth and Prijs, *Hebräische Handschriften*, no. 98
After qof peh zayin: 187+1240=1427

A 5

Zurich, Zentralbibliothek Heidenheim 51, f. 9r–10v (middle)
Title: "liqqutim min sefer hasidim"
Explicit f. 10v (middle): "liqqutin min sefer ha-hasidim siyyamti ve-lo ahat
minni elef qiyyamti ki kol yamai lo ra'iti ad she-katavti ve-otah ashmor ki
qodem lakhen ta'iti."
IMHM F 2613
PUSHD
Published: Soloveitchik, "Appendix to 'Pietists and Kibbitzers,'" #4 in JQR
96:1 (2006): [6–11] No page numbers are indicated in the online edition of
these texts. There are errors of transcription.
NLI: 14th century
Ashkenazic
Italian cursive hand
One column; divided into paragraphs by indentations
No paragraph numbers
Allony and Kupfer II, no. 73
In PUSHD there are nine paragraphs.
Of these, pars. 1, 5, 6, 7, 8, also have parallels in former JTS Boesky 45
and SHB; pars. 2 and 3 have parallels only in SHB; par. 4 has only a SHP
parallel.

Soloveitchik, "Appendix to 'Pietists and Kibbitzers,'" divides the long [PUSHD [9]] into many paragraphs, and he indicates their parallels in SHP or SHB or both.

A 6
Oxford, Bodleian Library Opp. 614 (Neubauer 2275), f. 30r–31v
Titles: f. 30r: "Liqqutin mi-sefer hasidim"
f. 30v: "gam zeh mi-sefer hasidim"
IMHM F 20967
Spaces but no numbers to mark off paragraphs
Published by Soloveitchik, "Appendix to 'Pietists and Kibbitzers,'" #2
14th century
Ashkenazic square
Quarto vellum
·Oxford I, 791

A 7
Oxford, Bodleian Library Or. 146 (Neubauer 782), f. 69av–70r
Title: f. 69r: "Liqqutin mi-sefer hasidim" [bottom of col. a]
f. 69v "gam zeh mi-sefer hasidim"
IMHM F 20319
PUSHD
Rhineland 1342/3
Oxford I, 154:
"Fol. 69. Aphorisms, headed 'liqqutim mi-sefer hasidim'
f. 70. Beg. the index, only 205 pars." "Ger. Rabb. Char.; 2 coll., fol., vellum, ff. 75 (slightly stained)."
Oxford II, 120:
"[Ashkenaz], 1342; Ashkenzic semi-cursive script."

A 8 (Short passages)
Oxford, Bodleian Library, Opp. Add. Fol. 39 (Neubauer 865), f. 1r–3r [in margins and very dark and hard to read]
IMHM F 21626

Not in PUSHD

Oxford I, 179:

"At beg[inning] of MS. extracts from the S. Hasidim (pale)" . . . "Germ. Rabb. char.; 2 coll., fol., vellum, ff. 381¾."

Oxford II, 135:

"Zurich 1386/7; Ashkenazic semi-cursive script."

A 9

Parma, Biblioteca Palatina H 2486; De Rossi 1420/5 f. [f. 45r]

Title: "katuv be-sefer hasidim"

IMHM F 13489

Not in PUSHD

14th century Italy

Richler, *Catalogue*, Parma, no. 1553

According to Richler, this is par. 54 in ed. Margoliot (!) of SHB. This passage is not the same as SHB 54 but has some overlap with it.

Richler catalog number 1553, p. 466: "4. 42r–45r massekhet semahot de-R. Hiyya . . . followed by an extract from Judah he-hasid's Sefer Hasidim (ed. Margoliot par. 52)."

Also contains: "qabbalat ha-rav r. yehudah hasid": f. 55r–56r.

Incipit: "katuv be-sefer hasidim: amru raboteinu ha-mevayyesh penei haveiro o mez'aro bifenei mi she-mitbayyesh u-mita'er, she-ilu hayah horego haya meqabel mitah kedei she-lo yehei mitbayyesh. Ve-khen mazinu be-aviah she-hokhiah et yerov'am ba-rabbim le-vayyesho ve-nuggaf. Vihudah she-heishiv et ha-zaqen."

A 10

Parma, Biblioteca Palatina H 3266, De Rossi 1131, f. 52r

Title: "Sefer Hasidim"

IMHM F 34168

Not in PUSHD

Ca. 1372/3

Ashkenazic square

Richler, *Catalogue*, Parma, no. 872, pp. 194–195

The quote is embedded in "Hilekhot beit Aaron." Ethical-religious work. Begins: "mi ha-ish he-hakham." At f. 52r, col. b, line 15 [end] is a quote from *Sefer Hasidim*:

"kakh nimza [line 16] be-sefer hasidim: ve-agra de-ta'anita zidqata ve-khol ta'anit she-molikhin ? bo zedaqah 'ad le-mahar ke-ilu shofekh damim."

B. *Manuscripts with small clusters of topical paragraphs*

B 1

Freiburg, Universitätsbibliothek Heb. MS 483/29, f. 4r–5v

IMHM F 11392

Striedl-Róth, *Verzeichnis,* 98, pp. 65–66:

"Sammlung von 5 Fragmenten . . . in 3 Gruppen . . . III kein Titel: kurze voneinander unabhängige Teile verschiedenen religiösen Inhalts."

These binding fragments consist of parallel paragraphs to small sections found in sequence in SHP and its parallels in former JTS Boesky 45, but Freiburg displays significant variants. It is not identical to SHP or to any other MS. There are no enlarged first words of paragraphs, and the beginnings are not lined up in the right margins, but there are spaces indicating new paragraphs most of the time. Although the editorial sequence is the same as SHP and former JTS Boesky 45, linguistically each paragraph has to be compared to other parallel witnesses.

14th century

Ashkenazic cursive

Two columns

Torn and so beginnings or endings of lines are missing;

4 ff.

Excerpts are parallel to topical sections: SHP 966–969, 979–986, 1056–1073;

Freiburg [966–969] are like SHP I on *kibbud av va-em* (honoring parents) (SHP 929–974); Freiburg [979–986] are like SHP I on *hasidut* (pietism) (SHP 975–1065); and Freiburg [1056–1073] are like SHP I on *shehitah ve-taharah* (ritual slaughter and purity) (SHP 1066–83).

B 2

Zurich Fragment, Zentralbibliothek, no shelf number

IMHM PH 5330 (bottom line/s not included in photograph)

PUSHD

15th century

1 page with two columns, edges with text missing on both sides

Indentations for paragraphs

No paragraph numbers

The text is a block of paragraphs starting from the very end of SHP 391 (SHB 750) to the middle of SHP 397/SHB 757.

It is from the first part of a collection on *tefillah* (prayer) in SHP 391–397/ SHB I (title before SHB 749: "be-khan katuv 'inyanei tefillah"; no title in SHP or in Zurich Fragment).

A comparison of the parallels shows that the Zurich Fragment agrees with SHP when SHB and SHP differ but it has variants from SHP too.

B 3

Oxford, Bodleian Library, Mich. 569 (Neubauer 1098), f. 104v

IMHM F 17293

Not in PUSHD

Published by Soloveitchik in "Appendix to 'Pietists and Kibbitzers,'" # 1

Oxford I, 303:

"Germ. Rabb. Char.; fol., vellum, ff. 120."

Oxford II, 172:

"[on Neubauer 1097] [Germany], c. 1288/9; Ashkenazic square, semi-cursive, and cursive script."

C. The three manuscripts just of Sefer ha-Hasidut (=SHB 1–152)

C 1

Oxford, Bodleian Library, Opp. 340 (Neubauer 875), f. 131r–151r

Title: "ve-zeh sefer ha-hasidut"

explicit: "siyyamti sefer ha-hasidut"

IMHM F 21834

PUSHD

Dated: 1299

Corresponds to SHB 1–152

Haym Soloveitchik notes [JQR 2002] it is missing SHM 103–116 [actually middle of 102–116]; these paragraphs are found, with variants to SHB parallels, in C 2 (Milan, Ambrosiana X.111) and C 3 (Moscow 103) as well as in E 1 (Cambridge, Add. 379).

There is also an entire passage at the end of Ox. Opp. 340 [102] that is not in SHB (end of 102), and the end of SHB 102 is not in Ox. Opp. 340.

Dated: 1299

Has enlarged initials, only one of which corresponds to new paragraphs in SHB.

Oxford I, 182:

"Fol. 131. *Sefer ha-Hasidut* (printed under the title S. Hasidim). The MS., which has no division into [paragraphs], ends with 154 [*sic*] of the edition [read: 152 of SHB]. More French glosses than in the edition" [SHB] . . . "Ger. Rabb. char.; quarto, vellum, ff. 161."

Oxford II, 138:

"[France?], 1299. Ashkenazic 'cursive' script."

No paragraph numbers

English translation in Singer

C 2

Milan, Ambrosiana X.111 sup, f. 166v–201v/a

Title: f. 166v/a: "Zeh niqra sefer ha-hasidim devarav mamtaqim ve-khulo mahmadim."

Explicit: f. 201v/a: "Hazaq. Zeh ha-sefer niqra sefer hasidim"

IMHM F 12336

PUSHD

Rubrics with spaces

No paragraph numbers

14th c. Ashkenaz

Bernheimer, no. 119, p. 175

Cat. Allony-Kupfer #43 (*Areshet* 4 [1966]: 254)

Par. 155 stops on fol. 201v.

It contains SHB 102 (all) –116 missing in Oxford Opp. 340.

C 3

Moscow, Russian State Library, Günzburg 103/4, f. 100r–124v

Title: "sefer ha-hasidim"

Explicit: "ve-salahta la-avoneinu u-le-hatateinu u-nehaltanu seliq seliq seliq."

IMHM F 6783

PUSHD

15th century

Ashkenazic

No paragraph numbers

Some of SHB parallel paragraphs are indented; others are not. SHB 7 "shoresh ha-hasidut" and SHB 9 "ve-'iqar hozeq ha-hasidut" are indented.

No rubrics

Some spaces before paragraphs

It contains parallels to SHB 102 (mid.) –116 not in Oxford Opp. 340.

D. Fragmentary MSS that are parallel to Sefer ha-Hasidut/SHB but end before SHB par. 153. There is no way to determine what text followed the break.

D 1

Nîmes, Bibliothèque municipale 26, f. 154v–174r (breaks off)

26 ff.

IMHM F 4424 (dark). Online scan from Nîmes, Bib. mun. is better than NLI microfilm.

PUSHD

See Simon, "Les manuscrits," 225–237, esp. 232–234:

"p. 231: long. 350 mm; larg. 260 mm; haut. 058 mm. 176 ff Parchmin. Ecriture carrée française. Texte en trois colonnes. Date probable XIII siècle. Premiers mots: 'eilu ha-mizvot asher tiqqen'; derniers mots: 'ba-mizvot hafez me'od.' Au verso de la garde anterieure, la liste des Thanaim et des Amoraim; 1 SMQ; 2 Sefer Tefillot; 3 Sefer ha-Hasidim."

On the French *le'azim,* see Simon, "Les manuscrits," who writes that there are more *le'azim* in D 1 (Nîmes 26) than in SHB, but that is true of all the manuscripts that contain all or part of this text. There are five more *le'azim* in MS Nîmes (and in most of the other 6 MSS) not in SHB.

Simon missed the single word "di" (=dieu) that is also in the other 6 MSS but not in SHB.

Simon thought that the SHB paragraph numbers referred to the paragraph above them instead of the one below and so his references to SHB are usually off by one.

No paragraph numbers

It may be the oldest manuscript of a version of *Sefer Hasidim* (see Chapter 2).

D 2

Oxford, Bodleian Library, Mich. 155 (Neubauer 1984), f. 279r–283v

IMHM F 19146

PUSHD

Parallels to SHB 1–16 (middle) (breaks off)

No paragraph numbers

Rubricated with enlarged initial words

Oxford I, 677:

"K. fol. 279. The printed *sefer hasidim* up to the paragraph:

'Te[no] R[abbanan] ve-nishmarta mi-kol davar ra' (by another recent hand, Span. Rabb. char.) Or. Rabb. char., quarto, paper, ff. 285."

Oxford II, p. 359:

"K (fols. 279–283): [Late 15th cent.]; Sephardic semi-cursive script."

One column, unnumbered sections

Unnumbered paragraphs do not line up with parallel SHB paragraph numbers:

f. 279r [1] [SHB 1] "ZEH NIQRA"

f. 279r [SHB 2] no rubric for "ve-amar ba'al zeh ha-sefer"; it is part of [1]

f. 279v [2] [SHB 3] "ZEKHER ZADIQ," etc.

E. These two compound manuscripts begin with Sefer ha-Hasidut (=SHB 1–152), continue with a version of SHB I, and conclude with a version of SHP II. The second and third blocks have fewer paragraphs than the parallels in SHB and SHP, respectively. Parallel numbered paragraphs do <u>not</u> have the same paragraph number much of the time.

E 1

Cambridge, Cambridge University Library, Add. 379, f. 1v–74r
Title: "zeh niqra sefer yere'im [dotted on top of letters to indicate error] ha-hasidim . . ."
IMHM F 16298
PUSHD
13th–14th century
Ashkenaz
This may be the earliest *Sefer Hasidim* manuscript to have numbered paragraphs that are contemporary to the manuscript and written in the same hand.
The MS has two sets of numberings of the folios. The first 1–28v is a *siddur.* The text of "an'im zemirot" is on new f. 1r; *Sefer Hasidim* is on new f. 1v–74 [text]; 86v–90 [indices in slightly later hand].
Reif, *Hebrew Manuscripts,* p. 222:
"Vellum; 20×15; 40ff. + 88 ff.; 2 cols; . . . Ashkenazi hands; 13th–14th c[entury]"

    1.   f. 1–40 Prayerbook
        [p. 223]:
    2.   f. 1r *Shir ha-Kavod*; "(ff. 1v–74r) *Sefer Hasidim* by Judah b. Samuel he-Hasid, divided into 579 sections numbered in the margins, here entitled "'Sefer yerei'im ha-hasidim' and at variance with other editions."
        "(f. 84v–88v) Table of contents for *Sefer Hasidim,* covering sections 1–536."

E 2

Oxford, Bodleian Library, Opp. Add. fol. 34 (Neubauer 641), f. 43v–57r
Truncated at beginning and end

Incipit f. 43r: "Alef. 'Iqar hozeq ha-hasidut" [=SHB 9]

IMHM F 20557

PUSHD

It contains same three blocks as Cambridge [E 1] but fewer paragraphs of each throughout.

New paragraph numbers 147–174 are parallel to some paragraphs in SHP II 1330–1923 in the same sequence.

Spaces before new paragraphs

Numbered in margins from 1 on, so Oxford Opp. Add. Fol. 34 1=SHB 9 but not the same exactly

Stops on f. 57r with new par. 174

Oxford I, 125:

"4. Fol. 43. R. Y'hudah ha-Hasid's S. Hasidim, with glosses and the index of 169 paragraphs."

Oxford II: 96:

"4. Compendium of Sefer Hasidim. Fols. 57v–58v: Laws of Repentance. End missing. Cf. Eleazar of Worms's Sefer Roqeah, laws of repentance . . . [Ashkenaz, 14th cent.]; Ashkenazic semi-cursive and cursive scripts."

Many paragraphs are missing including many with French *le'azim* in other manuscript parallels:

1=SHB 9

2=middle of SHB 10 [beginning lines of SHB 10 missing];

3=SHB 11

4=SHB 12 [SHB 13–14 omitted]

5=SHB 15–16, etc.

F. Two manuscripts contain different versions of topical notebooks in the same fourteen-book sequence as SHB I but with major sequence variations compared to SHB II and SHB III.

F 1

Parma, Biblioteca Palatina, Heb. MS 3280, De Rossi 1133, f. 2r–184r

IMHM F 13957

PUSHD

Ca. 1300

Ashkenaz

Enlarged rubrics and spaces on right margins until last few folios

Paragraphs were not numbered until at least the 15th century in an Italian hand.

Names of five topics also added in margins in a similar Italian hand, but the rubrics for the additional topics in SHP II are in the same hand as the original manuscript.

Facsimile edition, edited by Ivan G. Marcus, with Mavo, Jerusalem: Merkaz Dinur, 1985

De Rossi III, 72:

"R. Jehudae Chasid fil. R. Samuelis liber chasidim seu piorum, memb. Semirabb. In fol. 2 col. Sec. xiii. Vestutum apographum quod ab edito interdum dissidet suaque habet additamenta, libri moralis magnae inter judaeos existimationis magnique usus."

Richler, *Catalogue*, Parma no. 1367, pp. 387–388:

"Longer version than the Bologna 1538 edition. Printed from the MS by J. Wistinetzki (Berlin, 1891) and again by J. Freimann in 1924 . . .

184 ff. Parchment. 346x255 mm [Germany]. Ca. 1300.

Ashkenazic semi-cursive script

Owner (f. 2r): Jekutiel b. Uri Yaffe=Yequtiel ben HR"R Uri Yaffe Z"TZL [Heb.]

Bibliography: *Hebrew Manuscripts from the Palatine Library* [Jerusalem, 1985], 90–91, no. 41."

MS has 184 folios divided into 23 gatherings of four bi-folios each. It is written in two columns until f. 178r when it changes to one column. It is numbered in Hebrew letters. There are 1999 paragraphs, and the first word is written in enlarged letters. Defective numbering yields 1983 paragraphs. See Marcus, Mavo to facsimile edition, pp. 29–30.

F 2

Former JTS Boesky 45, f. 2r–207r

Sold to another private collector December 21, 2015

IMHM F 75736

PUSHD

Late 15th century

North Italy

Vellum in Ashkenazic semi-cursive script

This MS contains some censoring of Christian words like "komer" (priest) or "galah" (monk).

At the end, in same hand, is a description of the Trent blood libel of 1475. Former JTS Boesky 45 omits, adds, elides gaps in Parma, improves language, and renumbers the text, all signs of being edited later, though, as in all *Sefer Hasidim* manuscripts, it contains some paragraphs that offer better readings than parallel paragraphs elsewhere, including MS Parma.

PUSHD says that the end of MS former JTS Boesky 45 is not in SHP but is too faint to transcribe. PUSHD notes in its description of CUL Add. 379, but not in its description of the former JTS Boesky 45 manuscript, that the last part of former JTS Boesky 45 that is not in Parma, is found at the end of CUP Add. 379. PUSHD indicates some sections of former JTS Boesky 45 are not in SHP and some paragraphs in latter are not in former, but the blocks of listed paragraphs are neither accurate nor exhaustive, but only suggestive. There are many more of both categories. My former research assistant at JTS, now Rabbi Robert Kasman, went over both manuscripts line by line and marked photocopies of both as to variations between them. There are about two hundred passages in SHP that are not found in former JTS Boesky 45. Missing from SHP are the last two paragraphs in former JTS Boesky 45 but fewer than those mentioned in PUSHD.

G. Fragmentary MSS often with SHB paragraph number references, possibly copied from SHB.

G 1

Hamburg Staats- und Universität Bibliothek, Cod. Heb. 303, f. 24r–25v

IMHM F 26368; Fiche 221

Not in PUSHD

17th century (?)

Steinschneider, Hamburg 1878, n. 213, p. 86:

"303 (Uff. 224) 23 und 2 f. Qu., deutsch rabb. XVII J.? 24, 25 aus S. Hasidim [Heb.] (von Jehuda ha-Chasid) [*sic*] ohne Zaehlung (sehr klein und blass)."

Paragraph numbers from Hamburg paragraph 1059 to 1069 are off by one because SHB 1057 combines Hamburg 1057 and 1058 that form a question and answer (see below).

Other differences between Hamburg and SHB: when copying SHB pars. 1057 and 1058, the scribe of Hamburg 1056 added the word "she'eilah" at the beginning, not in SHB 1057, and in the middle of the next line skipped by *homoioteleuton* from "lezakkot aheirim" to "lezakkot aheirim" two lines below that, in the answer. He caught the mistake and resumed copying the rest of par. 1057. At the beginning of the answer, he added a new number, 1058, not in SHB. The result is that the numbers of the parallels from 1058 to the end are off by one compared to SHB.

The addition of the word "she'eilah" at the beginning of par. 1058 and the addition of the number 1059 to the answer likely are the scribe "improving" SHB. The text is nearly identical and likely is a modified copy of SHB.

The following is a comparison of the paragraph numbers of parallels in Hamburg and SHB:

Hamburg	SHB
1024 [mid]–1056	1024 [mid]–1056
1057–1058	1057
1059	1058
1060	1059
1061	1060
1062	1061
1063	1062
1064	1063
1065	1064
1066	1065
1067	1066
1068	1067 [SHB skips over par. 1068 and goes from 1067 to 1069]
1069	1069 (!)

MS Hamburg looks like a section of SHB, with some numbers hanging at the end of the paragraph that precedes the one numbered. So Soloveitchik, "Piety, Pieitsm." But sometimes the number is at the beginning of a paragraph, and the numbers are one less in Hamburg from paragraph 1059 to the end compared to the parallels in SHB. Comparison of some parallels indicates variations and some "improvements" in SHB, not a straight copy of or errors from SHB. *It may be a fragment of a numbered manuscript of what became SHB.* Compare Zurich Fragment (B 2) that seems to be a small section of what become SHP I and compare Freiburg with three sections that follow the sequences of SHP for all three and also three out of four paragraphs also parallel in SHB for the first block.

G 2

Oxford, Bodleian Library, Opp. 487 Neubauer 1943. f. 91v–93r

IMHM F 19105

PUSHD

Date: Rhineland 1677

Oxford I: 633:

"Ger. curs. char.; quarto, paper, ff. 142."

Oxford II: 346:

"[Ashkenaz], 1677; Ashkenazic cursive script."

The text starts with three consecutive paragraphs, numbered at the end of each, 204, 205, and 206, that correspond to SHB 204–206.

PUSHD claims: "MS Bodl. Lib. Opp. 487 contains three numbered paragraphs from Sefer Hasidim (204, 205, 206) fully corresponding to MS Parma, paragraphs 210, 211, 212." They do, but these three paragraphs have the same paragraph numbers as the parallel passages in SHB!

The readings in SHB are also nearly identical to those in this MS, including the *le'azim.*

The text is as follows:

f. 91v line 14:

Title: "sefer hasidim"

"IM [enlarged] ra'ita yehudi she-heimir mipnei zenut . . . Si[man] 204"=SHB 204

Title: "'od sham"

"Mi she-'oseq be-hashba'ot shel mal'akhim"=SHB 205

f. 92r ends: "ela bi-tefillah"

[no *siman* number at the end]

Title: "'od sham"

"IM [enlarged] tir'eh adam she-mitnabei 'al mashiah . . . ma'aminim bi-devarav. Siman 206"=SHB 206

[The next two passages are not from *Sefer Hasidim* itself. See explicit.]

"T[no] R[abbanan] [First letters enlarged]: kol ha-yodeia' shem M"B otiyot"

f. 92v (text continues) "le-havin u-le-horot"

"Ha-'OSEQ [enlarged] bi-shemot u-mishtamesh ba-hen"

f. 93r (text continues) ". . . 'a[l] k[en] yishmor 'azmo meihem"

Explicit: f. 93r: "'a[d] k[an] mazati ve-rubo katuv be-sefer hasidim be-siman 205 u-ve-siman 469 u-ve-siman 1178." [Not copied in PUSHD]

"Ve-ani ha-kotev mazati be-sefer me'irat 'einayim u-me'od [enlarged] me'od yesh lo la-adam lizaher bi-khvod ha-sh[em] y[itbarakh]."

G 3

Oxford, Bodleian Library, Opp. 677 (Neubauer 1167)

IMHM F 16626

Not in PUSHD

17th century Ashkenazic

4 ff.

See SHB 171 and 485

Oxford I, 371:

[refers to text in SHB 171 and 485]

"Germ. curs. char. without vowel points; quarto, paper, ff. 4."

Oxford II, 187:

"[Ashkenaz, early 17th cent.]; Ashkenazic cursive script."

G 4 [fragment from SHB?]

Leeds–Brotherton Library, MS Roth 46, f. 27v–35r

Description: "Liqqutim mi-sefer hasidim"

IMHM F 15278

62 ff.

Not in PUSHD

18th–19th century Mizrahit

Corfu

Roth, C., *Catalogue*, no. 46.

Refers to *siman* numbers that correspond to SHB:

f. 27v: "katuv be-sefer hasidim siman resh mem bet: ha-neheneh min ha-ma'ot" [SHB 242]

"'od sham be-siman tav tav (?) [800]: "adam she-mitpalel 'al"[SHB 803]

"'od siman tav 'ayin zayin (?): "shenei ahim . . . lo yazlihu" [SHB 477]

f. 29v "tav zadeh bet: bahur she-ba" [SHB 492]

"siman tav zadeh gimel: ishah she-meitah ahotah" [SHB 493]

"siman shin 'ayin tet: al teshadekh lehasi na'arah" [SHB 379]

f. 30v: "siman shin pe tet: ketiv ve-a'avor 'alekha" [SHB 389]

f. 31r: "siman shin zadeh: mi she-eino yakhol le-hizdaqeq 'im" [SHB 390]

f. 31v: "siman tav shin kaf het: "ma'aseh be-hasid ehad . . . shokhev 'al par'oshim" [SHB 528]

f. 32r: "siman tav qof kaf tet: hinei amru yissurin shel ahavah" [SHB 529]

f. 32v: "siman tav qof kaf tet" (continued)

"siman tav qof lamed: . . . ki et kol ma'asei elohim (!) yavi ba-mishpat" [SHB 530]

Ends f. 35r

G 5

Oxford, Bodleian Library, Or. 608 Neubauer 453, f. [231] (129)

Title: "Sefer niqra hasidim"

IMHM F 18597

Not in PUSHD

15th–16th centuries

Sephardic

Oxford I, 98:

"3. Ethical fragm.: a. Fol. 123. darkhei ha-teshuvah . . . b. fol. 129.

Sefer ha-Hasidim (incomplete) . . . Span. Rabb. char. (different hands); Quarto, paper, ff. 201, (stained and injured.)"

A change in the folio numbers given in Neubauer's catalog entry 453:

No. 2=f. 211 (not 109)

No. 3a=f. 224 (not 123)

No. 3b=f. 231 (not 129)

No. 4=f. 257 (not 155)

Actually 3a=f. 225r–230v

And 3b=f. 231r

Oxford II, 70:

"fols. 225r–237v, "'darkhei ha-teshuvah' based on Sefer Hasidim."

"[Sepharad, late 15th cent.]; Sephardic semi-cursive script."

G 6

Cincinnati, Hebrew Union College 269, f. 13v–14r

IMHM F 18220

Not in PUSHD

17th–18th centuries, Italian hand

16 ff.

Excerpt with paragraph numbers 235, 236, 237:

f. 13v line 6: "be-sefer hasidim siman resh lamed heh: im ro'eh adam halom o ru'ah" [SHB 235 reads: im adam ro'eh halom"]

f. 13v line13: "u-ve-siman resh lamed vav" [SHB middle of 236, from line 6] "y[esh] o[merim] she im nireh le-adam sheid yikhfof godelo" [ends f 14r line 8 with end of SHB 236]

f. 14r, line 9: "u-ve-siman resh lamed zayin ha-ro'eh goy ba-halom o goyim" [SHB 237]

G 7

Los Angeles, University of California, Los Angeles, Rosenberg Library

Rosenberg Collection Includes qame'ot. Notes on *Sefer Hasidim*

779 bx 9.15

IMHM F 32406

Not in PUSHD

Viyunti, David Abraham, attributed author

4 pages of notes on different numbered paragraphs

[24] pages

1 page says note is on par. 779=SHB 781 "lo yeizei adam mi-b[eit] ha-[keneset] 'ad she-yesayemu kol ha-tefillah."

G 8

New York, JTS Mic. 2507

Title: "Qehal Hasidim"

19th Mizrahi

On *Sefer Hasidim*, quotes from Brit Olam by HIDA and other books

92 ff.

IMHM 28760

Not in PUSHD

Paper

Commentary on a set of passages from printed ed. with many omissions, but otherwise in numbered sequence. Starts with middle of SHB par. 4, then 10, etc. and has many blank pages and parts of pages.

G 9

New York, JTS Mic. 5402, f. 139r–142v

IMHM 34963?

IMHM 18597

Not in PUSHD

Qahal Hasidim?

Hagahot 'al Sefer Hasidim

Drashot, HIDA

Quntres Livorno 176 ff. Printed in Lev David

G 10

Montréal, Elberg 66 Cf. Hamburg.

From the collection of Shindle and Yehuda Elberg

IMHM 40699 [only first and last five pages filmed]

Not in PUSHD

477+1240=1717

Possibly copied from SHB or SHK

f. 1v title page ends: "ne'etaq po Q"Q Radaa' [Yemen] yod ayin"alef
shenat 'ani B'TH [1717] ahishena' LP"Q"
[Text]
Numbered paragraphs
f. 2r to f. 6r text of SHB pars. 1–middle of 18
f. 2r "be-shem rahaman"/ZEH [initial]/Niqra Sefer Hasidim [initial]
2 cols.
f. 4rb: *le'azim* like those in SHB and so omits "dei" as does SHB
par. 15 omits *la'az* and writes in margin instead: "kan la'az ve-lo ra'iti
le-khotevo"
f. 5ra bottom–f. 5rb top: par. 18 *la'az* garbled
f. 5rb 4 lines from bottom: omits "ris"
Ends: f. 6rb line 21: "magen avraham" middle of SHB par. 18.
[Fragment of Index of Paragraphs]
f. 118v starts with SHB 826
f. 122b ends index with SHB 1178
f. 123r colophon: "Yitzhaq ben he-hakham HR"R Aharon mi-Prostitz"

G 11
New York, JTS Mic. 5252, f. 93r–96r
IMHM F 30049
Not in PUSHD
f. 93r: "Mazati katuv ve-hu mu'ataq mi-sefer ha-hasidim mi-zava'ot rabbeinu
yehuda [alef at end] he-hasid zzh"h ve-hem shiv'im zivuyim."
It goes through #66, lists #67 without any text and stops in the middle of
#70.

G 12
New York JTS Mic. 2082
IMHM F 11180
Not in PUSHD
17 pp.
Title: "Sefer Hasidim"
Cursive, dark, not clear

G 13

Montréal, Elberg 52 f. [2r]

IMHM F 40703

Not in PUSHD

22 ff.

Yemenite

19th century

"Sefer Hasidim"??

"bi-she'at ha-'aqeidah hayah qitrug bein michael u-vein samael ki samael hayah meqatreig ve-omeir: 'Atidin she-ya'asu 'eigel u-???? menazho
be-qorbanuto-ma'aseh ha-mishkan ve-ha-qetoret. Ve-zehu: ne'ehaz bi-sevah
bi-qeranav': otiyot shniyot: 'li-sevakh 'eigel' ve-zehu ma'aseh."

f. [2v]

"ha-'eigel u-mikhael menazeah bi-qeranav shel ayil, she-[af al pi] she-yihte'u
be-'eigel, u-tekhaper la-hem be-qorbanot ke-nizkar le'eil, ve-zehu: 'bi-qeranav
'al ayil hashvu.'"

G 14

David, Avraham. "Pisqah nosefet le-'Sefer Hasidim,'" *Qiryat Sefer* 45 (1970):
627–628.

G 15

Passages attributed to *Sefer Hasidim* are found in:

Oxford Opp. 111=Neubauer 1566 [IMHM F 16934] [copy of Ox. Opp. 540
Neubauer 1567 IMHM F 16935]

Dan, *'Iyyunim*, 138–139 cites several, including two from *Sefer ha-Malakhim*.
In addition:

a. There are two paragraphs in Joseph Dan, *'Iyyunim* (1978) p. 140 from Oxford, Bodleian Library, Opp. 540 (Neubauer 1567) and Opp. 111 (Neubauer
1566) [copy of 1567]: 1566 f. 180v [from "Sefer ha-Ne'elam"];

b. f. 178r: "A hasid used to teach his daughters to write . . ." [compare to SHP
830's etc.; different but related];

c. (continuation): "kos shel berakhah. Once a woman poured the wine for
the cup (over which) a blessing (was to be recited) and the hasid did not want
to take it from her"

Oxford I: p. 547 on no. 1567:

"The same work, beg. Wanting. Old Germ. Curs. Char.; 4to, paper, ff. 316"

Oxford II on no. 1567:

"Frankfurt, 1637/8?; Ashkenazic semi-cursive script"

A passage in *Sefer Mizvot Qatan*, par. 3, quoted in *Jewish Political Tradition* Vol. II, but is not in the North French Miscellany, London, British Library Add. 11639.

Reference to *Sefer Hasidim* in R. Isaac b. Moses, *Sefer Or Zarua'* (vols. 1 and 2, Zhitomir, 1862; vols. 3 and 4, Jerusalem, 1887–1890), 1: 78c, Hilekhot Tefillin, par. 576.

II. Catalog of *Sefer Hasidim* Printed Editions (1538–2007)

Abbreviations

Ben-Yaakov: Ben-Yaakov, *Ozar ha-Sefarim* (het, #755-, p. 197)

Friedberg: Bernhard Friedberg, *Beit Eiqed Sefarim* [1474–1950], vol. 2:385 under "het" #1076

JTS: Library of the Jewish Theological Seminary of America

Kasher: Menachem Kasher, *Sarei ha-Elef*

NLI: National Library of Israel online catalog

Vinograd: Yeshayahu Vinograd, *Ozar ha-Sefer ha-'Ivri* [Thesaurus of the Hebrew Book]. [from 1469–1863]. 2 vols. Jerusalem: Ha-Makhon le-Bibliografiah Memuhshevet, 1994–1995.

First Edition

Bologna, 1538 (available at: Hebrewbooks.org; NLI online for PC users)

Vinograd, p. 102, Bologna #10: [27], [1], 121 f. Oct. Also in Ben-Yaakov, quarto [*sic*]; Kasher, p. 312

The edition begins with title page, and an index of all paragraphs prepared by Avraham b. Moses ha-Kohen (see last page). Numbered paragraphs with enlarged initials and spaces are found around the first word of each paragraph.

Numbers tend to "hang" to the left of the page, under the preceding paragraph.

The last paragraph number in SHB is 1178, but actually there are 1176 numbered paragraphs. The following refers to the numbers, not the text, of paragraphs mentioned: #145 appears twice and there is no #491. These cancel each other out. SHB skips #870 but #883 appears twice. These cancel each other out. But there is no #884 or #1068. So the rest are off by -2.

#1171 appears twice but there is no #1172. These cancel each other out.

Folio page numbers are also defectively numbered as follows: missing: #21, 22, 42, 119 (43 appears twice); 69 appears as 65; 118 appears twice.

There are the following headings:

[1] "zeh niqra sefer hasidim" (incipit in enlarged letters)

20: "hilekhot teshuvah"

162: "sefer ha-hasidim"

End of 478: "gam kan katav 'onshei adam" [cf. SHP II]

End of 586: "ha-kol be-sefer ha-kavod"

604: "ha'ataqah mi-megillat setarim"

606 (in middle): "'ad heina divrei rav nisim gaon zz"l/rabbeinu yitzhaq ha-alfasi" [in SHK, 'rav' is replaced by 'rabbeinu']

after 613: "'ad kan he'etaqti mi-sefer she-yasad rabbeinu saadia gaon z"l"

after 748: "be-khan katuv 'inyanei tefillah"

after 761: "zeh ketav shelaho le-ziqnei regensburg" [in SHK there is a gap between the second and third letters of the word "regensburg."]

768: "ZEH kemo khen mei-'inyan rosh ha-shanah ve-yom ha-kippurim ve-shayakh le'eil [rubric is par. 768]

before 770: "'atah hazarnu le-'inyan hazanut"

before 842: "'inyanei tefillot ve-'inyanei berakhot ketuvim kan"

Before 1136: "seliq berikh rahmana de-siyye'an/ zeh hu'ataq mi-sefer hasidim aher"

There are editorial changes. Compared to parallels in SHP, SHB sometimes replaces "le-hishtamed" with "le-hamir"; "goyim" with "nokhrim." But SHB 237: "goy"/"goyim." Some copies of this edition were expurgated (by printer) and in some copies offensive passages were censored (blacked out); other copies survive in near pristine condition. Each is unique.

Second Edition

Basel, 1580
Vinograd, p. 98, Basel #168; Ambrosio Frobinio, 1580; 116 [4] fols. Oct. Ben-Yaakov [quarto]; NLI; Prijs, Basel, 132; Kasher, p. 312
Published by Ambrosius Frobenius in the German Empire under rules of censorship.
Major variations from SHB by additions at beginnings of some paragraphs and omissions (see below).
Headers at the top of pages vary throughout; there are none in SHB.
By folios:
1r–83r: "sefer hasidim"
83v–84v: "'inyanei meitim"
85r: "'inyanei hazkarat shemot ha-zaddiqim"
85v–86r: "'inyanei tefillah"
86v: "'inyanei tefillah ve-hazanut yamim nora'im"
87r–87v: "ketav le-ziqnei Regensburg"
88r: "'inyanei b[eit] h[a-keneset] u-tefillah"
88v–89r: "kavanat ha-tefillah u-v[eit] h[a-keneset]"
89v–90v: "'inyanei tefillah"
91r: "kavanot q[eriyat] sh[ema'] u-tefillah"
91v: "neqiyut ha-guf u-qedushat s[efer] t[orah]"
92r: "taharat ha-guf u-rehizah"
92v: "sefer hasidim"
93r: "'inyanei tefillot u-verakhot"
93v: "mishnat masekhet terumah"
94r: "hazalah min ha-deliqah be-shabbat"
94v–97r: "qedushat ha-sefarim"
97v–98v: "qedushat s[efer] t[orah] u-sefarim"
99r: "qedushat ha-limmudiut"
99v: "qedushat ha-limmud"

100r: "'inyan 'asaqim"
100v: "'inyan ha-limmudim"
101r: "'inyan ha-rav 'im ha-talmidim"
101v: "'inyan hanhagot ha-lomdim"
102r–105v: "sefer hasidim"
106r: "'inyanei zadiq"
106v: "'inyanei ha-zedaqah"
107r: "'inyanei zedaqah"
107v–116r: "sefer hasidim" [end of book]

Titles in body of text:
[1r]: Title page: "zeh niqra sefer hasidim . . ."
[1v]: "Haqdamah be-mahalal? ha-sefer ve-ha-mehabber ZZ"L"
[2r–2v]: "Haqdamah le-sefer hasidim"
[3r–4v]: "Rimzei kelalei ha-sefer/ eilu hen ha-simanim doleleim she-be-sefer hasidim hainu 'al kol ha-dinim ve-ha-ma'asim asher nimza bo ve-ha-hiddushim ha-pratiyyim nikhlelim/ u-muvla'im ba-hen"
There follows a selected number of *simanim* in sequence.
Par. 20: "hilekhot teshuvah"
Par. 162: no title
End of par. 478 "gam kan katav 'onshei adam"
End of par. 586 same as SHB
604: "ha'ataqah mi-megillat setarim mei-rav nisim gaon z"l"
606 (middle): "'ad heina divrei rav nissim gaon zz"l/ ha'ataqat rabbeinu yizhaq ha-alfasi"
after 613: "'ad kan he'etaqti mi-sefer she-yasad rabbeinu saadia gaon z"l"
after 747: "be-khan katuv 'inyanei tefillah'"
after 763: "zeh ketav shelaho le-ziqnei Regensburg"
par. 768: no title
par. 770: no title
after 838: "'inyanei tefillot ve-'inyanei berakhot ketuvim kan"
after 1128: "seliq berikh rahmana de-siyy'an/ zeh hu'ataq mi-sefer hasidim aher"

In the text, Hebrew *siman* numbers are located in right margins. The first paragraph is not numbered, and the second paragraph starts the numbering with bet (2).

Has at end #1172 instead of #1178, and several irregularities result in this final number, among them:

Numbering of SHBasel is same as SHB from beginning until SHBasel 681=SHB 682 because the text of SHB 681, beginning "ketiv," is omitted in SHBasel. See below for other passages found in SHB but omitted in SHBasel.

The numbering catches up when SHBasel skips #700 and goes from #699 to #701, resulting in SHBasel 701=SHB 701 starting "benei adam"

SHBasel=SHB to par. 721

SHBasel has two paragraphs numbered 721 (SHB 721 and SHB 722)

SHBasel is off by one (-1)

Sequence of paragraphs varies from SHB around the question to and answer from the Beit Din of Regensburg (=SHB 762–763) as follows:

SHBasel 760=SHB 761

SHBasel 761=SHB 764

SHBasel 762=SHB 765

SHBasel 763=SHB 769

SHBasel 764=SHB 762 (question to *beit din*)

SHBasel 765=SHB 763 (answer from *beit din*)

SHBasel 766=SHB 766 with variants: ["ma'aseh hayah] ehad hayah ragil . . ."

SHBasel 767=SHB 767

SHBasel 768=SHB 770 (off by -2)

[Title found in SHB not found in SHBasel: "'atah hazarnu le-'inyanei hazanut"]

SHBasel #780 appears twice for both SHB 782 and SHB 783 (off by -3)

SHBasel 781=SHB 784

SHBasel 867 should be SHB 870 but SHB omits #870 and goes from #869 to #871:

SHBasel 867=SHB 871 (off by -4)

SHBasel 880=SHB 883bis (SHB repeats #883 and has no #884)

SHBasel 881=SHB 885 (still off by -4)

SHBasel 888=SHB 892 but then SHBasel has no number for SHB 893

SHBasel 889=SHB 894 (off by -5)

SHBasel 918=SHB 923 but then SHBasel omits #919 and #920

SHBasel 921=SHB 924 (off by -3)

SHBasel #941 appears twice:

SHBasel 941=SHB 944

SHBasel 941bis=SHB 945 (off by -4)

SHBasel 949=SHB 953 (with variation)

SHBasel 950=SHB 955 (Basel omits text of SHB 954) (off by -5)

SHBasel 987=SHB 992

SHBasel omits #988

SHBasel 989=SHB 993 (off by -4) . . .

SHBasel 1063=SHB 1067

SHB omits #1068

SHBasel 1064=1069 (off by -5)

SHBasel 1083=SHB 1088 (SHBasel omits #1084)

SHBasel 1085=SHB 1089 (off by -4)

SHBasel 1086=SHB 1090

SHBasel [no number]=SHB 1091 (SHBasel has no number for SHB 1091)

SHBasel 1087=SHB 1092 (off by -5)

SHBasel 1109=SHB 1114 (SHBasel omits text of SHB 1115)

SHBasel 1110=SHB 1116 (off by -6)

SHBasel 1128=SHB 1134 (SHBasel omits text of SHB 1135)

SHBasel 1129=SHB 1136 (off by -7)

SHBasel 1131=SHB 1137 (SHBasel omits #1130) (off by -6 to the end)

Friedberg, p. 385 notes that Basel has omissions.

Text in SHB that SHBasel omits:

SHBasel par. 621 omits text after the first word to SHB 621 fifth line, third word introduced by added "she-" ["adam . . . *she*-hitvadeh . . ."].

SHBasel omits text of SHB 681, beginning "ketiv"

SHBasel omits text of SHB 954

SHBasel omits text of SHB 1115

SHBasel omits text of SHB 1135

There is no *siman* index at the end.

There are also variants throughout the passages that are found in both. It is not clear if these are based on different sources or from editorial manipulations in the second printing. SHBasel contains some euphemisms for Christians. The 116 folio pages contain the heading "sefer hasidim" through p. 83a, after which there are topical headings which are not found in SHB as well as rubrics in the text itself.

Third Edition

Krakow, 1581 [Online NLI; defective: missing pages 2–4; other copies in Scholem Library NLI]

Vinograd, p. 634, Krakow #72: Yitzhaq Prostitz; 146 ff. 19 cm. Ben-Yaakov; NLI; Kasher, p. 312

#1178 at end but actually #1176:

#145 appears twice [f. 20r, 20v] (-1);

#1068 is omitted [f. 114v] (-1)

The headers throughout at top of the page: "sefer hasidim"

Index of paragraphs with numbers at the end, not beginning

End f. 122r:

"Yehi shem H mevorakh me-'atah ve-'ad 'olam/ she-gamarti sefer hasidim tam ve-nishlam//'im hasdo ha-gadol le-rov ha-shalom/ yezakkeini im zar'i le-qayyem kol devarav bi-ferat u-khelalam//ha-mevaqesh ze shemo ka-zeh Yitzhaq bHHR (?) Aharon mi-Prostitz lir'ot be-no'am H ve-shavu vanim li-gevulam./

Nishlam be-R[osh] H[odesh] Sivan she-nitnah bo Torah, yom d[aled] li-frat ASH"M [1581] lekha shal[o]m."

PUSHD says that Margoliot is based on the "second edition" but does not identify it. SHM has the same number of paragraphs as SHBasel: 1172, instead of 1178 as in SHB and SHK but how Margoliot got to that number is not the same as how SHBasel did.

Other Early Editions

[Krakow], 1639
Vinograd, p. 641, Krakow #408: with "Peirush Mishnat Hasidim." Ben-Yaakov: [Folio]; Kasher, p. 312

[Krakow], [1641]
Vinograd, p. 642, Krakow #422: with "Peirush Mishnat Hasidim." Reprint of above ed. 1639? Folio; Ben-Yaakov

Amsterdam, [1651]
Vinograd, p. 35, Amsterdam #187: Same as last two; Amsterdam, Immanuel Benveniste. Folio, 6 ff.; not completed in print; Ben-Yaakov, p. 197; NLI

Sulzbach, 1685
Vinograd, p. 292, Sulzbach #17: Moshe Bloch. 79 [1] fols.; Oct.; Ben-Yaakov; NLI; Kasher, p. 312

Frankfurt am Main, 1712–13
Vinograd, p. 585, Frankfurt am Main #302: Johann Köllner; [3], 66 ff. 19 cm; Ben-Yaakov, p. 197; NLI; Kasher, with some explanations by David Gruenhut, tav 'ayin gimel; Quarto

Frankfurt am Main, 1724
Vinograd, p. 588, Frankfurt am Main #437: Johann Köllner/David Aptrod; [4] 148 ff.; 20 cm; Ben-Yaakov, het 757, p. 197: with short commentary of David Aptrod and the *zava'ah* published by David Aptrod's son; Kasher, p. 312

[Zolkiew], 1775
Vinograd, p. 314, Zolkiew #363: [1], 4, 3–155; 52 ff.; Oct., NLI

Zolkiew, 1776
Vinograd, p. 314, Zolkiew #368, [1], 33 ff.; 23 cm.; Yiddish

Zolkiew, 1787
Vinograd, p. 316, Zolkiew #434; Quarto; Yiddish

Polnoya, 1792
Vinograd, p. 500, Polnoya #14; 4, 148 ff.; 20 cm, Shmuel ben Yisakhar bar
Segal; Ben-Yaakov, NLI

NP, 1794
Vinograd, p. 696, NP #82; Yiddish

[Lemberg], [1800]
Vinograd, p. 416, Lemberg #181: [1], 4, 3–145 ff.; Oct.; NLI

Zolkiew, 1805
Vinograd, p. 320, Zolkiew #637: Avraham Yehudah Leib Meirhaffer;
Ben-Yaakov; Oct.

Zolkiew, 1806
Vinograd, p. 321, Zolkiew #670; M. Rubinstein [37] ff.; Oct.; Yiddish

Ostraha, 1814
Vinograd, p. 4, Ostraha #69: 34 ff.; 23 cm; NLI

Hrubieszow, 1817
Vinograd, p. 167, Hrubieszow #5; Finkelstein, [32] ff.; Quarto; Yiddish

Poritzk, 1817
Vinograd, p. 503, Poritzk #39: Shlomo ben Hanina. 133 ff.; Quarto; Ben-Yaakov;
NLI

Vilna, 1819
Vinograd, p. 196, Vilna #124. 74 ff.; Yiddish

Polnoya, 1819
Vinograd, p. 502, Polnoya #116: 20 cm; NLI

NP, 1822
Vinograd, p. 697, NP #123: 83 ff.; Oct.; NLI

NP, 1826
Vinograd, p. 697, NP #126: 157 ff.; Oct.; NLI

NP, 1826
Vinograd, p. 697, NP #127, 144 ff.; Oct.; NLI

Sdilkov, 1826
Vinograd, p. 485, Sdilkov #100; Ben-Yaakov

[Russia-Polin], [1830]
Vinograd, p. 663, Russia-Polin #131: [86] ff.; 23 cm.; NLI

Sdilkov, 1832
Vinograd, p. 486, Sdilkov #160: Pinhas Eliezer Biltsh. [136] ff.; Oct.; Ben-Yaakov; NLI

Sdilkov, 1833
Vinograd, p. 486, Sdilkov #179: 144 ff.; Oct.; NLI

[Lemberg], [1840]
Vinograd, p. 427, Lemberg #672

[Russia-Polin], [1850]
Vinograd, p. 664, Russia-Polin #203: 144 [1] ff.; 21 cm

Lemberg, 1851
Vinograd, p. 435, Lemberg #1078: 15, 5–33 [V: should be 32], 27 ff.; Quarto; NLI

Zhitomir, 1856
Vinograd, p. 334, Zhitomir #154: Hanina Lippa and Yehoshua Heshel Shapira; 144 ff.; Oct.; NLI

Zhitomir, 1857
Vinograd, p. 334, Zhitomir #183; 116 pp.; Yiddish

Zhitomir, 1857
Vinograd, p. 334, Zhitomir #184: Haninah Lippa and Yehoshua Heschel Shapira; 144 pp.; 23 cm; NLI

Lemberg, 1858
Vinograd, p. 441, Lemberg #1369: David Zvi Shrentzel; [259] pp.; Oct.; Ben-Yaakov, NLI

Warsaw, 1859
Vinograd, p. 184, Warsaw #718: Natan Shriftgisser; [2], 61 ff.; Oct.; Yiddish

Yosvov, 1860
Vinograd, p. 352, Yosvov #187: David Saadia Yeshaya Wachs; 58 ff.; Oct.; Ben-Yaakov; NLI

Lemberg, 1863
Vinograd, p. 452, Lemberg #1902; Ben-Yaakov; NLI

Lemberg 1863
Vinograd, p. 452, #1903: Leib Madpis; 86 ff.; Oct.; NLI
Has SHB 185, not 191, 221, 407, 412, 425,464–465, 473, 686–687, 1117, 1146.

[Zolkiew], no date
Vinograd, p. 330, Zolkiew, #1092; Nizanim. 113 pp.; Oct.; Yiddish

Lemberg, 1865
Friedberg 2: 385, #18; Quarto; 80 ff.

Warsaw, 1865
Friedberg #34; 56 ff.; Yiddish

Zhitomir, 1870
Friedberg #21: 1, 114 ff.
"bi-defus yizhaq moshe baqst":
f. 2a haqdamah; f. 2b–3a: "zava'at rabbi yehudah he-hasid"; f. 3r–4r: "rimzei kelalei ha-sefer"; from f. 4b: text with "brit 'olam" and "peirush."

Lemberg, 1870
Friedberg #22

Lemberg 1872
Friedberg #23

Warsaw, 1873

Warsaw, 1874
Friedberg #24, 296 pp.

Warsaw, 1879
Friedberg #25, 224 pp.

Zhitomir, 1879
Defus R. Pesah Lebenson.

Warsaw, 1884
Friedberg #35, Oct.; 108 pp.; Yiddish

Zhitomir, 1885

Warsaw, 1902
Friedberg #26, Oct.

Warsaw, [1913]
"Bi-defus Levin-Epstein"

Modern Editions

Sefer Hasidim, edited by Jehuda Wistinetzki. Frankfurt am Main, 1891 [online at DAAT]

Sefer Hasidim, edited by Jehuda Wistinetzki and Jacob Freimann. Frankfurt am Main, 1924

Sefer Hasidim, edited by Reuven Margoliot. Lemberg, 1924 [SHM 1] Friedberg #27 with Reuven Margoliot's *Meqor Hayyim*; Oct., 540 pp.; Kasher, p. 132; reprinted Lemberg, 1935

Sefer Hasidim, edited by Abraham A. Price. 3 vols. Toronto: Yeshivat Torat Hayim, 1955–1964

Sefer Hasidim, edited by Reuven Margoliot. New edition. Jerusalem: Mosad Ha-Rav Kook, 1956/7 [SHM 2] reprinted many times. It is this edition most often referred to as "ed. Bologna" but the two are different throughout.

Sefer Hasidim K[tav] Y[ad] Parma H 3280. Introduction by Ivan G. Marcus. Jerusalem: Merkaz Dinur of the Hebrew University of Jerusalem, 1985

PUSHD (2007)
Nineteen versions of *Sefer Hasidim* with a search engine

Notes

Where a source appears in a shortened citation and is not in the Select Bibliography, it is listed in full earlier in the notes of the chapter where the shortened citation appears.

INTRODUCTION

Epigraph taken from Erich Auerbach, *Literary Language and Its Public in Late Latin Antiquity and in the Middle Ages,* translated from the German by Ralph Manheim (Princeton, N.J.: Princeton University Press, 1965), 20.

1. Among the early historical treatments, see Lucien Febvre and Henri-Jean Martin, *The Coming of the Book: The Impact of Printing, 1450–1800,* translated by David Gerard (London: Verso, 1976); Marshall McLuhan, *The Gutenberg Galaxy: The Making of Typographic Man* (Toronto: University of Toronto Press, 1962), and McLuhan, *Understanding Media: The Extensions of Man* (New York: McGraw-Hill, 1964); D. F. McKenzie, *Bibliography and the Sociology of Texts* [Panizzi Lectures, 1985] (Cambridge: Cambridge University Press, 1999); Bernard Cerquiglini, *In Praise of the Variant: A Critical History of Philology,* translated by Betsy Wing (Baltimore: Johns Hopkins University Press, 1999); Armando Petrucci, *Public Lettering: Script, Power, and Culture,* translated by Linda Lappin (Chicago: University of Chicago Press, 1993); Petrucci, *Writers and Readers in Medieval Italy: Studies in the History of Written Culture,* edited and translated by Charles M. Radding (New Haven, Conn.: Yale University Press, 1995); Roger Chartier, *The Order of Books: Readers, Authors, and Libraries in Europe Between the Fourteenth and Eighteenth Centuries,* translated by Lydia G. Cochrane (Stanford, Calif.: Stanford University Press, 1994); Chartier, *Forms and Meanings: Texts, Performances, and Meanings from Codex to Computer* (Philadelphia: University of Pennsylvania Press, 1995); Chartier, "Crossing Borders in Early Modern Europe: Sociology of Texts and Literature," *Book History* 8 (2005): 37–50; Chartier, *The Author's Hand and the Printer's Mind,* translated by Lydia G. Cochrane (Cambridge: Polity Press, 2014).

For early studies of Hebrew book history, see Abraham M. Habermann, *Toledot ha-Sefer ha-'Ivri* (Jerusalem: Reuven Mass, 1945); Raphael Posner and Israel Ta-Shma, eds., *The Hebrew Book: An Introduction* (New York: Leon Amiel, 1975); Yaakov Spigel, *'Amudim be-Toledot ha-Sefer ha-'Ivri*, 2 vols. (Ramat Gan: Bar Ilan University Press, 1996–2005), as well as the ongoing work of the Institute of Hebrew Paleography founded by Malachi Beit-Arié with Colette Sirat in 1965. Continuing updates are available online by registering with "SfarData."

2. See Baer, "Ha-Megamah"; Soloveitchik, "Three Themes," 311–357; Marcus, *Piety and Society*; and Marcus, *Dat ve-Hevrah*. On Judah he-hasid's life, see Chapter 3.

3. See Marcus, "Jewish-Christian Symbiosis," 448–516, reprinted in Marcus, *Jewish Culture and Society*.

4. See Soloveitchik, "Midrash, *Sefer Hasidim*," 170.

5. Dan, *R. Yehudah he-Hasid*, 15.

6. See Güdemann, *Geschichte des Erziehungswesens*, 1:281.

7. See Catalog.

8. See Select Bibliography, Secondary Sources.

9. Cf. McLuhan, *Understanding Media*, 7–21, for the related phrase "The medium is the message."

10. For recent studies of the *mise-en-page* and other matters related to Hebrew scribal cultures, see Nicholas de Lange and Judith Olszowy-Schlanger, eds., *Manuscrits hébreux et arabes: Mélanges en l'honneur de Colette Sirat* [*Bibliologia*, 38] (Turnhout: Brepols, 2014).

11. Marcus, "Mavo," viii–ix and, in Hebrew section, 29–30.

12. For patterns of topical notebooks in the two texts, based on analysis of the parallels according to their content, see Marcus, "Recensions and Structure," 131–153. Reprinted in Marcus, *Jewish Culture and Society*.

13. See Marcus, "Recensions and Structure."

14. For the method of textual criticism that assumes an author wrote one original composition that scholars try to reconstruct from manuscript remains, see Paul Maas, *Textual Criticism*, translated from the German by Barbara Fowler, 3rd ed. (Oxford: Clarendon Press, 1958), and Martin L. West, *Textual Criticism and Editorial Technique Applicable to Greek and Latin Texts* (Stuttgart: B. G. Teubner, 1973).

15. Umberto Eco published his original essay on "texta aperta" in 1962 and expanded it several times. See Umberto Eco, "The Poetics of the Open Work," in Umberto Eco, *The Open Work,* translated by Anna Cancogni, with an introduction by David Robey (Cambridge, Mass.: Harvard University Press, 1989), 1–23. My appreciation to Peter Lehnhardt for the reference.

For an application of Eco's term with the meaning of polysemic readings of text in Jewish sources, see Giuseppi Sermoneta, "'Le-Reah Shemanekha Tovim'—Rabbi Yehudah Romero ve-Shitat 'ha-Yezirah ha-Petuhah,'" *Mehqarei Yerushalayim be-Mahshevet Yisrael 9* [*Sefer ha-Yovel li-Shelomo Pines bi-Melot lo Shemonim Shanah,* II] (1990): 77–113.

16. Israel Ta-Shma, "The 'Open' Book in Medieval Hebrew Literature: The Problem of Authorized Editions," *Bulletin of the John Rylands Library* 75:3 (1993): 17–24. For "open book" in the sense of "accessible book," see Robert Bonfil, "Reading in the Jewish Communities of Western Europe in the Middle Ages," in *History of Reading in the West,* edited by Guglielmo Cavallo and Roger Chartier, translated by Lydia G. Cochrane (Cambridge: Polity Press, 1999), 149–178, 404–413.

17. Ta-Shma, "'Open' Book," 20. For Ashkenazic books that conform to Ta-Shma's model of an "open book" in the sense of an author revising one or more times his original version, such as *Sefer ha-Terumah* and *Sefer Mizvot Gadol,* see Chapter 4.

18. Israel Ta-Shma himself refers to this kind of Ashkenazic parallel book composition, such as the Italian Talmud commentator R. Isaiah di Trani, who studied in Ashkenaz, writing four or five editions of his Talmud commentary from scratch. On di Trani, see Israel Ta-Shma, *Ha-Sifrut ha-Parshanit la-Talmud,* 2 vols. (Jerusalem: Magnes Press, 1990–2000), 2:178–179.

19. David Konstan, "The *Alexander Romance*: The Cunning of the Open Text," *Lexis* 16 (1998): 123, redefined the term independently, without any linkage to Eco's original Italian essay of 1962. See, too, Joachim Bumke, "The Fluid Text: Observations on the History of Transmission and Textual Criticism of the Thirteenth-Century Courtly Epic," in *Visual Culture and the German Middle Ages,* edited by Kathryn Starkey and Horst Wenzel (New York: Palgrave MacMillan, 2005), 99–113, esp. 104–107.

20. Konstan, "*Alexander Romance,*" 123.

21. Ibid., 125, 126.

22. Ibid., 126.

23. Ibid., 127.

24. Both quotations, ibid., 128.

25. I owe the comparison to Professor Simcha Emanuel of the Hebrew University of Jerusalem in a conversation in 2014. See the interview with Lego CEO Joergen Vig Knudstorp in the PBS documentary *Inside Story: Lego,* 2014.

26. On Ashkenazic scribal activism, see Malachi Beit-Arié, *Hebrew Manuscripts of East and West: Towards a Comparative Hebrew Codicology* [Panizzi Lectures, 1992] (London: British Library, 1993). On rabbinic authorship, see Catherine Hezser, "Classical Rabbinic Literature," in *The Oxford Handbook of Jewish Studies,* edited by Martin Goodman et al. (Oxford: Oxford University Press, 2004), 135. For the relationship between *heikhalot*

traditions and German Pietist manuscripts, see Klaus Herrmann, "Rewritten Mystical Texts: The Transmission of the Heikhalot Literature in the Middle Ages," *Bulletin of the John Rylands University Library* 73:3 (Autumn 1993): 97–116.

27. On anthologizing in Hebrew literature, see David Stern, ed., *The Anthology in Jewish Literature* (Oxford: Oxford University Press, 2004). Robert Bonfil points to the genre of medieval historiography as anthological, though the three 1096 Hebrew chronicles were variant compositions based on written sources and oral reports that three different writers composed in different ways in their own words. See Robert Bonfil, *History and Folklore in a Medieval Jewish Chronicle: The Family Chronicle of Ahima'az ben Paltiel* (Leiden: E. J. Brill, 2009), 31–32 and below. One needs to distinguish between writing local history, composed in segmented texts, and world histories, written as anthologies.

28. Moshe Bar-Asher, "Matbea' she-Tav'u Hakhamim bi-Verakhah ('Iyyun Rishon)," in *Kenishta: 'Iyyunim 'al Beit ha-Keneset ve-'Olamo* 4, edited by J. Taboury (Ramat Gan and Jerusalem: Bar-Ilan University Press, 2010), 24–49.

29. See Jean-Baptiste Frey, ed., *Corpus Inscriptionum Judaicarum* [Corpus of Jewish Inscriptions], vol. 1, *Europe,* 1936, reprinted with a Prolegomenon by Baruch Lifshitz (New York: Ktav Publishing House, 1975), 24.

30. See Güdemann, *Geschichte des Erziehungswesens*, vol. 1; Bonfil, "Can Medieval Story Telling Help Understanding Midrash?" 228–254; and Marcus, *Rituals of Childhood,* introduction.

31. Marcus, *Rituals of Childhood*, introduction; Israel Jacob Yuval, *Two Nations in Your Womb: Perceptions of Jews and Christians in Late Antiquity and the Middle Ages* (Berkeley: University of California Press, 2006); Elisheva Baumgarten, *Practicing Piety in Medieval Ashkenaz: Men, Women, and Everyday Religious Observance* (Philadelphia: University of Pennsylvania Press, 2014); Ephraim Shoham-Steiner, *On the Margins of a Minority: Leprosy, Madness and Disability Among the Jews of Medieval Europe* (Detroit: Wayne State University Press, 2014). These studies owe their inspiration to the *Annales* approach of Robert Bonfil.

32. See Colette Sirat, "Le livre hébreux: Rencontre de la tradition juive et de l'esthétique française," in *Rashi et la culture juive dans la France du Nord au Moyen Age,* edited by Gilbert Dahan, Gérard Nahon, and Elie Nicolas (Paris and Louvain: Peeters, 1994), 243–259; Sirat, "En vision globale: Les juifs médiévaux et les livres latins," in *La tradition vive: mélanges D'histoire des textes en l'honneur de Louis Holtz,* edited by Pierre Lardet [*Bibliologia* 20] (Turnhout: Brepols, 2000), 197–219, 15–20; Sirat, *l'examen des écritures, l'oeil et la machine, essai de méthodologie* (Paris: Editions du Centre national de la recherche scientifique, 1981); Sirat, *Hebrew Manuscripts of the Middle Ages,* edited and

translated by Nicholas de Lange (Cambridge: Cambridge University Press, 2002), 170–203; Edna Engel, "Between France and Germany: Gothic Characteristics in Ashkenazi Script," in *Manuscrits hébreux et arabes: Mélanges en l'honneur de Colette Sirat*, edited by Nicholas de Lange and Judith Olszowy-Schlanger [*Bibliologia*, 38] (Turnhout: Brepols, 2014), 197–219; and Justine Isserles, "Les parallèles esthétiques des manuscrits hébreux ashkenazes de type liturgico-légal et des manuscrits latins et vernaculaires médiévaux," in *Manuscrits hébreux et arabes: Mélanges en l'honneur de Colette Sirat*, edited by Nicholas de Lange and Judith Olszowy-Schlanger [*Bibliologia*, 38] (Turnhout: Brepols, 2014), 77–113; Javier del Barco, ed., *The Late Medieval Hebrew Book in the Western Mediterranean* (Leiden: Brill, 2015).

33. For Sephardic impact on eighteenth-century German Jewry, see Morris M. Faierstein, "The Liebesbrief: A Critique of Jewish Society in Germany," *Leo Baeck Year Book* 27 (1982): 219–241. On the "Sephardic Mystique" in modern Germany, see Ivan G. Marcus, "Beyond the Sephardic Mystique," *Orim* 1:1 (Autumn 1985): 35–53, Ismar Schorsch, "The Myth of Sephardic Supremacy," *Leo Baeck Year Book* 34 (1989): 47–66, and John M. Efron, *German Jewry and the Allure of the Sephardic* (Princeton, N.J.: Princeton University Press, 2016), 16.

34. See Yisrael Mordecai Peles, "Sefer 'Maharil' [='Minhagei Maharil'] 'al pi Kitvei ha-Yad ha-Otografiyyim shelo ve-Yihudo ke-'Hibbur Merubeh 'Arikhot'" (PhD diss., Bar-Ilan University, 2005), especially chapter 10.

35. On the combination of *hasidut* and *halakhah* in Judah's Regensburg court decision, see Kanarfogel, "R. Judah he-Hasid and the Rabbinic Scholars of Regensburg," 19–21 and 34–36.

36. See, for example, Wineman, "Agnon's Use of Narrative Motifs," 175–118.

CHAPTER 1

Epigraph taken from Gershom Scholem, *Major Trends in Jewish Mysticism*, 83.

1. Joseph Dan also noted correctly that *Sefer Hasidim* is made up of disjunctive passages even in the topical blocks. Remove some, and no one would know. See Dan, *R. Yehudah he-Hasid*, 29.

2. The earliest *Sefer Hasidim* manuscript with contemporary numbering may be Cambridge Add. 379. The numbers in SHP were added later in an Italian hand as were the five topical titles found in the margins of the first part of SHP. See Marcus, "Mavo." Colette Sirat is right that most of the early manuscripts were originally unnumbered, and that includes SHP. See Sirat, *La conception du livre*, Annexes, 149–150. My appreciation to

Malachi Beit-Arié and Edna Engel for their assistance in dating paragraph numbers in SHP.

3. See Catalog, Part G.

4. On the way the *Zohar* developed before and after printing, see Daniel Abrams, *Kabbalistic Manuscripts and Textual Theory: Methodologies of Textual Scholarship and Editorial Practice in the Study of Jewish Mysticism*, 2nd ed. (Jerusalem: Magnes Press; Los Angeles: Cherub Press, 2013), esp. 224–438. About the status of a complete, reliable manuscript of the *Zohar*, Daniel Matt comments: "Unfortunately no such manuscript exists anywhere in the world; in all likelihood it never did, since from the start the *Zohar* was circulated in sections or booklets." See Daniel Matt, "Translator's Introduction," in *The Zohar, Pritzker Edition*, translated by Daniel Matt, vol. 1 (Stanford, Calif.: Stanford University Press, 2004), xvii and xviii; on the idea of an original text of the *Zohar*, Matt adds: "There may never have been any such thing" (xviii). See, too, Joseph Dan, *Toledot Torat ha-Sod ha-'Ivrit: Yemei ha-Beinayyim* 11, *Sefer ha-Zohar* (Jerusalem: Merkaz Zalman Shazar, 2015), 11–13.

5. Leopold Zunz, *Zur Geschichte und Literatur* (Berlin, 1845), 126, and Güdemann, *Geschichte des Erziehungswesens* 1: 281–288.

6. See the translation in Singer, *Medieval Jewish Mysticism*.

7. See Catalog, Part G. For example, Hamburg, Hamburg Staats- und Universitätsbibliothek, Cod. Heb. 303, f. 24r–25v is a modified copy of SHB, 1024–1068. The text and the paragraph numbers do not always agree with SHB. The location of the paragraph numbers in Hamburg 303 is not consistent, pace Soloveitchik, "Appendix to 'Pietists and Kibbitzers,'" n. 84.

8. Haym Soloveitchik, "Appendix to 'Pietists and Kibbitzers.'"

9. As of the publication of this book, they are: (1) Vatican, ebr. 285, f. 150r–152r (not in Hershler, *Genuzot* 1); (2) Hamburg Staats- und Universitätsbibliothek, Cod. Heb. 303, f. 24r–25v; (3) Oxford, Bodleian Library, Mich. 569 (Neubauer 1098), f. 104v; and (4) Oxford, Bodleian Library, Opp. Add. Fol. 39 (Neubauer 865), f. 1r–3r, in the margins.

10. Soloveitchik, "Piety, Pietism," 456n.3.

11. Judah b. Samuel *he-hasid, Sefer Hasidim K[tav] Y[ad] Parma H 3280*, introduction by Ivan G. Marcus.

12. R. Moses b. Eleazar ha-Kohen, *Sefer Hasidim Qatan=Sefer ha-Maskil*, pt. II, par. 8, p. 45.

13. Simcha Emanuel, *Shivrei Luhot: Sefarim Avudim shel Ba'alei ha-Tosafot* (Jerusalem: Magnes Press, 2007), 6–12.

14. Vatican, Vatican Library, ebr. 285/26, f. 108v–127v; Title: f. 108v: "liqqutim"; Vatican, Vatican Library, ebr. 285, f. 150r–152r; title: f. 150r: "gam eilu liqqutim mi-sefer

hasidim"; Frankfurt am Main, Stadt- und Universitätsbibliothek, Oct. 94/3, f. 270r–272r (formerly Merzbacher 56); title: f. 270r: "Liqqutim neʿetaqu mi-sefer hasidim"; Zurich, Zentralbibliothek, Heidenheim 51/4, f. 9r–10v (middle) title: "liqqutim min sefer hasidim"; Oxford, Bodleian Library, Opp. 614 (Neubauer 2275), f. 30r–31va; title: f. 30r: "Liqqutin mi-sefer hasidim"; Oxford, Bodleian Library, Or. 146 (Neubauer 782), f. 69av–70r; title: f. 69r: "Liqqutin mi-sefer hasidim" (bottom of col. a).

15. This is the better reading from the Moscow 82 manuscript, f. 64v, as opposed to the reading in Hebrew manuscript Strasbourg 3970 (Landauer, *Katalog*, no. 44), that Jacob Freimann quotes in his introduction to the Wistinetzki edition, p. 11: "two books of Sefer Hasidim" (*shenayim kerakhim shel sefer hasidim*). See Lange, *Peirushei ha-Torah*, in the uncensored and censored editions, 17.

16. SHP 700. The parallel in SHB 281 is missing a line by *homoioteleuton* (*al yahtokh . . . al yahtokh*).

17. SHB 932. The parallel in SHP 667 omits a line by *homoioteleuton* (*torah she-beʿal peh . . . torah she-beʿal peh*). The comparison of a text to weaving is familiar from the Latin etymology of *textus* (weaving). See, for example, D. F. McKenzie, *Bibliography and the Sociology of Texts* (Panizzi Lectures, 1985) (Cambridge: Cambridge University Press, 1999), 13–14.

18. There are fourteen topical blocks that follow the initial section that consists of a short work on the fear of God (*Sefer ha-Yirʾah*) attributed to Judah *he-hasid*'s father, Samuel *he-hasid* (SHB 153–166). The fourteen topical blocks of SHB I and SHP I are as follows: Atonement, The Dead, Harmful Spirits, Prayer, Sabbath, Books, Study, Charity, Honoring Parents, Pietism, Ritual Slaughter and Purity, Women, (Business) Trustworthiness, Bans and Oaths.

This corrects the omission of a block on Atonement in Marcus, "Recensions and Structure," 147. It is the first topical block in SHB I (167–230) and in SHP I (18–26, 37–265) but lacks any title in SHP II. My reference to the abbreviation "SHB I" as the first topical edition in the Bologna edition, follows Marcus, "Recensions and Structure," 145. Cf. the confusing terminology of "SH I" in Soloveitchik, "Piety, Pietism." The first 152 paragraphs of SHB should properly be referred to as *Sefer ha-Hasidut* (ShH) and not "SH I" since it is strictly speaking not *Sefer Hasidim* per se but a northern French rewriting of it. See Chapter 2.

19. SHB, par. 1.

20. R. Eleazar b. Judah of Worms, *Sefer ha-Roqeah* (1960), par. 316, end of "Hilekhot Aveilut." Despite this reference to a topical notebook (*mahberet*) that R. Judah *he-hasid* wrote, no single topical notebooks have survived among the manuscripts of *Sefer Hasidim*, only combinations of the fourteen notebooks. After Judah redacted topical notebooks

more than once, he presumably destroyed them, much as working copies of manuscripts were usually destroyed when they were printed for the first time.

21. Kogut, "Ha-Mishpat ha-Murkav." When Kogut compared SHM2 to SHP, he
assumed that ed. Margoliot (SHM2) was the same text as SHB. He made his own table
of paragraph numbers between SHB and SHM2 but did not publish it.

Although scholars repeatedly claim that Rabbi Reuven Margoliot's edition is the
same as the first edition, with slightly different numbering, it is not a word for word
reiteration of ed. Bologna, and one must use PUSHD and ed. Bologna, now online at
Hebrewbooks.org and from the National Library of Israel scanned rare books data base,
to compare parallels and get at its exact text and not rely on ed. Margoliot. A simple word
for word comparison of ed. Margoliot and ed. Bologna for a paragraph of *Sefer Hasidim*
Bologna, such as 153, shows *homoioteleuta*, omissions, additions, and variations totaling
forty differences that one would find between two manuscript copies of the same text.

22. See Kogut, "Ha-Mishpat ha-Murkav," 5–13; Kogut, "Language of 'Sefer Hasidim,'" 97–98.

23. Kogut, "Language of 'Sefer Hasidim,'" 100–101. Dan, *R. Yehudah he-Hasid*, 30,
cites Kogut but ignores his view that the syntax of Mittelhochdeutsch did not influence
the Hebrew syntax of *Sefer Hasidim*. Soloveitchik, "Piety, Pietism," 462 does not cite
Kogut and assumes medieval German syntactic influence without any linguistic evidence.

24. Dan, *'Iyyunim*, 9–25 and 138–141; Dan, *R. Yehudah he-Hasid*, 29–30; David,
"Pisqah nosefet," 627–628; and see a story attributed to Judah *he-hasid* that appears in
the anonymous *Sefer ha-Asufot*, former London, Montefiore 134 [Halberstam 115], f. 157r
col. a, that is also found in *Sefer Hasidim*, as in SHP 327 and former JTS Boesky 45, 144;
Vat. 285, [104] and JTS 2499, [104]; SHB 236 and Cambridge Add. 379, 237. The attribu-
tion to Judah is in *Sefer ha-Asufot* f. 156v col. d. See SHP 63 and parallels in former JTS
Boesky 45, par. 51; Vatican 285 [56] and JTS 2499 [56]; SHB 169 and Oxford, Opp. Add.
Fol. 34 (Neubauer 641), f. 49r col. c, par. 65. The paragraph is not included in the near
twin to Oxford, Opp. Add. Fol. 34 (Neubauer 641), namely, Cambridge, Cambridge Add.
379, and compare Yassif, *Me'ah Sippurim Haser Ehad*, #59 p. 223 and his note on p. 280.
In addition, see a quotation from *Sefer Hasidim* (*be-sefer hasidim katuv*) found in none of
the manuscripts. It is cited by Judah *he-hasid*'s student, R. Isaac b. Moses of Vienna,
Sefer Or Zarua', vols. 1 and 2 (Zhitomir, 1862); vols. 3 and 4 (Jerusalem, 1887–1890), 1:78c,
Hilekhot Tefillin, par. 576. My thanks to Ephraim Kanarfogel for the reference.

25. Dan, *R. Yehudah he-Hasid*, 28.

26. Frankfurt [33] has a parallel in SHB 136 in addition to SHP 706 and Oxford
614 (Neubauer 2275)/Oxford 146 (Neubauer 782) [1].

27. This is clear from the notes in Soloveitchik, "Appendix to 'Pietists and Kibbitzers.'" The numbering of the paragraphs in Zurich Heid. 51 differs in PUSHD and the

"Appendix" starting with par. [5]: PUSHD [5]="Appendix" [5–6]; PUSHD [6]="Appendix" [7–8], although there is space and two marks at the end of "Appendix" [7]; PUSHD [7–8]="Appendix" [9], even though there is a space and two marks at the end of PUSHD [7]; PUSHD [9]="Appendix" [10–39] even though there are clear markers of individual paragraphs. As a result, parallels to this part of the Zurich manuscript are available only in the footnotes to the text as presented in "Appendix" but not in PUSHD.

28. Soloveitchik, "Appendix to 'Pietists and Kibbitzers'" and see f. 74r: "zeh shir ha-kavod she-yasad rabbeinu yehudah hasid mei-Regensburg zz"l." On the manuscript, see Malachi Beit-Arié, comp., and R. A. May, ed., *Catalogue of the Hebrew Manuscripts in the Bodleian Library*, Supplement of Addenda and Corrigenda to Vol. 1 (Neubauer's catalog) (Oxford: Clarendon Press, 1994), under nos. 1098 and 1097.

29. See Marcus, "Recensions and Structure," 145–147.

30. In the second and third block of parallel text in Freiburg and SHP, there are only a few single parallels in SHB, not parallel blocks.

31. On the fragmentary texts in Nîmes 26 and Oxford, Mich. 155 (Neubauer 1984), a fifth pair of manuscript texts with similar structures, see Chapter 2 on "Sefer ha-Hasidut." One may compare the editions of *Sefer Hasidim* with two manuscripts each, to the six groupings of twenty-two manuscripts in Jacob b. Moses Ha-Levi Mölln (Maharil), *Sefer Maharil: Minhagim*, edited by Shlomo Spitzer (1989; reprinted with corrections, Jerusalem: Makhon Yerushalayim, 2005), "Mavo," 12–13.

32. See Marcus, "Recensions and Structure."

CHAPTER 2

Epigraph taken from Edward Fram, "German Pietism," 468.

1. On rabbinic texts, see Catherine Hezser, "Classical Rabbinic Literature," in *The Oxford Handbook of Jewish Studies,* edited by Martin Goodman et al. (Oxford: Oxford University Press, 2002), 128 and 131; on Heikhalot texts, see Peter Schäfer et al., eds., *Synopse zur Hekhalot-Literatur* (Tübingen: J.C.B. Mohr [Paul Siebeck], 1981), and Peter Schäfer, "Tradition and Redaction in Hekhalot Literature," *Journal for the Study of Judaism* 14:2 (1983): 176, 180–181.

2. On Judah, see Ta-Shma, *"Zekher 'Asah le-Nifleotav,"* 123. On Eleazar, see Marcus, "Hasidei Ashkenaz Private Penitentials," 57–83, and Liss, "Copyright im Mittelalter?," 81–108.

3. Dan pointed to several quotations from *Sefer Hasidim* in the two related Oxford manuscripts. He was not able to find three of the quotations, but he correlated others with specific passages in the editions. See Dan, *'Iyyunim,* 138–139, for his theory of how

these passages got into *Sefer Hasidim*. More likely, Judah wrote and rewrote short passages and hundreds of stories and put them into whatever compositions he was working on at the time.

4. For passages in *'Arugat ha-Bosem*, see Freimann, "Mavo," 15–16, and Ephraim E. Urbach's corrections in Abraham b. 'Azriel, *Sefer 'Arugat ha-Bosem* 4: 114n.39.

5. Dan, *R. Yehudah he-Hasid*, 109–111.

6. Ibid., 111.

7. For an earlier review of Dan's thinking on this problem, see his "Book of Divine Glory," 15.

8. Dan, *R. Yehudah he-Hasid*, 105, refers to the main composition titled "Sefer ha-Kavod" in the two Oxford manuscripts as a chaotic work (*hibbur kaoti*) made up of independently written passages. I agree. This is what I have been calling an "open" or "segmented book," typical of Ashkenazic Hebrew book composition.

9. See SHP 1589; former JTS Boesky 45, 671; Cambridge Add. 379, 480.

10. See Malachie Beit-Arié, comp., and R. A. May, ed., *Catalogue of the Hebrew Manuscripts in the Bodleian Library*, Supplement of Addenda and Corrigenda to vol. 1 (Neubauer's catalog) (Oxford: Clarendon Press, 1994), no. 1566.

11. For the former, see SHP 198 and FJTSB 45, 101, and SHB 197; SHP 495 and FJTSB 45, 214; SHP 512 and FJTSB 45, 325, and SHB 811; SHP 1533 and FJTSB 45, 641, and SHB 449; SHP 1535 and FJTSB 45, 642; for the latter, see SHP 430 and FJTSB 45, 181; SHP 880 and FJTSB 45, 355 and SHB 321.

12. R. Eleazar b. Judah of Worms, *Sefer ha-Roqeah* (1960), "Hilekhot Aveilut," par. 316.

13. On the *Zava'ah*, see Shvat, "Zava'at Rabbi Yehudah he-Hasid: Hashva'at Mahadurot Qedumot," 82–152; Shvat, "Zava'at Rabbi Yehudah he-Hasid 'al pi Mahadurot Yeshanot," and Kahana, "Meqorot ha-Yeda'," 223–262. On interrelations between *Sefer ha-Kavod* and the *Zava'ah* of Judah *he-hasid*, see R. Jacob b. Moses Ha-Levi Mölln (Maharil), *She'eilot u-Teshuvot Maharil*, edited by Yitzhaq Satz (Jerusalem: Makhon Yerushalayim, 1979), par. 111: "*ra'iti be-sefer ha-kavod she-hibber he-hasid ve-khatav sham be-zava'ato.*"

14. See the quotation in Simcha Emanuel's introduction to his edition of R. Eleazar b. Judah of Worms, *Derashah le-Fesah*, 35n.135.

15. See Beit-Arié and May, *Catalogue of the Hebrew Manuscripts in the Bodleian Library*, Supplement, to Neubauer 1567. Part of the *Zava'ah* was first printed in Savionetta, 1551.

16. See Shvat, "Zava'at Rabbi Yehudah he-Hasid 'al pi Mahadurot Yeshanot," 4n.9. This practice continues even in recent scholarship as in Lifshitz, *Ehad be-Khol Dimyonot*, 145 and n. 44, where he refers to "Sefer Hasidim" but cites the *Zava'ah* printed in Reuven Margoliot's edition of *Sefer Hasidim* [SHM 2].

17. The text goes through #66, lists a #67 without any text, and stops in the middle of #70.

18. See R. Jacob b. Moses Ha-Levi Mölln (Maharil), *She'eilot u-Teshuvot Maharil*, par. III, p. 208, cited by Emanuel in "Hibburav ha-Hilkhatiyim," 223n.83.

19. See *Zava'at R. Judah he-Hasid*, printed in *Sefer Hasidim*, edited by Reuven Margoliot (1956), and Emanuel, "Hibburav ha-Hilkhatiyim," 223n.83.

20. On the Songs of Divine Unity (*shirei ha-yihud*), see Dan, *'Iyyunim*, 72–79, and Habermann, *Shirei ha-Yihud*. For Judah's lost commentaries on the prayer book and for Eleazar's extant prayer commentaries, see Dan, *R. Yehudah he-Hasid*, 137–141. On Judah's *piyyutim*, see Kanarfogel, *Intellectual History*, 415.

21. See Stal, *Amarot Tehorot Hizoniyot u-Fenimiyot*, "Mavo," 6–7, for a list of passages. On this text, see Shyovitz, *Remembrance of His Wonders*.

22. See Marcus, "Hasidei Ashkenaz Private Penitentials," 57–83.

23. Paris, Bibliothèque Nationale de France, héb. 363; Fano, 1505.

24. See R. Eleazar b. Judah of Worms, *Derashah le-Fesah*, 41, 51, and 63n.248.

25. Ibid., 62–67.

26. On more than one version of Eleazar's prayer book commentary, see Dan, *R. Yehudah he-Hasid*, 138, and R. Eleazar b. Judah of Worms, *Derashah le-Fesah*, 60–61nn.238–239. On Eleazar's commentary on Psalms, compared to passages in his prayer book commentaries, see Simcha Emanuel, *Mi-Ginzei Eiropa* I (Jerusalem: Meqizei Nirdamim, 2015), 183–203. On Eleazar's *piyyutim*, see Kanarfogel, *Intellectual History*, 416–420.

27. On Rabbeinu Tam's poetry and Spanish meter, see Leon J. Weinberger, ed. and trans., *Twilight of a Golden Age: Selected Poems of Abraham Ibn Ezra* (Tuscaloosa: University of Alabama Press, 1997), 6–7, and Isaac Meiseles, *Shirat Rabbeinu Tam: Piyyutei Rabbi Yaakov ben Rabbi Meir* (Jerusalem: Isaac Meiseles, 2012), 8 and 11.

28. On R. Meir's lament, see "Sha'ali serufah ba-esh," in *Seder Kinot le-Tish'ah be-Av*, edited by Daniel Goldschmidt (Jerusalem: Mosad ha-Rav Kook, 1972), no. 42, pp. 135–137. For English translations, see Robert Chazan, *Church, State, and Jew in the Middle Ages* (New York: Behrman House, 1980), 229–231, and Susan Einbinder, *Beautiful Death: Jewish Poetry and Martyrdom in Medieval France* (Princeton, N.J.: Princeton University Press, 2002), 76–78.

29. Michael Stanislawski, "The Yiddish Shevet Yehudah: A Study in the 'Ashkenization' of a Spanish-Jewish Classic," in *Jewish History and Jewish Memory: Studies in Honor of Yosef Hayim Yerushalmi,* edited by Elisheva Carlebach, John M. Efron, and David N. Myers (Hanover, N.H. and London: Brandeis University Press, University Press of New England, 1998), 134–149, and see Elisabeth Hollender, "Adoption and Adaptation: Judah ha-Levi's 'Zion ha-Lo Tishali li-Shelom Asirayikh' in Its Ashkenazic Environment," in

Entangled Histories: Knowledge, Authority, and Jewish Culture in the Thirteenth Century, edited by Elisheva Baumgarten, Ruth Mazo Karras, and Katelyn Mesler (Philadelphia: University of Pennsylvania Press, 2017), 248–262, 332–337. On *Shevet Yehudah*, see Jeremy Cohen, *A Historian in Exile: Solomon ibn Verga, "Shevet Yehudah," and the Jewish-Christian Encounter* (Philadelphia: University of Pennsylvania Press, 2017).

30. See Ephraim Kanarfogel, "The Origin and Orientation of *Sefer Huqqei ha-Torah*," in his *Jewish Education and Society in the High Middle Ages* (Detroit: Wayne State University Press, 1992), 101–115, for the Hebrew text, and Kanarfogel, "A Monastic-like Setting for the Study of Torah," in *Judaism in Practice: From the Middle Ages Through the Early Modern Period*, edited by Lawrence Fine (Princeton, N.J.: Princeton University Press, 2001), 191–202, for an English translation.

31. For the phrase "common Judaism" from an earlier period, see E. P. Sanders, *Judaism: Practice and Belief: 63 BCE–66 CE* (Philadelphia: Trinity Press International, 1992).

32. See Catalog, Part C.

33. Soloveitchik, "Piety, Pietism," 456n.3.

34. For the Maimonidean references, see Azulai, *Brit 'Olam*, 80a–143a; Zunz, *Zur Geschichte und Literatur*, 126; Reifmann, *Arba'ah Harashim*, 7; Wertheimer, *Leshon Hasidim*; Freimann, "Mavo," 17–18.

35. Marcus, "Recensions and Structure," 153n.57.

36. My thanks to Cyril Aslanov for pointing out this possibility in a private conversation.

37. See Güdemann, *Geschichte des Erziehungswesens* 1:287–288; Freimann, "Mavo," 15; Marcus, "Recensions and Structure," 153n.57; Cyril Aslanov, "The Juxtaposition Ashkenaz/Tzarfat vs. Sepharad/Provence Reassessed—A Linguistic Approach," *Jahrbuch des Simon-Dubnow-Instituts* 8 (2009): 49–65.

38. Soloveitchik, "Piety, Pietism," 457. The concept of the hidden divine will has no content. It is definitional of different expressions of pietism, compared to piety. *Sefer Hasidim* and Judah *he-hasid*'s *Zava'ah*, for example, fill in that content uniquely as did other forms of Jewish pietism that also demand more of a Jew than rabbinic Judaism and piety. For this reason, "the will of the Creator" cannot be definitional of German *hasidut* per se.

39. Compare Soloveitchik, "Three Themes," 350n.8, where references to the elaboration of the "will of the Creator" are attributed to passages in *Sefer ha-Hasidut*. For the phrase "rezon ha-borei," see SHB 14, 53 (both in *Sefer ha-Hasidut*), 300, 374, 542, 848, 927; for "rezon ha-QBH," see SHB 153; for "rezon boreinu," see SHB 46 (part of *Sefer ha-Hasidut*). In SHP, for "rezon ha-borei," see pars. 27, 114, 302, 815, 1076, 1114, 1703.

40. Soloveitchik, "Piety, Pietism," 458. In SHP, under "gimatria": SHP 2, 33, 45, 440, 452, 554, 637, 704, 742, 780, 794, 949, 971, 1009, 1143, 1176, 1476, 1510, 1514, 1737, 1906, and

1980; under "gmatria": SHP 1906. In SHB "gimatria" appears in pars. 156, 173, 343, 389, 393, 942, 964, 1175; "be-gimatria" in SHB 260, 346; "bi-gmatria" in SHB 143. "Gmatria" is found in SHB 106 (part of *Sefer ha-Hasidut*).

41. Soloveitchik, "Piety, Pietism," 460.

42. Ibid., "Piety, Pietism," 458, made more clearly in Soloveitchik, "The Midrash, *Sefer Hasidim*," 167.

43. For an example of family customs that the pietist authors sometimes referred to as "minhag avoteinu" (a custom of our ancestors), see Marcus, *Rituals of Childhood*, 26, and R. Eleazar b. Judah of Worms, *Derashah le-Fesah*, 51.

44. See R. Eleazar b. Judah of Worms, *Hilekhot Teshuvah;* SHP pars. 52–53 *passim*. These struggles suggest the moral quandaries of a wealthy population living in an expanding boomtown such as Regensburg.

45. SHP par. 36.

46. Soloveitchik, "Piety, Pietism," 465.

47. In light of the sources adduced below, it is necessary to revise my original view that private confession succeeded sage confession because the latter failed. See Marcus, *Piety and Society*, 121. That some Jews did oppose personal confession as Christians did is clear from David Berger, ed. and trans., *The Jewish-Christian Debate in the High Middle Ages: A Critical Edition of the Nizzahon Vetus* (Philadelphia: Jewish Publication Society of America, 1979), 22–23, 223–224, and 339.

48. R. Moses b. Eleazar ha-Kohen, *Sefer Hasidim Qatan*, part 2, par. 33, pp. 66–67.

49. See Marcus, *Piety and Society*, 75–86.

50. See Stal, *Derashot limei ha-Teshuvah*, par. [24], 17–18, and par. [34], 23–26, and n. 130.

51. See R. Eleazar b. Judah of Worms, *Teshuvot Rabbeinu Eleazar mi-Vermaiza ha-"Roqeah."*

52. See R. Zidqiyah b. Abraham, *Shibbolei ha-Leqet*, edited by Samuel K. Mirsky (New York: Sura, 1966), 267 [*sic*; 276], cited by Soloveitchik, "Piety, Pietism," 471.

53. See Ivan G. Marcus, "Performative Midrash in the Memory of Ashkenazi Martyrs," in *Midrash Unbound: Transformations and Innovations*, edited by Michael Fishbane and Joanna Weinberg (Oxford: Littman Library of Jewish Civilization, 2013), 187–199.

54. See R. Meir b. Barukh of Rothenburg, *Sefer Sha'arei Teshuvot*, edited by Moses A. Bloch (Berlin, 1891), 346–347 (Koblenz on April 2, 1265).

55. R. Meir b. Barukh of Rothenburg, *Responsa* (Prague, 1608), #132 and see #485.

56. See Simcha Emanuel, ed., *Teshuvot Maharam mi-Rotenburg ve-Haveirav*, 2 vols. (Jerusalem: World Union of Jewish Studies, 2012), #394, 2:768–769.

57. *Sefer ha-Neyar*, edited by Gershon Appel (New York: Sura, 1960), 166–167.

58. Joseph b. Moses, *Sefer Leqet Yosher,* edited by Amihai Kahati, 2 vols. (Jerusalem: Mahon Yerushalayim, 2010), 2, Hilekhot Teshuvah, 90, #1.

59. R. Jacob b. Moses Ha-Levi Mölln (Maharil), *Sefer Maharil: Minhagim,* edited by Shlomo Spitzer (1989; reprinted with corrections, Jerusalem: Makhon Yerushalayim, 2005), Shabbat #1. In addition, see the application of German Pietist penances by rabbinical courts, following confessions, in Keil, "Rituals of Repentance," 164–176.

60. Cf. Marcus, *Piety and Society,* 121–129.

61. We also find several stories about R. Judah *he-hasid* involving confession of sins and dispensing penances in thirteenth-century Hebrew stories about Samuel and Judah. See Yassif, *Me'ah Sippurim Haser Ehad,* no. 29 (195–196); no. 30 (196–197); and no. 31 (197), where Judah dispenses penances.

62. Similarly, R. Eleazar of Worms's addition of *Hilekhot Hasidut* to the beginning of his legal compendium *Sefer ha-Roqeah* may have been suggested by Maimonides' prefacing *Sefer ha-Madda'* to the *Mishneh Torah,* but the form of Eleazar's work was segmented and not Iberian. See Ephraim E. Urbach, *Ba'alei ha-Tosafot* (Jerusalem: Mosad Bialik, 1980), 393.

63. On the editions, see the Catalog. For abundant numbers of quotations from *Sefer Hasidim,* see Fram, "German Pietism," and Jacob Elbaum, "Traces of Sefer Hasidim within the Literature of Early Modern Polish and Ashkenazic Jews," a paper delivered at the international conference "Sefer Hasidim in Context," held in Jerusalem, March 19–22, 2017.

64. See Soloveitchik, "Three Themes," 335n.74 (end) and 336–337n.82, where he refers to Maimonides' approach in *Sefer ha-Hasidut* but considers it to be from *Sefer Hasidim.*

CHAPTER 3

Epigraph taken from R. Isaac b. Moses, *Sefer Or Zarua',* vols. 1 and 2 (Zhitomir, 1862), 2:9d Hilekhot, par. 42.

1. Ta-Shma, "Le-Toledot ha-Yehudim be-Folin," 367, claims that there is little one can say about his biography, and Dan, *R. Yehudah he-Hasid,* 11, maintains that the only reliable source is his son's report about his father's death. For a statement of a cultural historian's use of stories, see Robert Bonfil, *History and Folklore in a Medieval Jewish Chronicle: The Family Chronicle of Ahima'az ben Paltiel* (Leiden: E. J. Brill, 2009), 55n.27.

2. Simhoni, "Ha-Hasidut ha-Ashkenazit bimei ha-Beinayim," reprinted in Marcus, *Dat ve-Hevrah,* 47–79, referred to many of the stories about Judah *he-hasid,* but he did

not deal with the implications of the genre or their historical credibility. See, too, Ka-melhar, *Hasidim ha-Rishonim*. Cycles of stories about Samuel and Judah are found in the Hebrew manuscript Jerusalem, National Library of Israel, Oct. 3182, the Ninety-nine stories. The stories date back to the thirteenth century and were published in Eli Yas-sif, *Me'ah Sippurim Haser Ehad*. Reworked Yiddish versions appear in the *Mayseh Bukh* (1602), reprinted thirteen times from 1602 to 1763 in Old Yiddish and in an East Euro-pean Yiddish adaptation another twenty-one times from 1807 to 1925. See Sara Zfat-man, *"Mayseh Bukh,"* 126–152, and Bamberger, "Sippurei ha-Shevahim shel Hasidei Ashkenz," chapter 1, 21. On the oral source of a story associated with R. Judah *he-hasid* that begins, "A story they heard from the mouth of R. Judah *he-hasid* who said," see Yassif, *Me'ah Sippurim Haser Ehad*, #4, p. 176.

3. For R. Isaac's principal halakhic teachers, see Ephraim E. Urbach, *Ba'alei ha-Tosafot*, 2 vols. (Jerusalem: Mosad Bialik, 1980), 436–447.

4. Compare the students' passive role in SHP 303=FJTSB 45, 129; Vatican 285 [85] and JTS 2499 [85] to Jerusalem Oct. 3182 published in Yassif, *Me'ah Sippurim*, nos. 25 and 35.

5. R. Isaac b. Moses, *Sefer Or Zarua'*, par. 147, 2: 39d. See also *Sefer Or Zarua'*, par. 89, 2: 24a: "But I heard from the mouth of my teacher R. Judah hasid . . . and my teacher R. Judah *hasid* zz"l said to me."

6. In a comparison of different versions of parallel stories from southern Italy and *Sefer Hasidim*, Robert Bonfil has shown how tensions in the synagogue are more typical of Germany than southern Italy. See Bonfil, "Can Medieval Story Telling Help Under-standing Midrash?," 228–254, and Marcus, "Historical Meaning of Hasidei Ashkenaz," 103–114, the latter reprinted in Marcus, *Jewish Culture and Society*.

7. R. Isaac b. Moses, *Sefer Or Zarua'*, par. 114, 1: 21a. Compare SHP 1595.

8. R. Jacob b. Asher, *Arba'ah Turim*, Orah Hayim 113 in standard edition.

9. R. Isaac b. Moses, *Sefer Or Zarua'*, *Hilekhot Shabbat*, par. 42, 2: 9d for the three stories. The gloss to SHP 427 begins: "I heard in the name of Rabbei[nu] Judah *hasid* zz"l." Both versions of these stories seem to be independent witnesses.

10. SHP gloss to 427.

11. On German "zipfel," see Kogut, "Ha-Mishpat ha-Murkav," 38n.18, who refers to "zepfe" (sheaves of wheat). The Polish is from "kwietny wieniec," a wreath of flowers. My thanks to my colleague Timothy Snyder.

12. R. Barukh b. Samuel of Mainz (early fourteenth century) in R. Samson b. Zadoq's *Sefer Tashbez* (Cremona, 1556; Lemberg, 1858), par. 219. See Urbach, *Ba'alei ha-Tosafot*, 426, and R. Abraham b. 'Azriel, *'Arugat ha-Bosem*, 4: 92–95. The reference to "weddings" may be to the "shabbat hatan," the "Groom's Sabbath," the Sabbath morning

celebration following a wedding, as suggested by Ephraim Kanarfogel, when reciting special *piyyutim* lengthened the service. For example, see the *piyyut* composed by R. Meir b. Barukh of Rothenburg for this Sabbath in Jacob b. Moses Ha-Levi Mölln (Maharil), *Sefer Maharil: Minhagim*, edited by Shlomo Spitzer (1989; reprinted with corrections, Jerusalem: Makhon Yerushalayim, 2005), Hilekhot Nesu'in, 470, cited by Lifshitz, *Ehad be-Khol Dimyionot*, 202n.49.

13. R. Samson b. Zadoq, *Sefer Tashbez* (Cremona, 1556; Lemberg, 1858), par. 248.

14. See also SHP 52–53 and former JTS Boesky 45, 45; Vatican 285 [3] but the passage is missing in JTS 2499. It is translated from SHP in Marcus, "Narrative Fantasies from Sefer Hasidim," 220–223. See, too, the discussions about *din shamayim* (law of heaven or equity) in Baer,"Ha-Megamah," 12–13, Soloveitchik, "Three Themes," 320–322, and Marcus, *Piety and Society*, 24, 26. Resisting sinful urges that one stimulates oneself is a feature of German pietism. Such situations have been compared to the moral dilemma constructed in medieval French romances of the mainly unfulfilled love quest for a married woman. See Harris, "Concept of Love in *Sefer Hasidim*."

15. SHP 1575; former JTS Boesky 45, 665.

16. R. Isaac of Corbeil, *Sefer 'Amudei Golah=Sefer Mizvot Qatan* (New York: Edison, 1959), par. 3, translated in *The Jewish Political Tradition*, vol. 2, edited by Michael Walzer et al. (New Haven, Conn.: Yale University Press, 2006), 95.

17. SHP 211; former JTS Boesky 45, 103; Oxford Opp. 487 (Neubauer 1943), 205; Oxford Opp. 614 (Neubauer 2275) [13]; Oxford Opp. 146 (Neubauer 782) [13]; SHB 205. SHP and SHB are cited in connection with the passage in *Sefer Mizvot Qatan* in Kanarfogel, *"Peering,"* 86.

18. The rabbinic prohibition of committing suicide is found in B. Bava Qama 91b based on Genesis 9:5.

19. Spitzer, ed., "She'eilot u-Teshuvot Rabbeinu Yehuda he-Hasid be-'Inyanei Teshuvah," 201, from Oxford, Opp. 312 (Neubauer 682), f. 369r–v, and see SHP 18 (end) and former JTS Boesky 45, 21; SHP 163 and SHB 675. The passage on Yaqim Ish Zerurot is in *Midrash Bereishit Rabbah*, edited by J. Theodor and Chanokh Albeck, 3 vols. (Jerusalem: Wahrmann, 1965), 2: 742–743.

20. See Soloveitchik, "Three Themes," 337n.86, quoted from *Sefer Hasidim*, Zurich, Heid. 51, f. 9v beginning of par. [10]. The manuscript reads "al ya'anu," in the plural, not "al ya'aneh." Compare Soloveitchik, "Appendix to 'Pietists and Kibbitzers,'" where he published *Sefer Hasidim* Zurich, Heid. 51 as an example of a manuscript lacking any characteristics of *Sefer Hasidim* or of German Pietism.

21. See Marcus, "Exegesis for the Few and for the Many," and Soloveitchik, "Two Notes."

22. See R. Moses b. Isaac ha-Levi (Maharam) Mintz, *She'eilot u-Teshuvot* (Krakow, 1617), par. 76.

23. See SHP 1592–1593, former JTS Boesky 45, 673–674, SHB 763–764, and Ephraim Kanarfogel, "Religious Leadership During the Tosafist Period: Between the Academy and the Rabbinic Court," *Jewish Religious Leadership: Image and Reality*, edited by Jack Wertheimer, 2 vols. (New York: Jewish Theological Seminary of America, 2004), 1: 272; Kanarfogel, "R. Judah he-Hasid and the Rabbinic Scholars of Regensburg."

The three rabbis of the Regensburg court are also mentioned elsewhere. See Simcha Emanuel, *Shivrei Luhot: Sefarim Avudim shel Ba'alei ha-Tosafot* (Jerusalem: Magnes Press, 2007), 224n.24, from a newly found book of customs in Oxford, Bodleian Library, Opp. 672 (Neubauer 1150), f. 18r.

24. Although Ephraim E. Urbach viewed Judah *he-hasid* as grounding his decision here solely on pietism, Ephraim Kanarfogel has shown that Judah based himself both on Jewish legal principles as well as on pietism. See Urbach, *Ba'alei ha-Tosafot*, 391–392, and Kanarfogel, "R. Judah he-Hasid and the Rabbinic Scholars of Regensburg." *Sefer Hasidim* sometimes offers guidelines to a sage who could function as a religious authority on Jewish law as well as on pietism, similar to Judah's serving on the religious court in Regensburg. See, for example, SHP 1569 and cf. SHP 17.

25. See Steiner, "The Ma'aseh Book and the Pietists."

26. See Marcus, "Hierarchies, Religious Boundaries and Jewish Spirituality," 13–15, and cf. Katz, *Exclusiveness and Tolerance*, 93–105.

27. See Simhoni, "Ha-Hasidut ha-Ashkenazit," in Marcus, *Dat ve-Hevrah*, 61, and Urbach, *Ba'alei ha-Tosafot*, 212–214, where the letter is quoted from Meir b. Barukh of Rothenburg, *Responsa* (Lemberg, 1860), no. 112. A parallel is found in R. Isaac b. Moses, *Sefer Or Zarua'*, par. 113, 1: 40d.

28. See Joseph Hacker, "Li-Gezeirot Tatnu," *Zion* 31 (1966): 229–231; SHP 198; former JTS Boesky 45, 101; SHB 196 and SHP 1922; Cambridge Add. 379, 541. Cf. A. M. Habermann, ed., *Sefer Gezeirot Ashkenaz ve-Zarfat* (Jerusalem: Ophir, 1971), 56, and Eva Haverkamp, ed., *Hebräische Berichte über die Judenverfolgungen während des ersten Kreuzzugs* (Hannover: Hahn, 2005), 481.

29. Avraham David, "Sibbuv R. Petahiah mi-Regensburg: Nusah Hadash," *Qovez 'al Yad*, n.s. 13 (1996): 239–243, and see Kanarfogel, "R. Judah he-Hasid and the Rabbinic Scholars of Regensburg," 17–37, and Galit Hasan-Rokem, "Homo viator et narrans judaicus: Medieval Jewish Voices in the European Narrative of the Wandering Jew," in *Europäische Ethnologie und Folklore im internationalen Kontext: Festschrift für Leander Petzoldt*, edited by Ingo Schneider (Frankfurt am Main: Peter Lang, 1999), 93–102.

30. See Yassif, *Me'ah Sippurim Haser Ehad*, no. 95, p. 264 (text) and comments on 115–117; Meitlis, *Di Shvohim*, 142–143 (text) and comments on 88–91.

31. Lange, *Peirushei R. Yehudah he-Hasid*, 17, based on Moscow, Russian State Library, Günzburg Hebrew 82, f. 64v: beginning of "lekh lekh" (Gen. 12:1–14:27). A second, less reliable version is Strasbourg, Bibliothèque Nationale et Universitaire 3970, f. 65; the passage on Genesis is not found in Cambridge, Cambridge University Library, Hebrew MS 669.2. For the Strasbourg manuscript, see Landauer, *Katalog*, no. 44, 64–65. In 1217, 1 Adar was a Friday and Saturday night was 3 Adar. See Eduard Mahler, *Handbuch der Jüdischer Chronologie* (Leipzig: G. Fock, 1916), 564.

32. Lange, *Peirushei R. Yehudah he-Hasid*, 116, based on Moscow, Russian State Library, Günzburg Hebrew 82, f. 80v, end of "tezaveh" (Exod. 27:20–30:10). Cambridge, Cambridge University Library 669.2, f. 45v has some variants, including the scribal error of 1216 instead of 1217 (a *vav* for a *zayin*). See Lange, *Peirushei R. Yehudah he-Hasid*, 116n.34. The passage in Moscow 82 and Cambridge 669 begins with the year 1217 and does not mention "9 Adar." The text quoted in *Kerem Hemed* 7 (1843), 71 is Cambridge 669. On the Cambridge manuscript, see Stefan C. Reif, *Hebrew Manuscripts at Cambridge University Library: A Descriptive Introduction* (Cambridge: Faculty of Oriental Studies, University of Cambridge, 1997), 86–87. It is not clear to what manuscript Jacob Freimann refers in his "Mavo," 4n.13. The text in *Ozar Tov* (Berlin, 1878), 45 reads: "Mazati katuv mei-hiddushei humash le-R. Yehudah he-hasid be-farashat ve-atah tezaveh: eshtaqad, bi-shenat tav tav qof 'ayin zayin hayetah parashat zakhor be-f[arashat] ve-atah tezaveh ve-halah avi holo asher met bo ve-sha'alnu lo. . . .'" This is a variation on the comment as recorded in Moscow 82.

33. Lange, *Peirushei R. Yehudah he-Hasid*, 17, included the date at the end but not the abbreviation, based again on Moscow, Russian State Library, Günzburg Hebrew 82, f. 64v that ends with the word "and he passed away" (*va-yinnafash*). On that meaning, see B. Beiza 16a. Strasbourg, Bibliothèque Nationale et Universitaire, 3970, f. 65, adds: "13 Adar. H[a-] R[av] R[abbi] M[oshe] b[en] R[abbi] Y[ehudah] H[asid]." For a transcription of the whole passage in the Strasbourg manuscript, see Landauer, *Katalog*, 64–65.

34. *Haqdamah* (Introduction) to *Sefer ha-Hokhmah* from Oxford, Bodleian Library, Opp. 506 (Neubauer 1812), f. 54r. See Eleazar ben Judah of Worms, "Sefer ha-Hokhmah," 169; Dan, *'Iyyunim*, 45. Rabbi David Segal has argued that *Sefer ha-Hokhmah*, including the *Haqdamah*, is a sixteenth-century forgery. See R. Eleazar b. Judah of Worms, *Sefer Sodei Razei Semukhin*, edited by David Segal, 35, 51–52. For problems connected with claims made in the *Haqdamah*, see Dan, *'Iyyunim*, 51–52. For a nuanced reassessment of Segal's analysis see Idel, "'Al ha-Peirushim," 212n.398 and 213–216.

35. See SHP par. 1528, 1052, and 1620 and Dan, "Book of Divine Glory," 3–5; Dan, *R. Yehudah he-Hasid*, 13–14.

36. SHP 631.

37. In MS Jerusalem, National Library of Israel, Oct. 3182, no. 94, f. 162r; Yassif, *Me'ah Sippurim Haser Ehad,* no. 94, p. 263 (text) and 77–78.

38. Meitlis, *Di Shvohim,* 140–141 (text) and 84–86; Gaster, *Maaseh Book,* no. 183, 395–396.

39. SHP 1356; former JTS Boesky 45, 552; SHB 432.

40. See Stith Thompson, *Motif-Index of Folk-Literature.* 6 vols., rev. and enlarged ed. (Bloomington: Indiana University Press, 1952–1958), 2:269 D1552.6. "Gate or wall opens or closes, letting saint through," cited in Raspe, *Jüdische Hagiographie,* 229n.39, where she discusses the traditions about the synagogue wall in Worms bending to prevent harm to the mother of either Rashi or of Judah *he-hasid* in different traditions. In Worms, an actual physical niche in the wall generated different etiological stories. Were the stories about the Regensburg wall and gate similarly generated about R. Isaac and R. Judah *he-hasid*?

41. All the stories about Judah in the Hebrew cycle place him in Regensburg, not Speyer. See Ta-Shma, "Le-Toledot ha-Yehudim be-Folin," 368. Although the stories about Judah in the *Mayseh Bukh* also place Judah in Regensburg, the story about the rich Jew who shaved takes place in Speyer, and it was added late to the Regensburg cycle there. See Zfatman, "*Mayseh Bukh,*" 144–145, and Bamberger, "Sippurei ha-Shevahim shel Hasidei Ashkenaz," chapter 1, 59–61.

42. See *Sefer ha-Gan* (Venice 1606), f. 9b–10a. This story does not appear in the Ninety-nine stories Hebrew cycle about Judah in Jerusalem, National Library of Israel, Oct. 3182, but it is in the *Mayseh Bukh,* Meitlis, *Di Shevohim,* no. 170, p. 116; Gaster, *Maaseh Book,* no. 170, pp. 353–354. In addition, Simcha Emanuel sent me by email on July 23, 2012, a different version of the story from a privately held Hebrew manuscript that a dealer showed him. It was titled (f. 1a) "Sod ha-'Ibbur" and on (f. 3v) "Sod ha-Ne'arim ve-ha-Bahurim she-Meitim Qodem 'Esrim Shanah." The story is on f. 7r.

43. SHP 1575; former JTS Boesky 45, 665.

44. On R. Jacob b. Meir (Rabbeinu Tam) and the Count of Troyes see Avraham (Rami) Reiner, "Bible and Politics: A Correspondence Between Rabbennu Tam and the Authorities of Champagne," in *Entangled Histories: Knowledge, Authority, and Jewish Culture in the Thirteenth Century,* edited by Elisheva Baumgarten, Ruth Mazo Karras, and Katelyn Mesler (Philadelphia: University of Pennsylvania Press, 2017), 59–72.

45. This text from the unique thirteenth-century manuscript of *Sefer ha-Asufot,* f. 162r, is quoted by Moritz Güdemann, *Geschichte des Erziehungswesens,* vol. 1, 1880,

24n.2, where he misread the last word as "from Toul" instead of the correct reading: "menuval" (unkempt).

46. R. Isaac b. Moses, *Sefer Or Zarua'*, Bava Qama, par. 460, 3:37c; also in R. Meir b. Barukh of Rothenburg, *Responsa* (Prague, 1608), no. 932. R. Qalonimos b. Meir of Speyer was the father of R. Judah ben Qalonimos of Speyer, who wrote the rabbinic work *Seder Tannaim ve-Amoraim* and who was R. Eleazar of Worms's teacher. R. Eleazar of Worms's father, R. Judah ben Qalonimos b. Moses of Mainz, and R. Qalonimos ben Meir of Speyer were brothers-in-law, apparently having married sisters. See the family tree in Marcus, "Mavo," 17.

47. See Yassif, *Me'ah Sippurim Haser Ehad*, no. 37, p. 202 from Jerusalem MS Oct. 3182, f. 135v–136r.

48. See Oxford, Bodleian Library, Opp. 160 (Neubauer 1204), f. 259, quoted with other cases in Kamelhar, *Rabbeinu Eleazar ben Yehudah mi-Germaiza ha-Roqeah*, 13n.2.

49. SHP 1344; former JTS Boesky 45, 547.

50. SHP 1272; former JTS Boesky 45, 508; Vatican 285 [77]; JTS 2499 [77]. On this passage, see Soloveitchik, "Three Themes," 335 and n. 74.

51. SHP 116; former JTS Boesky 45, 78; SHB 93 and other paraphrases of part of SHB. See PUSHD.

52. The responsum is found in his *She'eilot u-Teshuvot Maharshal* (Lemberg, n.d.), 23r–23v, quoted in Joseph Shlomo Delmedigo, *Mazreif la-Hokhmah* (Warsaw, 1890; reprinted Jerusalem, n.d.), f. 32r.

53. A proposal that Samuel, Judah's father, and not Judah was the subject of the story of the migration from Speyer to Regensburg contradicts all the evidence that places Samuel and Judah's older brother Abraham only in Speyer, not in Regensburg. Except for one story that places Judah in Speyer, all the stories and other biographical sources associate Judah, not Samuel, with Regensburg. See Shoham-Steiner, "Mi-Speyer le-Regensburg," 149–176.

54. Soloveitchik, "Three Themes," 350n.125.

55. On the question of why he relocated, see Marcus, "Political Dynamics," 122–123; Ta-Shma, "Le-Toledot ha-Yehudim be-Folin," 367–368 and especially n. 73; Zimmer, *'Olam*, 296–297; Dan, *R. Yehudah he-Hasid*, 52; and Dan, *Toledot Torat ha-Sod ha-'Ivrit: Yemei Ha-Beinayim*, V, 73. Cf. Israel Jacob Yuval, *Two Nations in Your Womb: Perceptions of Jews and Christians in Late Antiquity and the Middle Ages* (Berkeley: University of California Press, 2006), 171.

56. On Judah's view that Jews should not move around, see Liberles Neuman, "Merhav u-Merhaq be-*Sefer Hasidim*."

57. See Ta-Shma, "'Inyanei Erez Yisrael," 81–82 (compare the transcription of Judah *he-hasid*'s responsum here to the text in MS Montefiore 104 f. 2r); Ta-Shma, "'Al Odot Yahasam shel Qadmonei Ashkenaz," 315–318.

58. See Ephraim Kanarfogel, "The Aliyah of 'Three Hundred Rabbis' in 1211: Tosafist Attitudes Toward Settling in the Land of Israel," *Jewish Quarterly Review* 76 (1986): 191–215.

59. For the annotated text, see Bonfil, *History and Folklore in a Medieval Jewish Chronicle*, [42] pp. 311–313. In the earlier edition, Benjamin Klar, ed., *Megillat Ahimaaz* (Jerusalem, 1944; 1974), the passage is on p. 30. On menstrual impurity and desecration of sacred objects in Christian and Jewish circles, see Robert Bonfil, "Reading in the Jewish Communities of Western Europe in the Middle Ages," in *History of Reading in the West,* edited by Guglielmo Cavallo and Roger Chartier, translated by Lydia G. Cochrane (Cambridge: Polity Press, 1999), 150–151, esp. 405n.5. On the Christian idea of the female pollution of cult objects, see, for example, Gratian, *Decretum*, dist. 23, chapter 25 (prohibiting women from touching sacred utensils) and Rufinus's commentary on denying women entry into church, a prohibition established by Gregory the Great and reiterated by Gratian: "Because woman is the only animal to menstruate, in contact with her blood fruit fails to mature, wine sours, the grass wilts, the trees drop their fruit, iron rusts, the air darkens, and if dogs lick that blood they are stricken with rabies." For this quotation and remarks on related passages, see Alain Boureau, *La Papesse Jeanne* (Paris: Flammarion, 1993), 44–45.

60. On Samuel *he-hasid* as a wanderer in exile, see Yassif, *Me'ah Sippurim Haser Ehad,* no. 25, p. 192 (text) and 110–115, 272 (discussion); Jerusalem, National Library of Israel, Hebrew MS Oct. 3182, f. 130v.

61. On R. Ephraim of Regensburg and his problems getting along in Speyer, see Urbach, *Ba'alei ha-Tosafot*, 199–207.

62. See Yassif, ed., *Me'ah Sippurim Haser Ehad*, no. 36, p. 202, from Jerusalem, National Library of Israel, Hebrew MS Oct. 3182, f. 135v.

63. On Hillel, see B. Pesahim 66a and for R. Moses, Abraham Ibn Daud, *The Book of Tradition (Sefer ha-Qabbalah)*, edited by Gerson D. Cohen (Philadelphia: Jewish Publication Society of America, 1967), 47 (Hebrew) and 65 (English).

64. See Marcus, "History, Story, and Collective Memory," 375–379. Another such story is about an early Ashkenazic rabbinical founder in Mainz from Italy, R. Meshulam b. Qalonimus, about whom there is an important rivalry story, explicitly between Mainz and Babylonia but implicitly also between Mainz and northern French Talmud glossators (Tosafists) in Yassif, *Me'ah Sippurim Haser Ehad* #39, on which also see Sara Zfatman, *Rosh va-Rishon: Yissud Manhigut be-Sifrut Yisrael* (Jerusalem: Magnes, 2010), 440–445.

That the German pietists did not see tosafist (dialectical) study of the Talmud and Hasidism as mutually exclusive, see Marcus, *Piety and Society*, 102–104 and notes. Cf. Ta-Shma, "Mizvat Talmud Torah," 98–113, reprinted in Marcus, *Dat ve-Hevrah*, 237–252, whose position is not supported by *Sefer Hasidim* and other German pietist sources.

65. See R. Isaac b. Moses, *Sefer Or Zarua'*, 'Avodah Zarah, pars. 199–200, 4: 27d. Another report attributes the story to R. Baruch b. Isaac of Regensburg. See R. Samuel b. Zadoq, *Sefer Tashbez* (Lemberg, 1858), par. 352. On the report in *Sefer Or Zarua'* see Kanarfogel, "R. Judah he-Hasid and the Rabbinic Scholars of Regensburg," 29–30, and Kanarfogel, *Intellectual History*, 465n.76 and the sources cited there.

66. Yassif, *Me'ah Sippurim Haser Ehad*, no. 85 pp. 253–254, from Jerusalem, National Library of Israel, Hebrew MS Oct. 3182, f. 157v–158r; Meitlis, *Di Shvohim*, 119–121 (text) and comments on 65–66; Gaster, *Maaseh Book*, no. 172, pp. 358–362.

67. R. Isaac b. Moses, *Sefer Or Zarua'*, Rosh Hashanah par. 275, 2: 63a has a chain of tradition going from R. Eleazar of Worms back to Rabbenu Gershom b. Yehudah (d. 1028) in which Eleazar says that his father, R. Judah b. Qalonimos (b. Moses of Mainz), learned it from R. Judah *he-hasid*, apparently in Speyer.

68. See Kanarfogel, *Intellectual History*, 418–419.

69. Yassif, *Me'ah Sippurim Haser Ehad*, no. 34, p. 200–201; Jerusalem, National Library of Israel, Hebrew MS Oct. 3182, f. 134v–135r; Meitlis, *Di Shvohim*, 121–124; Gaster, *Maaseh Book*, no. 173, pp. 363–367.

70. Eleazar claims his father as well as R. Judah *he-hasid* as sources of his esoteric learning. See R. Eleazar b. Judah of Worms, *Derashah le-Fesah*, 67; R. Eleazar b. Judah of Worms, *Peirush H[a-rav] R. E[leazar] mi-Germaiza 'al Sefer Yezirah* (1888), f. 2b and 22b, and Eleazar's comment in his prayer commentary to "yishtabah" in Oxford, Bodleian Library Opp. 160 (Neubauer 1204), f. 54v. In his commentary on the prayer book, R. Eleazar of Worms also traces his knowledge of esoteric prayer lore to his father and to R. Judah *he-hasid*. See Joseph Shlomo Delmedigo, *Mazreif la-Hokhmah*, chapter 24, f. 32b and f. 33a, and see Urbach, *Ba'alei ha-Tosafot*, 388–389, who quotes the tradition about his father but not the one about R. Judah *he-hasid*. The passage from Paris, Bibliothèque Nationale, héb. 772, f. 60r, is quoted in Dan, *Torat ha-Sod*, 16, and translated in Marcus, *Piety and Society*, 67.

71. These claims make the point of the story all the more striking as an attempt to emphasize only R. Judah *he-hasid* as Eleazar's teacher of magic and esoteric lore despite his father's wishes. It tells us about how Regensburg wanted to remember Judah as the source of Eleazar's magical and esoteric lore: Eleazar had to disobey his father and go to Judah in Regensburg, the new center of Jewish mystical learning.

72. See Mark Verman and Shulamit H. Adler, "Path Jumping in the Jewish Magical Tradition," *Jewish Studies Quarterly* 1:2 (1993–1994): 131–148, especially 136–137.

73. Several of the stories are in Yassif, *Me'ah Sippurim Haser Ehad*, and in the *Mayseh Bukh*.

74. On the *Zava'ah* of R. Judah *he-hasid* and the Hatam Sofer, see Kahana, "Meqorot ha-Yeda' u-Temurot ha-Zeman," 223–262. The great popularity of R. Judah *he-hasid's Zava'ah* and the story cycles about him that lasted at least into the seventeenth century belie my earlier proposal that Eleazar of Worms's institutional and legal authority replaced Judah's charismatic authority. See Marcus, "Judah the Pietist and Eleazar of Worms," 97–126. Judah's charisma continued to influence people for centuries through the *Zava'ah*, *Sefer Hasidim* penitential practices, and especially his prophetic aura as a Jewish saint in Regensburg.

75. Eli Yassif, *The Hebrew Folktale: History, Genre, Meaning,* translated from the Hebrew by Jacqueline S. Teitelbaum (Bloomington: Indiana University Press, 1999), 284.

76. On the limited circulation outside of German lands of even the hagiographical stories about Samuel and Judah, see Raspe, *Jüdische Hagiographie,* 331 and 229n.39.

77. That Judah *he-hasid's* radical social vision did not outlive him, see Marcus, *Piety and Society,* 130–132; Dan, "Li-Demuto ha-Historit," 389–398, especially 398; Gruenwald, "Normative und volkstümliche Religiosität," 117–126; Dan, "Ashkenazi Hasidim, 1941–1991," 87–101; and Marcus, "Historical Meaning of Hasidei Ashkenaz," 103–114, reprinted in Marcus, *Jewish Culture and Society.*

78. See R. Eleazar b. Judah of Worms, *Derashah le-Fesah,* 51–52, 101, and 127; Marcus, *Rituals of Childhood.* The first mention that Jews should avoid eating legumes (*qitniyot*) on Passover is found as an accepted practice, at least among *hasidim,* in R. Eleazar b. Judah of Worms, *Derasha le-Fesah,* 90, and in Simcha Emanuel's "Mavo," 51–52. R. Jacob b. Judah Landau (d. 1493), who studied in Ashkenaz but lived and wrote in Italy, remarks: "and I, the writer, saw German pietists and sages (*hasidei ashkenaz ve-hahamehah*) avoid eating any kind of legume (*qitniyot*) on Passover." See his *Sefer ha-Agur* (Rimini, 1526), par. 745, f. 58a, and in *Sefer ha-Agur ha-Shalem,* edited by Moshe Hershler (Jerusalem: Moznayim, 1960), 121.

79. See, for example, Kanarfogel, *"Peering,"* 45–46n.35, on standing throughout the night of Yom Kippur and reciting hymns, as a pietistic custom recorded in R. Jacob b. Asher, *Arba'ah Turim,* Orah Hayyim, par. 619 and other practices discussed by Kanarfogel in his learned monographs, *"Peering"* and *Intellectual History.*

80. See Mendel Piekerz, *Bimei Zemihat ha-Hasidut: Megamot Ra'ayoniyot be-Sifrei Drush u-Musar* (Jerusalem: Mosad Bialik, 1978); Fram, "German Pietism," 50–59; Gershon Hundert, *The Jews in Poland-Lithuania in the Eighteenth Century: A Genealogy of Modernity* (Berkeley: University of California Press, 2004). Cf. Soloveitchik, "Piety, Pietism," 455–493, and Soloveitchik, "Pietists and Kibbitzers," 60–64.

On the ongoing Jewish legal authority of *Sefer Hasidim*, compared to Judah *he-hasid*'s *Zava'ah*, see Shvat, "Zava'at Rabbi Yehudah he-Hasid 'al pi Mahadurot Yeshanot ve-Khitvei ha-Yad," 4n.9, and Rabbi Abraham A. Price's edition of *Sefer Hasidim*, 3 vols. (Toronto: Yeshivat Torat Hayim, 1955–1964). A historical study of the cultural impact of *Sefer Hasidim* and other German pietist writings on Jewish practice remains to be undertaken.

81. See Marcus, *Rituals of Childhood*, introduction.

CHAPTER 4

Epigraph taken from David Konstan, "The *Alexander Romance*: The Cunning of the Open Text," *Lexis* 16 (1998): 127.

1. My thanks to Peter Lehnhardt for the observation about Aesop, on which see B. E. Perry, *Aesopica* (Urbana: University of Illinois Press, 1952), and N. Holzberg, "Der Aesop-Roman: Eine Struckturanalystische Interpretation," in *Der Aesop-Roman: Motivgeschichte und Erzählstrucktur*, edited by N. Holzberg (Tübingen: Gunter Narr, 1992), 33–75. And see esp. Konstan, *"Alexander Romance,"* 123–138.

2. On rabbinic literature, see Catherine Hezser, "Classical Rabbinic Literature," in *The Oxford Handbook of Jewish Studies*, edited by Martin Goldman et al. (Oxford: Oxford University Press, 2002), 115–140, and Martin S. Jaffee, *Torah in the Mouth: Writing and Oral Tradition in Palestinian Judaism 200 B. C. E.–400 C.E.* (Oxford: Oxford University Press, 2001).

3. On Ben-Sira, see Seth Schwartz, *Were the Jews a Mediterranean Society? Reciprocity and Solidarity in Ancient Judaism* (Princeton, N.J.: Princeton University Press, 2010), chapter 3.

4. On Philo, see Harry A. Wolfson, *Philo: Foundations of Religious Philosophy in Judaism, Christianity, and Islam* (Cambridge, Mass.: Harvard University Press, 1947), and Mireille Hadas-Lebel, *Philo of Alexandria: A Thinker in the Jewish Diaspora,* translated by Robyn Frechet (Leiden: E. J. Brill, 2012). On Josephus, see Shaye J. D. Cohen, *Josephus in Galilee and Rome: His Vita and Development as a Historian* (Leiden: E. J. Brill, 1979), and Seth Schwartz, *Josephus and Judaean Politics* (Leiden: E. J. Brill, 1990).

5. Azariah de' Rossi, *The Light of the Eyes* (*Meor Eynayim*), translated and edited by Joanna Weinberg, Yale Judaica Series 31 (New Haven, Conn.: Yale University Press, 2001).

6. See David Flusser, ed., *Sefer Yosippon: Ha-Nusah ha-Meqori* (Jerusalem: Merkaz Shazar, 1979), "Haqdamah," and David Flusser, *Sefer Yosippon*, 2 vols. (Jerusalem: Mosad Bialik, 1978–1980).

7. See Hezser, "Classical Rabbinic Literature," 135; Martin Jaffee, "Rabbinic Authorship as a Collective Enterprise," in *The Cambridge Companion to the Talmud and Rabbinic Literature*, edited by Charlotte Fonrobert and Martin S. Jaffee (Cambridge: Cambridge University Press, 2006), 17–37; Jaffee, *Torah in the Mouth;* and Hermann L. Strack and Günter Stemberger, eds., *Introduction to the Talmud and Midrash*, translated and edited by Markus Bockmühl, 2nd ed. (Minneapolis: Fortress Press, 1996), 46.

8. Saul Lieberman, "How Much Greek in Jewish Palestine?," in *Biblical and Other Studies*, edited by Alexander Altmann (Cambridge, Mass.: Harvard University Press, 1963), 123–141; Hayim Lapin, *Rabbis as Romans: The Rabbinic Movement in Palestine: 100–400 C.E.* (Oxford: Oxford University Press, 2012); Jacob Neusner, *Talmudic Judaism in Sasanian Babylonia: Essays and Studies* (Leiden: E. J. Brill, 1976); Yaakov Elman, "Middle Persian Culture and Babylonian Sages: Accommodation and Resistance in the Shaping of Rabbinic Legal Tradition," in *The Cambridge Companion to the Talmud and Rabbinic Literature,* edited by Charlotte Fonrobert and Martin S. Jaffee (Cambridge: Cambridge University Press, 2006), 165–197; Shai Secunda, *The Iranian Talmud: Reading the Bavli in Its Sasanian Context* (Philadelphia: University of Pennsylvania Press, 2014); Robert Brody, "Irano-Talmudica: The New Parallelomania?," *Jewish Quarterly Review* 106:2 (Spring 2016): 209–232.

9. On Saadia, see Robert Brody, *Saadia Gaon*, translated from the Hebrew by Betsy Rosenberg (Portland, Ore.: Littman Library of Jewish Civilization, 2013); and Rina Drory, *Models and Contacts: Arabic Literature and Its Impact on Medieval Jewish Culture* (Leiden: E. J. Brill, 2000).

10. On Rapoport, see Isaac Barzilay, "The Scholarly Contribution of Shelomo Judah Leib Rapoport (Shir) (1790–1867)," *Proceedings of the American Academy for Jewish Research* 35 (1967): 1–41; and Robert Bonfil, *History and Folklore in a Medieval Jewish Chronicle: The Family Chronicle of Ahima'az ben Paltiel* (Leiden: E. J. Brill, 2009), 42, 206, plate 13. Scholars argue over the sources in Palestine or Babylonia of European *legal* traditions, but are agreed about the Palestinian-Italian-Ashkenazic path of liturgical poetry (*piyyut*) and mystical lore (*heikhalot*), for example. For a recent summary, see Israel Ta-Shma, "Rabbinic Literature in the Middle Ages: 1000–1492," in *The Oxford Handbook of Jewish Studies*, edited by Martin Goodman et al. (Oxford: Oxford University Press, 2004), 219–240, and the earlier literature cited there. The way Ashkenazic books were written has not been linked historically to Palestinian or Babylonian traditions, and it seems likely to be derived, like *piyyut* and *heikhalot* traditions, from Byzantine Palestine and Italy in contrast to the Babylonian Geonic book that was part of the Arabic book milieu.

11. Jacob Mann, "*Sefer ha-Ma'asim* li-Venei Erez Yisrael," *Tarbiz* 1:3 (1930): 1–14. The quotation is on 1.

12. See Mordecai Margoliot, ed., *Ha-Hilluqim she-Bein Anshei Mizrah u-Venei Erez Yisrael* (Jerusalem: Reuven Mass, 1948), 59.

13. Chaim Horowitz, ed., *Uralte Tosefta's (Borajta's)* [*Tosefta 'Atiqta be-Agadeta u-ve-Hilkheta*] (Frankfurt am Main, 1880–1890), and Evyatar Marienbad, ed., *La Baraita de Niddah: Un texte juif pseudo-talmudique sur les lois religieuses relatives à la menstruation* (Turnhout: Brepols, 2012), and Marienbad, *Niddah: Lorsque les juifs conceptualisent la menstruation* (Paris: Les Belles Lettres, 2003), 295.

14. See Jacob Elbaum, "Bein 'Arikhah le-Shikhtuv: Le-Ofyah shel ha-Sifrut ha-Midrashit ha-Me'uheret," in *Proceedings of the Ninth World Congress of Jewish Studies,* Division C: 57–62 (Jerusalem: World Union of Jewish Studies, 1985). On *Tanhuma*-type literature, see Marc Bregman, *The Tanhuma-Yelammedenu Literature: Studies in the Evolution of the Versions* (Piscataway, N.J.: Gorgias Press, 2003). My thanks to Steven Fraade for the reference. Fragments of *Midrash Tanhuma*-type texts that differ from all known versions have been found in European book bindings. See Simcha Emanuel, *Mi-Ginzei Eiropa* I (Jerusalem: Meqizei Nirdamim, 2015), 49, and Jacob Elbaum, "From Sermon to Story: The Transformation of the Akedah Author(s)," *Prooftexts* 6:2 (May 1986): 97–116. On *Pirqei de-Rabbi Eliezer*, see Elbaum, "Ha-Melizah, ha-Motiv ve-ha-'Inyan: Le-Derekh 'Izuvo shel ha-Sippur be-Firqei de-Rabbi Eliezer," in *Mehqerei Yerushalayim be-Folklor ha-Yehudi* 13–14 *li-Khvod Dov Noy*, edited by Tamar Alexander and Galit Hasan-Rokem (Jerusalem: Hebrew University of Jerusalem, 1992), 99–126.

15. See Bonfil, *History and Folklore in a Medieval Jewish Chronicle,* 45–86, especially 83. Bonfil notes that the manuscript's "sections are separated by small blank spaces," 224, and are "relatively brief," 225. See Plates 1–4.

16. Like the unique Toledo manuscript of *Ahima'az*, Jerusalem, National Library of Israel, MS Oct. 41280 of *Sefer Yosippon* also has no headings or divisions other than spaces between sections. In the Jerusalem MS there is also a single dot between sections; in the Toledo MS of *Ahima'az*, there is a single dot between phrases. See Flusser, *Sefer Yosippon: Ha-Nusah ha-Meqori,* "Haqdamah," and Flusser, *Sefer Yosippon.*

17. Israel Ta-Shma, "Le-Toledot ha-Qesharim ha-Tarbutiyyim bein Yehudei Byzantion ve-Ashkenaz," in *Me'ah She'arim: 'Iyyunim be-'Olamam ha-Ruhani shel Yisrael bimei ha-Beinayim le-Zekher Yizhaq Tversky*, edited by Ezra Fleisher et al. (Jerusalem: Magnes Press, 2001), 61–70.

18. See Strack and Stemberger, *Introduction to the Talmud and Midrash,* 346.

19. See Peter Schäfer, ed., *Synopse zur Hekhalot-Literatur* (Tübingen: Mohr-Siebeck, 1981), on which see reviews of Joseph Dan, in *Tarbiz* 53 (1983): 313–317; Rachel Elior, in

Jewish Quarterly Review 77:2–3 (October 1986–January 1987): 213–217; Itamar Gruenwald, in *Journal of Biblical Literature* 103:1 (March 1984): 135–137; and Philip Alexander, in *Journal of Jewish Studies* 34:1 (1983): 102–106.

There are some similarities between the *heikhalot* corpus and *Sefer Hasidim* traditions. This should not be too surprising in light of the provenance of some of the most important *heikhalot* manuscripts in *hasidei ashkenaz* scribal culture. See Klaus Herrmann, "Rewritten Mystical Texts: The Transmission of the Heikhalot Literature in the Middle Ages," *Bulletin of the John Rylands University Library* 73:3 (Autumn 1993): 97–116.

By viewing the manuscripts, rather than literary texts, as the data, Schäfer adopted an empirical approach toward the *heikhalot* corpus that I have followed here with *Sefer Hasidim*. In practice, though, it is difficult to sustain this posture. See Daniel Abrams, *Kabbalistic Manuscripts and Textual Theory*: *Methodologies of Textual Scholarship and Editorial Practice in the Study of Jewish Mysticism*, 2nd ed. with new chapter (Jerusalem: Magnes Press; Los Angeles: Cherub Press, 2013), 40n.105.

20. On the genre of historical biographical essays on medieval Ashkenazic authors, see Ivan G. Marcus, "Israeli Medieval Jewish Historiography: From Nationalist Positivism to New Cultural and Social Histories," *Jewish Studies Quarterly* 17:3 (September 2010): 1–42.

21. Even when an Ashkenazic book follows the order of a master text, such as the Hebrew Bible or the Talmud, there is a surprising amount of disorder in the paragraph units within any particular section of the Ashkenazic book. See below.

22. On Hebrew books that have not survived, see Simcha Emanuel, *Shivrei Luhot: Sefarim Avudim shel Ba'alei ha-Tosafot* (Jerusalem: Magnes Press, 2007).

23. For some examples, see Yaakov Spigel, *'Amudim be-Toledot ha-Sefer ha-'Ivri*, 2 vols. (Ramat Gan: Bar Ilan University Press, 1996–2005), 2:523–534.

24. The only complete manuscript of R. Eliezer b. Samuel of Metz's *Sefer Yerei'im* is Paris, Bibliothèque Nationale, héb. 1309, f. 16r–254r [IMHM F 34247 (also online)]. See Emanuel, *Shivrei Luhot*, 23. This Paris manuscript is the basis of the first edition by A. A. Shif, Vilna, 1892–1902. It has enlarged initial words, and each division has a title and a list of topics. It is numbered both within each of seven "pillars" (*amudim*) and also consecutively throughout, perhaps in a later hand, reaching number 464. For a page found in a manuscript fragment in Munich of a different version, see Emanuel, *Mi-Ginzei Eiropa* I, 54 and 55n.179. On the book's arrangement, see Ephraim E. Urbach, *Ba'alei ha-Tosafot*, 2 vols. (Jerusalem: Mosad Bialik, 1980), 159–162, and especially Judah D. Galinsky, "The Significance of Form: R. Moses of Coucy's Reading Audience and his *Sefer ha-Mizvot*," *AJS Review* 35:2 (November 2011): 305–308.

25. The manuscript has been sold at public auction more than once since 2004 and is now in private hands. It was f. 1r–f. 169v of former London, Montefiore 134 [Halberstam

115], a codex that also contains several short additional texts [IMHM F 7304]. Moses Gaster published a detailed list of its contents and several pages in "The Sepher Assufoth" in *Report for the Year 1892–1893, Judith "Montefiore" College* (London: 1893), 33–74, reprinted in his collection *Texts and Studies* 2 (1928): 711–724. Avraham Yitzhaq Dzubas published a section of the manuscript as *Sefer ha-Assufot* (London: Y. Naroditski, [1942]). He erroneously attributed the work to R. Elijah of Carcassonne. It was the work of one of R. Eleazar b. Judah of Worms's students, possibly later edited by a grandson of R. Eliezer b. Joel Halevi (Ravyah), who is quoted throughout. See Avigdor Aptowitzer, *Mavo le-Sefer Raviah* (Jerusalem: Meqizei Nirdamim, 1938), 150.

26. See Avraham Grossman, *Hakhmei Ashkenaz ha-Rishonim* (Jerusalem: Magnes Press, 1981), 175–210, especially 196, and R. Judah b. Meir ha-Kohen, *Sefer ha-Dinim*, introduction by Avraham Grossman (Jerusalem: Merkaz Zalman Shazar, 1977), and Simcha Emanuel, "Seridim Hadashim mi-Sefer ha-Dinim le-R. Yehudah ha-Kohen," *Qovez 'al Yad* 20 (2010): 81–103. For other early collections of responsa that are short texts assembled often without clear patterns of organization, see Joel Müller, ed., *Teshuvot Geonei Mizrah u-Ma'arav* (Berlin, 1888), and Müller, ed., *Teshuvot Hakhmei Zarfat ve-Lotir* (Vienna, 1881; reprint, Jerusalem, 1992).

27. The only complete manuscript of *Even ha-'Eizer* is Wolfenbüttel, Herzog Augustus Library Codex Guelf Fol. 5.7 [IMHM F2130], and it is earlier than the manuscript on which the first edition (Prague, 1610) was based. Later editions include Shalom Albeck, ed., with an introduction (Warsaw, 1905); Shlomo Zalman Ehrenreich (Shamloya, 1927; reprint, Jerusalem, 1975). See Emanuel, *Shivrei Luhot,* 52n.2 and 52–59. On R. Eliezer b. Nathan, see Aptowitzer, *Mavo*, 49–57, Chaim Tchernowitz, *Toledot ha-Poseqim*, 3 vols. (New York: Jubilee Committee, 1946–1947), 2:76–78, and Urbach, *Ba'alei ha-Tosafot*, 173–184.

That *Even ha-'Eizer* has problems of order, see Tchernowitz, *Toledot ha-Poseqim*, 2:45 ("ein seder le-mishnato"), and Urbach, *Ba'alei ha-Tosafot*, 178–179. Emanuel, *Mi-Ginzei Eiropa I,* 51, and nn. 162–163 points to a few pages recovered from bindings of archival records in Modena and environs that differ from the familiar text.

28. See Rella Kushelevsky, *Siggufim u-Fituyim: Ha-Sippur ha-'Ivri be-Ashkenaz k. y. Parma 2295, De Rossi 563* (Jerusalem: Magnes Press, 2010), and Yassif, *Me'ah Sippurim Haser Ehad*; "Ma'asim shel Hasidim," JTS Microfilm 2374, f. 110b–124b [IMHM F 28627]. On medieval Hebrew stories in general, see Joseph Dan, *Ha-Sippur ha-'Ivri bimei ha-Beinayim* (Jerusalem: Keter, 1975), and Eli Yassif, *The Hebrew Folktale: History, Genre, Meaning,* translated by Jacqueline S. Teitelbaum (Bloomington: Indiana University Press, 1999).

29. See Josef Bamberger, "Sippurei ha-Shevahim shel Hasidei Ashkenaz: Qavvei Yesod la-Hagiografiah ha-Yehudit be-Ashkenaz bimei ha-Beinayim" (PhD diss., Bar Ilan University, 2005), 42–43.

30. See Anat Shapira, ed., *Midrash 'Aseret ha-Dibrot: Teqes, Midrash, u-Feirush* (Jerusalem: Mosad Bialik, 2005). On *The Canterbury Tales*, see Matthew Spencer et al., "Analyzing the Order of Items of Manuscripts of *The Canterbury Tales*," *Computers and the Humanities* 37 (2003): 97–109: "Our results support the idea that there was no established order when the first manuscripts were written" (from the abstract).

31. Although scholars have claimed that French but not German scholars collected their own responsa until R. Meir b. Barukh of Rothenburg (d. 1293), Simcha Emanuel has argued that they existed but were lost. See Emanuel, *Shivrei Luhot,* chapter 1, a revision of Israel Ta-Shema, "Rabbinic Literature in the Middle Ages: 1000–1492," in *The Oxford Handbook of Jewish Studies,* edited by Martin Goodman (Oxford: Oxford University Press, 2004), 224. See, too, Ephraim Kanarfogel, "Religious Leadership During the Tosafist Period: Between the Academy and the Rabbinic Court," *Jewish Religious Leadership: Image and Reality,* edited by Jack Wertheimer, 2 vols. (New York: Jewish Theological Seminary of America, 2004), 1:297.

32. Simcha Emanuel, ed., *Teshuvot Maharam mi-Rotenburg ve-Haveirav,* 2 vols. (Jerusalem: World Union of Jewish Studies, 2012), especially 1:29–30 for the role Abraham played in collecting many of his brother's responsa.

33. Jacob b. Meir (Rabbeinu Tam) (d. 1171) probably wrote two versions of *Sefer ha-Yashar.* See Avraham (Rami) Reiner, "Sefer ha-Yashar le-Rabbeinu Tam: Structure and Coherence of the Book," in a conference volume in honor of Zev Gries, Ben-Gurion University of the Negev, forthcoming. My appreciation to the author for a pre-publication copy. The two main manuscripts are Jerusalem, NLI, 4° 370 [IMHM #B 252] and Oxford, Bodleian Library Opp. Add. Fol. 50 (Neubauer 2355) [F 21419], and they differ in order and content.

Hayyim Yosef David Azulai (Hida) used the Jerusalem manuscript to which he added an index at the end, and it was the basis of the first edition (Vienna, 1811). It is dated to the sixteenth century and written in a Sefaradit Rabbanit hand. Paragraphs have enlarged initials and spaces, and it is not clear when they were numbered. In addition to ed. Vienna, Rabbeinu Tam's responsa were published a second time based on f. 163r–224r of the Jerusalem manuscript as *Sefer ha-Yashar: Heleq She'eilot u-Teshuvot,* edited by Shraga Rosenthal (Berlin: Meqizei Nirdamim, 1898). See pp. vii–viii. The manuscript has rubrics for the questions and answers. Sometimes there is space of three or four lines between texts. No numbers are visible after #546 f. 190v. The *simanim* are hardly separated by spaces although there often are enlarged initials. The *novellae* (*hiddushim*) were published a second time based mainly on Oxford, Bodleian Library Opp. Add. Fol. 50 (Neubauer 2355) [IMHM F 21419], with additions from the Jerusalem manuscript, f. 1r–162r, wherever the Oxford manuscript is missing, as *Sefer ha-Yashar le-Rabbeinu Tam: Heleq ha-Hiddushim,* edited by Simon Shlomo Schlesinger (Jerusalem,

1959). The *simanim* only sometimes have spaces or enlarged initials between them. A shorter collection, Montefiore 98, has some of the responsa in *Sefer ha-Yashar* but arranged in a different order. See Avraham (Rami) Reiner, "Rabbeinu Tam u-Venei Doro: Qesharim, Hashpa'ot ve-Darkhei Limmudo ba-Talmud" (PhD diss., Hebrew University of Jerusalem, 2002), 23–28.

34. On R. Baruch b. Isaac of Worms's *Sefer ha-Terumah*, a northern French rabbinic work, see Urbach, *Ba'alei ha-Tosafot*, 347–354; Simcha Emanuel, "'Ve-Ish 'al meqomo mevo'ar shemo': le-Toledotav shel R. Barukh b. Yizhaq," *Tarbiz* 69 (2000): 423–440; Emanuel, *Shivrei Luhot*, 5–6, Galinsky, "Significance of Form," 305; Yoel Friedman, "Sefer ha-Terumah le-Rabbeinu Barukh b. R. Isaac: Megammot, Mivneh, ve-Nusah" (PhD diss., Hebrew University of Jerusalem, 2013); Friedman, "Mivneh 'Sefer ha-Terumah' u-Mashma'uto li-Fesiqat ha-Halakhah," *Ha-Ma'ayan* 54:4, no. 210 (2014): 93–99. Friedman shows that R. Barukh b. Isaac produced one edition of his work and revised it himself, and it is an example of what Israel Ta-Shma meant by an "open book."

For the best manuscripts of the author's different editions, see Friedman, "Mivneh 'Sefer ha-Terumah.'" For recent editions, see R. Barukh b. Isaac of Worms, *Sefer ha-Terumah,* vols. 3–4, edited by David Avraham (Jerusalem: Makhon Yerushalayim, 2010), on which, see the critical review, Yoel Friedman, Review, "'Al ha-Mahadurah ha-Hadashah shel Sefer ha-Terumah," *Ha-Ma'ayan* (March 4, 2017). See, too, R. Barukh b. Isaac of Worms*, Sefer ha-Terumah le-Rabbeinu Barukh b. Isaac,* Hilekhot Hallah, Erez Yisrael, edited by Yoel Friedman (Shavei Darom: Makhon ha-Torah ve-ha-Arez, 2016).

35. At first, the editor of *Sefer Mizvot Gadol* wrote that the author revised the book once and that there were two editions. See Yisrael Mordechai Peles et al., eds., *Sefer Mizvot Gadol ha-Shalem,* 2 vols. (Jerusalem: Makhon Yerushalayim, 1993–2003), 1:19–23. He subsequently revised himself and concluded that there were three versions, an original one and two that the author modified. See Yisrael Mordechai Peles, "Sefer 'Maharil' [='Minhagei Maharil'] 'al pi Kitvei ha-Yad ha-Otografiyyim shelo ve-Yihudo ke-'Hibbur Merubeh 'Arikhot'" (PhD diss., Bar-Ilan University, 2005), 325, and see Peles, "Nusah ha-SMG ha-Shalem," in *Sefer Mizvot Gadol ha-Shalem*, vol. 2 (Jerusalem: Makhon Yerushalayim, 2003).

Manuscripts include: Parma, Biblioteca Palatina, H 3278, Giovanni Bernardo De Rossi, *MSS Codices Hebraici in Bibliothecae I. B. De-Rossi,* 3 vols. (Parma, 1808), 93; Benjamin Richler, *Hebrew Manuscripts in the Biblioteca Palatina in Parma: Catalogue,* Palaeographical and codicological descriptions Malachi Beit-Arié (Jerusalem: Hebrew University of Jerusalem, Jewish National and University Library, 2001), no. 790; [IMHM F 12322] is dated 1285. Features include: 3 columns; Ashkenazic semi-cursive hand; no initials, but spaces between paragraphs. See Yisrael Mordechai Peles, "Ha-Semag u-

Mahadurotav," *Moriah* 18:9–10 (1993): 105–110. A second manuscript is Zurich, Braginsky
Collection 274 [formerly Jerusalem, Schocken Library 13869], 2 columns, large rubric
MIZVAT ASEH (positive commandment) plus numbered paragraphs [IMHM F 74047].
Paris, Bibliothèque Nationale, héb. 370, dated 1293, is apparently a copy of Zurich, Bragin-
sky [IMHM F 20241]. On this book, see Galinsky, "Significance of Form," 293–321.

36. See Avraham Y. Havazelet, "Sefer Simanei Mizvot le-Rabbeinu Avraham
b. Ephraim," in *Sefer ha-Zikkaron li-Khvodo u-le-Zikhro shel R. Yizhaq Yedidya Frankel,*
edited by David B. Lau and Yosef Buksbaum (Jerusalem: Makhon Yerushalayim,
1992), 281–304, and Judah D. Galinsky, "Between Ashkenaz (Germany) and Tsarfat
(France): Two Approaches Toward Popularizing Jewish Law," in *Jews and Christians in
Thirteenth-Century France,* edited by Elisheva Baumgarten and Judah D. Galinsky
(New York: Palgrave Macmillan, 2015), 80–81. See Paris, Bibliothèque Nationale héb.
392 [IMHM F 20243], dated 1271; an index to paragraphs 1–533; enlarged initials and
space between numbered paragraphs; Paris, Bibliothèque Nationale, héb. 1408, f. 175r–
195v [IMHM F 15770 or F 24886]; no index; numbered paragraphs 1–186 (breaks off);
Paris, Bibliothèque Nationale héb. 393 [IMHM F 4428]; 15th-century Italy; f. 2r–numbered
paragraphs 1–365; Colophon f. 55r: "nishlam sefer ha-mizvot."

37. See the online Catalogue of the National Library of Israel, under "Isaac b. Joseph
of Corbeil" (d. 1280) (not under the title).

38. On *Sefer Mizvot Qatan,* also known as *'Amudei Golah,* the oldest manuscript is
London, British Library Add. 11639, George Margoliouth, *Catalogue of the Hebrew and
Samaritan Manuscripts in the British Museum,* 4 vols. (London, 1899–1935), no. 1056, known
as the "Northern French Miscellany." See Malachi Beit-Arié, "The Making of the Miscellany," in *North French Hebrew Miscellany (British Library Add. MS 11639) Companion
Volume to an Illuminated Manuscript from Thirteenth Century France in Facsimile,* edited
by J. Schoenfeld (London: Facsimile Editions, 2003), 47–73; Emanuel, *Shivrei Luhot,* 199
and n. 55; Tchernowitz, *Toledot ha-Poseqim,* 2:93–95, especially 94; and Urbach, *Ba'alei
ha-Tosafot,* 572, who noted problems of order. On the author's publicity campaign to have
his text copied everywhere, see Urbach, *Ba'alei ha-Tosafot,* 573, Emanuel, *Shivrei Luhot,*
198, and notes 51–52 for other early manuscripts. See, too, Galinsky, "Between Ashkenaz
(Germany) and Tsarfat (France)," 81.

39. R. Isaac b. Moses, *Sefer Or Zarua',* Amsterdam, Bibliotheca Rosenthaliana Hs.
Ros. 3 (online) [IMHM F 10455; on the film every other page is upside down]. See L.
Fuks and R. G. Fuks-Mansfeld, eds., *Hebrew and Judaic Manuscripts of the Bibliotheca
Rosenthaliana, University Library of Amsterdam* (Leiden: E. J. Brill, 1973), 48–49; E. G. L.
Schrijver, "Some Light on the Amsterdam and London Manuscripts of Moses of Vienna's
Or Zarua'," *Bulletin of the John Rylands University Library of Manchester* 75:3 (1993): 53–82.

It has 3 columns, is from Ashkenaz, and has numbered paragraphs and enlarged initial words with space all around. The beginning has a summary index up to paragraph 211. It is the basis of the first two parts published in Zhitomir, 1862.

London, British Library Or. 2859 and 2860 [IMHM F 6408 and F 6409] in Margoliouth, *Catalogue*, 2:137, nos. 530–531. The London manuscript is the basis of vols. 3 and 4 published in Jerusalem, 1887–1890. In his introduction, the author refers to his "liqqutim" or notebooks in which he recorded different traditions that he preserved. See Tchernowitz, *Toledot ha-Poseqim*, 2:56, and Emanuel, *Shivrei Luhot*, 250–252, and Simcha Emanuel, "The Manuscripts of Rabbi Isaac ben Moses of Vienna's Or Zarua'," at http://www.misrachi.at/idex.php/geschichte-der-juden-in-wien/82-handschriften-und -drucke-des-or-sarua. Some of the lack of coherence of the individual passages he copied was transferred to the book. On the differences in the order in the two manuscripts, see also Uziel Fuchs, "'Iyyunim be 'Sefer Or Zarua'' le-R. Yizhaq b. Moshe mi-Veena" (M.A. thesis, Hebrew University of Jerusalem, 1993), 68.

40. Vatican, Hebrew MS 301, f. 1r–176r, and index on f. 191r–191v [IMHM F 8702]; Richler, *Hebrew Manuscripts in the Vatican Library*, p. 241, 191ff. It is written on parchment in 2 columns; quaternions (Ashkenazic); in a late 13th-century Ashkenazic semi-cursive script. A description of this manuscript is found in Abraham b. 'Azriel, *'Arugat ha-Bosem*, 4:128–129, and it is the basis of the edition. The editor notes (4:114) that the author composed it more than once. It has 53 lines on page. There are some spaces following two short lines at end of passages [″]; it is numbered with enlarged initial words with space all around. Numbered sections go to 71 (f. 127r–132v) with some headers of paragraph numbers and enlarged initials without paragraph numbers f. 133r–138r; then new numbering f. 137v–157r (to #65); f. 191r index of 1–71 (first set of numbers).

A second manuscript, with major differences, is Frankfurt am Main, Hebrew MS Fol. 16 (Merzbacher 95) (online catalog and facsimile) [IMHM F 41160]. It has 2 columns; enlarged initial words; segments end with spaces and two lines [″]; numbers are not always clear in beginning of the text.

41. R. Simcha b. Samuel of Vitry, *Mahzor Vitry*, edited by Simon Halevy Horowitz (Berlin: Meqizei Nirdamim, 1892; 2nd ed., Nürnburg, 1922). This edition is based on London, British Library 27200 and 27201. Margoliouth, *Catalogue of the Hebrew and Samaritan Manuscripts in the British Museum*, no. 655 [IMHM F 5872 and F 5873]. It was edited again by Aryeh Goldschmidt, 3 vols. (Jerusalem: Makhon Ozar ha-Posqim, 2004–2009). Paris, Klagsbald [former Sassoon 535] is the earliest manuscript [IMHM F 9278] [f. 52r: Aleinu] [f. 104v lion with dog on its tail]. It has no paragraph numbers and begins with continuous text with two little lines after divisions [″]. A second MS is Ox-

ford, Bodleian Opp. Add. Fol. 14 (Neubauer 1101) [IMHM F 17707]. The paragraphs are numbered 1–155, then 1–540 and again 1–284.

See Tchernowitz, *Toledot ha-Poseqim* 2:18–20; Israel Ta-Shma, "'Al Kamah 'Inyanei Mahzor Vitry," *'Alei Sefer* 11 (1984): 81–89; Simcha Emanuel, "Le-'Inyano shel Mahzor Vitry," *'Alei Sefer* 12 (1986): 129–130; and Israel Ta-Shma, "Teguvah le-He'arah," *'Alei Sefer* 12 (1986): 131–132. The last two are summarized in Ta-Shma's revision of his original article in his *Keneset Mehqarim: 'Iyyunim be-Sifrut ha-Rabbanit bimei ha-Beinayim*, vol. 1, *Ashkenaz* (Jerusalem: Mosad Bialik, 2004), 64, 73–76. See also Justine Isserles, "Mahzor Vitry: Étude d'un corpus de manuscrits hébreux ashkénazes de type liturgico-légal du XII au XIV siècle [The Production and Textual Transmission of a Corpus of Liturgical Manuscripts: Mahzor Vitry]" (PhD diss., École des Hautes Études, 2012), with her summary in *Revue des études juives* 173:1–2 (January-June 2014): 191–194.

42. On *Sefer ha-Oreh*, see Tchernowitz, *Toledot ha-Poseqim*, 2:14–16 and 2:45; for the name, meaning "collection," see 2:45, based on M. Shevi'it 2:2 and B. Shabbat 73b; for *Sefer ha-Pardes*, see 2:16–17; and on *Siddur Rashi*, see 17–18.

43. See David Berger, ed. and trans., *The Jewish-Christian Debate in the High Middle Ages: A Critical Edition of the Nizzahon Vetus* (Philadelphia: Jewish Publication Society of America, 1979), 373–382, and Mordechai Breuer, ed., *Sefer Nizzahon Yashan* (Ramat Gan: Bar Ilan University Press, 1978), 23–26. For earlier observations, see E. E. Urbach, "Études sur la littérature polémique au moyen âge," *Revue des études juives* 100 (1935): 49–77. Munich Hebrew MS 147 f. 1r–29r on Genesis [IMHM F 25963] has numbered paragraphs from 34 (f. 10v) to 134 (f. 28v). See Berger, *Jewish-Christian Debate*, 374; New York, JTS Mic. 2221 [IMHM F 2847]; a copy of Wagenseil edition that has headings between paragraphs; Harvard, Hebrew MS 57 [IMHM F 34466]. It has enlarged headings but no paragraph numbers; Milan, Biblioteca Ambriosiana, Hebrew X.191 Sup. *Nizzahon* f. 1r–14r [IMHM F 12640]. This MS is not in either modern edition. It has very light, small script; paragraphs have no numbers, and it has enlarged headings.

44. See David Berger, "How, When, and to What Degree Was the Jewish-Christian Debate Transformed in the Twelfth and Thirteenth Centuries?," in *Jews and Christians in Thirteenth-Century France*, edited by Elisheva Baumgarten and Judah Galinsky (New York: Palgrave Macmillan, 2015), 129.

45. *Sefer Nizzahon* of Yom Tov Lipmann-Mühlhausen (d. after 1420) (Altdorf, 1644); reprint, with an introduction by Frank Talmage (Jerusalem: Merkaz Dinur of the Hebrew University of Jerusalem, 1984), "Amar ha-mehabber" (author's introduction). The book contains 354 paragraphs. On the book, see Yehuda Kaufman (Even-Shmuel), *R. Yom Tov Lipmann Muehlhausen Ba'al ha-Nizzahon, ha-Hoqer ve-ha-Mequbbal* (New York, 1927), and Ora Limor and Israel Jacob Yuval, "Scepticism and Conversion: Jews,

Christians and Doubt in Sefer ha-Nizzahon," in *Hebraica Veritas?: Christian Hebraists and the Study of Judaism in Early Modern Europe*, edited by Allison Coudert and Jeffrey S. Shoulson (Philadelphia: University of Pennsylvania, 2004), 159–179.

46. Lange, *Peirushei ha-Torah le-Rabbi Yehudah he-Hasid* (published in uncensored and censored editions). The two best manuscripts are "Peshatim mei-H. R. Yehudah he-hasid": Moscow, Russian State Library, Günzburg Hebrew MS 82, f. 62r–97r [F 6762 and F 7247] and Cambridge, Cambridge University Library, Add. 669.2, f. 1r–71v (incomplete) [IMHM F 15890]. See description in Solomon Marcus Schiller-Szinessy, ed., *Catalogue of the Hebrew Manuscripts Preserved in the University Library, Cambridge* (Cambridge: Cambridge University Press, 1876–1878; reprinted 2012), no. 53, pp. 159–165, especially 159: "Paper in quarto, 6 7/8 in × 5 ¼ in.; 72 leaves, 4-sheet quires, 28–31 lines; Rabbinic character, fine German Ashkenazic handwriting of the XIV century"; Stefan C. Reif, *Hebrew Manuscripts at Cambridge University Library* (Cambridge: Cambridge University Press, 1997), no. SCR 97. On their different sequencing, see Brin, "Qavvim le-Feirush ha-Torah shel R. Yehudah *he-hasid*," 215. A less important manuscript is Strasbourg, Bibliothèque Nationale et Universitaire, Hebrew MS 3970, Landauer, *Katalog*, 44, f. 21v–80r.

47. See Yitzhaq Lange, ed., *Ta'amei Masoret ha-Miqra le-R. Yehudah he-hasid* (Jerusalem: Y. Lange, 1980), Judah *he-hasid's* other Pentateuchal commentary, 11: "within the sections (*parshiyot*) themselves, there is no order, and sometimes a comment was even put in an adjacent section. To make it easier for the reader, I have rearranged the comments in the order of the verses." The edition is based primarily on Moscow, Russian State Library, Günzburg Hebrew 82 f. 62r–97v [IMHM F 7247 and F 6762]; and Oxford, Bodleian Library, Opp. 31 (Neubauer 271), f. 90r–99v. [IMHM F 16739]. Fourteenth-fifteenth century; Ashkenazic hand.

48. R. Jacob b. Moses Ha-Levi Mölln (Maharil), *Sefer Maharil: Minhagim*, edited by Shlomo Spitzer (1989; reprinted with corrections, Jerusalem: Makhon Yerushalayim, 2005), "Mavo," 12.

49. R. Abraham Klausner, *Sefer Minhagim*, edited by Yonah Yosef Dissen (Jerusalem: Makhon Yerushalayim, 1978), and Abraham Klausner, *Sefer ha-Minhagim le-Rabbeinu Avraham Klausner*, edited by Shlomo Spitzer, 2nd ed. (Jerusalem: Makhon Yerushalayim, 2006).

Joseph Juspa b. Pinhas Seligmann Hahn, *Yosef Omez* (Frankfurt am Main, 1928; reprint, Jerusalem, 1965), sometimes refers to title divisions (p. 84, par. 403) or to paragraph numbers (p. 223, par. 1005) or to both (p. 223, par. 1006). Numbered paragraphs about the rules of Purim are interrupted by two paragraphs that describe the "Frankfurt Purim" of 1614 (p. 242, pars. 1107 and 1109), and rules about fasting are the occasion for a separate paragraph about the same local event (p. 211, par. 953).

On Tyrnau, see Isaac Tyrnau, *Sefer ha-Minhagim le-Rabbeinu Izaaq Tyrnau,* edited by Shlomo Spitzer, 2nd ed. (Jerusalem: Makhon Yerushalayim, 2000), introduction, about two important and very different manuscripts. It was the most popular customs book in Ashkenaz. See Rachel Zohn Mincer, "Liturgical Minhagim Books: The Increasing Reliance on Written Texts in Late Medieval Ashkenaz" (PhD diss., Jewish Theological Seminary, 2012).

50. R. Jacob b. Judah Landau, *Sefer ha-Agur* (Rimini, 1526); Jacob b. Judah Landau, *Sefer ha-Agur ha-Shalem,* edited by Moshe Hershler (Jerusalem: Moznaim, 1960).

51. R. Samson b. Zadok, *Sefer Tashbez* (Cremona, 1556; Lemberg, 1858). Among the early manuscripts of *Sefer Tashbez* are: MS Giessen, Germany, Universitätsbibliothek, Codex 892, f. 192v–233v [IMHM F 39878 or F 1287]. See E[rnst] Róth, *Verzeichnis der Orientalischen Handschriften in Deutschland,* Teil VI, 2, no. 153. There are headings throughout at the top or in the middle of the pages; it has enlarged initial letters, not words; continuous paragraph numbers from 6 to 279. The beginning and end are missing: it starts with par. 6.

Parma H 2592, De Rossi no. 392, Richler, *Catalogue,* Parma, no. 875 [IMHM F13293] 199 ff. parchment Ashkenaz, mid-late fourteenth century; Ashkenazic semi-cursive script. It has paragraphs numbered 1–314; f. 159v–199r, with glosses by R. Perez b. Elijah, index of contents, not index of incipits, before the text of *Sefer Tashbez* (f. 159r–163r), but the index is separated from the text of *Sefer Tashbez* by the insertion on f. 163v–166r of a poem, "qe'arat kesef" by Jehoseph Ezobi and prose by same author on 166v–167r. It has enlarged initial letters (not words) of each paragraph.

Paris, Bibliothèque Nationale héb. 643 (online) [IMHM F11539] f. 20v–36v with index of contents on f. 37r; Ashkenazic thirteenth century; numbered only from 1 to the low 200s.

52. R. Joseph b. Moses, *Sefer Leqet Yosher,* edited by Jacob Freimann (Berlin: Meqizei Nirdamim, 1903; reprint, Jerusalem, 1964), in two parts, based on MS Munich, Bayerische Staatsbibliothek, Cod. Heb. 404–405 [IMHM F 1645 and F 1646]; and R. Joseph b. Moses, *Leqet Yosher,* edited by Amihai Kinarti, 2 vols. (Jerusalem: Makhon Yerushalayim, 2010).

53. On Israel b. Petahya Isserlein, *Terumat ha-Deshen,* see MS New York, Jewish Theological Seminary Mic. 7148 [F 43423], 285ff. Ashkenazit, early sixteenth century; and compare the first edition, Venice, 1519.

54. See Eva Haverkamp, ed., *Hebräische Berichte über die Judenverfolgungen während des ersten Kreuzzugs* (Hannover: Hahn, 2005), "Einleitung" and the synoptic tables. On medieval Jewish historiography as made up of episodic collections of small sources, see Bonfil, *History and Folklore in a Medieval Jewish Chronicle,* 32.

55. See Yaakov Spigel, '*Amudim be-Toledot ha-Sefer ha-'Ivri*, 2 vols. (Ramat Gan: Bar Ilan University Press, 1996–2005), esp. 2:523–564. My thanks to Simcha Emanuel for this important reference.

56. Jehuda Wistinetzki provided a content index at the end of his edition of the Parma manuscript of *Sefer Hasidim* in 1891.

57. See Richard H. Rouse and Mary A. Rouse, "*Statim Invenire*: Schools, Preachers, and New Attitudes Toward the Page," in *Renaissance and Renewal in the Twelfth Century,* edited by Robert L. Benson and Giles Constable (Cambridge, Mass.: Harvard University Press, 1982), 201–225.

58. *Sefer Nizzahon* of Yom Tov Lipmann-Mühlhausen, "Amar ha-mehabber" (author's introduction).

59. R. Eliezer b. Samuel of Metz, *Sefer Yerei'im ha-Shalem*, edited by A. A. Shif (Vilna, 1892–1902), introduction.

60. R. Isaac b. Joseph of Corbeil, *Sefer 'Amudei Golah=Sefer Mizvot Qatan* (New York: Edison, 1959), introduction.

61. R. Isaac b. Eliezer, *Sefer ha-Gan* (Venice, 1606). This book from fourteenth-century German Ashkenaz is to be distinguished from the Tosafist Torah commentary of the same name edited by M[itchel] Orlian (Jerusalem: Mosad ha-Rav Kook, 2009).

Select Bibliography

Manuscripts of *Sefer Hasidim* are described in the Catalog. Many other important *hasidei ashkenaz* manuscripts are listed at the end of Joseph Dan, *Torat ha-Sod shel Hasidut Ashkenaz* (Jerusalem: Mosad Bialik, 1968). Manuscripts of penitential texts by Eleazar of Worms are described in Marcus, "Hasidei Ashkenaz Private Penitentials." A complete annotated catalog of *hasidei ashkenaz* writings in manuscript remains to be done. In addition, a census of which texts were copied in the same manuscripts needs to be carried out. The sources listed in the bibliography are cited in the book in short form; other sources are cited in full the first time they appear in each chapter and in short form thereafter.

This multitiered bibliography is divided into primary sources and secondary sources. Primary sources are further subdivided into important manuscripts of *hasidei ashkenaz* writings; published texts ascribed to Judah; published texts of Eleazar's; and other primary texts related to *hasidei ashkenaz*.

PRIMARY SOURCES

Selected Manuscripts of Hasidei Ashkenaz Writings

Australia, Private MS 1 [IMHM 43104] contains *Sefer Hilekhot ha-Emunah* of "Sodei Razayya heleq 2." *Sefer ha-Shem* (except for 8 missing pages), *Peirush 'al Sefer Yezirah,* and *Hokhmat ha-Nefesh.* Dated: 1342; Ashkenazic.

Cambridge, University Library, Add. 669, f. 1r–11v (incomplete) [IMHM F 15890]. Judah *he-hasid* Humash commentary published by Yitzhaq Lange.

Frankfurt am Main, Goethe Universität, Universitätsbibliothek Johann Christian Senkenberg (formerly Stadt- und Universitätsbibliothek), Hebrew Oct. 35 (end).

Online: http://sammlungen.ub.uni-frankfurt.de/mshebr/content/titleinfo/1831880.
Ten stories about Samuel *he-hasid*.

Jerusalem, National Library of Israel, Hebrew Oct. 3182 includes cycles of stories about Samuel and Judah. Published in Brüll, "Sagen," and Yassif, *Me'ah Sippurim*.

London, British Library, Add. 27199 Margoliouth Cat. No. 737 [IMHM F 5871]. Copied for Cardinal Egidio da Viterbo in 1516 (see colophon). Contains all five parts of Eleazar of Worms' *Sodei Razayya*.

Moscow, Russian State Library, Günzburg Hebrew 82, f. 62r–17r [F 6762 and F 7247] Judah *he-hasid* Humash commentary published by Yitzhaq Lange.

Moscow, Russian State Library, Günzburg Hebrew 511, f. 3r–187v [F 47854]. Eleazar b. Judah of Worms: *Peirush ha-Tefillot* (Commentary on Prayers); f. 187v–103r *Derashah le-Fesah*.

Munich, Bayrische Staatsbibliothek, Hebrew 81 [IMHM 23129] is a copy of London, British Library, Add. 27199. It contains all five parts of Eleazar of Worms, *Sodei Razayya*.

Oxford, Bodleian Library, Mich. 365 (Neubauer 1208) [F 16668]. "Zeher 'Asah le-Nifle'otav" See Ta-Shma, below.

Oxford, Bodleian Library, Mich. 448 (Neubauer 2215), f. 30r [F 20498] Avraham Meir Habermann, ed. *Sefer Gezeirot Ashkenaz ve-Zarefat*, 165–166. See Marcus, "Mothers," below.

Oxford, Bodleian Library, Opp. 111 (Neubauer 1566, a copy of N. 1567) [F 16934] dated 1700. See Joseph Dan, *'Iyyunim*, below.

Oxford, Bodleian Library, Opp. 160 (Neubauer 1204), 254r–175r [F 16664].

Oxford, Bodleian Library, Opp. 540 (Neubauer 1567) [F 16935], dated 1639. See Dan, *'Iyyunim*, below.

Oxford, Bodleian Library, Opp. 757 (Neubauer 2289), f. 25v–16v [F 20981] Yisrael Kamelhar, R. Eleazar of Worms, 17–19. See Marcus, "Mothers," below.

Paris, Bibliothèque Nationale, héb. 772 [F 12330] Eleazar b. Judah of Worms, *Peirush ha-Tefillot* (Commentary on Prayers). See Hershler, Moshe.

Paris, Bibliothèque Nationale, héb. 1408 [F 24886]. See Sirat, Colette.

Strasbourg, Bibliothèque Nationale et Universitaire, 3970 (Landauer, *Katalog*, no. 44), f. 21v–10r [IMHM F 2864].

Published Texts Attributed to Judah he-hasid

Titles marked with an asterisk contain translated excerpts from *Sefer Hasidim*.

Abrams, Daniel, and Israel Ta-Shma, eds. *Sefer Gematriyot*. Los Angeles: Cherub Press, 1998.

*Beek, Martinus Andrianus, ed. Judah b. Samuel *he-hasid*. *Het Boek der vromen: Fragmenten*. Amsterdam: Arbeiderspers, 1954.

*Borchers, Susanne. *Jüdisches Frauenleben im Mittelalter: Die Texte des Sefer Chasidim*. Frankfurt am Main: Peter Lang, 1998.

*Cassuto, Umberto. "Dal Sefer Chasidim." *La Rassegna Mensile di Israel* 12 (1938): 51–57 (*Scritti in onore di Dante Lattes*).

*Cohn-Sherbok, Dan. *Jewish Mysticism: An Anthology*. Oxford: Oneworld Publications, 1995. From Eleazar of Worms' Secret of Secrets (90–95); from *Sefer Hasidim* (95–98); a prayer (98–100).

*Cronbach, Abraham. "Social Thinking in the *Sefer Hasidim*." *Hebrew Union College Annual* 22 (1949): 1–149.

Dan, Joseph. "'Sefer Malakhim' le-Rabbi Yehudah he-hasid.'" *Da'at* 2–3 (1978–79): 99–120.

*Dan, Joseph. "Qeta' mi-sefer ha-kavod le-Rabbi Judah he-hasid." *Sinai* 71 (1972): 118–120 [MS Paris, Bibliothèque Nationale, héb. 1032, fols. 28r–19r].

Dan, Joseph. "Sippurim Dimonologiyyim mi-Kitvei R. Yehudah he-Hasid." *Tarbiz* 30:3 (1961): 273–289. Reprinted in Marcus, *Dat ve-Hevrah*, 165–181.

*David, Avraham. "Pisqah nosefet le-'Sefer Hasidim.'" *Qiryat Sefer* 45 (1970): 627–628.

*Finkel, Avraham Yaakov, trans. *Sefer Chasidim: The Book of the Pious by Yehuda Ha-Chasid* [*sic*]. Northvale: Jason Aronson, 1997.

*Gourévitch, Edouard, trans. *Jehudah ben Chemouel le Hassid. Sefer Hassidim. Le Guide des Hassidim*. Paris: Les Editions du Cerf, 1988.

*Güdemann, Moritz. *Geschichte des Erziehungswesens und der Cultur der abendländischen Juden*. 3 vols. 1880–1988. Reprinted. Amsterdam: Philo Press, 1966.

Habermann, Avraham M., ed. *Shirei ha-Yihud ve-ha-Kavod*. Jerusalem: Mosad ha-Rav Kook, 1948.

*Hershler, Moshe. "*Sefer Hasidim* le-Rabbeinu Yehudah Hasid." *Genuzot* [1], 125–162. Jerusalem: Shalem, 1984.

Hershler, Moshe. "She'eilot u-Teshuvot le-Rabbeinu Yehudah he-Hasid." *Sinai* 70 (1972): 34–38.

*Judah b. Samuel *he-hasid*, *Zava'ah*. Sabionetta, 1553.

*Kozma, Emese, trans.; Kornélia Koltai, ed. *Széfer Haszidim*, 1–2. Budapest: L'Harmatan, 2016. (Translation into Hungarian of Parma and some passages not in SHP.)

Lange, Yitzhaq, ed. *Peirushei ha-Torah le-Rabbi Yehudah he-Hasid*. Jerusalem: Y. Lange, 1975. (Published in uncensored and censored editions).

Lange, Yitzhaq, ed. *Ta'amei Masoret ha-Miqra le-R.Yehudah he-Hasid*. Jerusalem: Y. Lange, 1980.

*Leviant, Curt. *Masterpieces of Hebrew Literature: A Treasury of 2000 Years of Jewish Creativity*, 380–388. New York: Ktav Publishing House, 1969.

*Marcus, Ivan G. "Narrative Fantasies from Sefer Hasidim." In *Rabbinic Fantasies: Imaginative Narratives from Classical Hebrew Literature*, edited by David Stern and Marc Mirsky, 215–238. 1990. Reprint, New Haven, Conn.: Yale University Press, 1998. Reprinted in Marcus, *Jewish Culture and Society*.

*Maier, Johann. *Fremdes und Fremde in der Jüdischen Tradition und im Sefär Chasidim*: 4. Arye Maimon-Vortrag an der Universität Trier, 7. November 2001. Trier: Kliomedia, 2002.

*Marcus, Jacob R. *The Jew in the Medieval World: A Source Book, 315–1791*. 1938. Reprinted with biboiographical updates by Marc Saperstein, 377–378. Cincinnati: Hebrew Union College Press, 1999.

Sefer Hasidim K[tav] Y[ad] Parma H 3280. Introduction by Ivan G. Marcus. Jerusalem: Merkaz Dinur of the Hebrew University of Jerusalem, 1985.

Sefer Hasidim, edited by Reuven Margoliot. Lemberg, 1924.

Sefer Hasidim, edited by Reuven Margoliot. New edition. Jerusalem: Mosad Ha-Rav Kook, 1956/7.

Sefer Hasidim, edited by Abraham A. Price. 3 vols. Toronto: Yeshivat Torat Hayim, 1955–1964.

Sefer Hasidim, edited by Jehuda Wistinetzki. Frankfurt am Main, 1891.

Sefer Hasidim, edited by Jehuda Wistinetzki and Jacob Freimann. Frankfurt am Main, 1924.

*Singer, Sholom Alchanan. *Medieval Jewish Mysticism: The Book of the Pious*. Northbrook, Ill.: Whitehall Co., 1971.

*Sirat, Colette, et al. *La conception du livre chez les piétistes ashkenazes au moyen âge*. Genève: Droz, 1996.

Soloveitchik, Haym. "Appendix to 'Pietists and Kibbitzers.'" *Jewish Quarterly Review* 96:1 (Winter 2006). https://muse.jhu.edu/article/190747.

Spitzer, Shlomo, ed. "She'eilot u-Teshuvot Rabbeinu Yehuda he-Hasid be-'Inyanei Teshuvah." In *Sefer ha-Zikkaron . . . Rabbi Shmuel Verner*, edited by Yosef Buksbaum, 199–205. Jerusalem: Moriah, 1996.

Stal, Yaakov, ed. *Amarot Tehorot Hitzoniyot u-Fenimiyot . . . be-'Inyanei Emunot ve-De'ot ve-Sod ha-Yihud*. Jerusalem: Yaakov Yisrael Stal-Yefeh Nof, Y. Pozen, 2006.

Stal, Yaakov Israel. "Derashah le-Brit Milah le-Talmid Rabbeinu Yehudah he-Hasid." *Yerushateinu* 4 (2010): 39–62.

Stal, Yaakov Israel. "Hora'ot ve-Hanhagot le-Rabbeinu Yehudah he-Hasid." *Moriah* 32:3–5 (Shevat 2003): 3–22.

*Stal, Yaakov Israel. "Qeta'im Hadashim mi-Khtav Yad mi-Peirushei Rabbeinu Yehudah he-Hasid 'al ha-Torah." *Hazi Gibborim-Pelitat Soferim* 10 (Nisan 2017): 134–151.

Stal, Yaakov, ed. *Sefer Gematriyot.* 2 vols. Jerusalem: Yaakov Stal, 2006.

Stal, Yaakov, ed. [Judah b. Samuel *he-hasid* and students.] *Sodei Humash u-Sh'ar* [Shir ha-Shirim, Iyyov, Ruth]. Jerusalem: Yaakov Stal, 2009.

*Sulzbach, A., ed. and trans. *Die Ethik des Judentums: Auszüge aus dem "Buch der Frommen" (Sefer Hasidim) des R. Jehuda Hachassid.* Frankfurt am Main: Verlag von Sänger & Friedberg, 1923.

Ta-Shma, Israel. "Quntresei 'Sodot ha-Tefillah' le-Rabbi Yehudah he-Hasid." *Tarbiz* 65:1 (1996): 65–78.

Ta-Shma, Israel, ed. *"Zekher 'Asah le-Nifleotav."* *Qovetz 'al Yad* 12 (1994): 121–146.

*Zunz, L. *Zur Geschichte und Literatur,* 135–142. Berlin, 1845.

Published Texts Attributed to R. Eleazar b. Judah of Worms

Bregoli, Francesca, ed. [Eleazar b. Judah of Worms's *Sod Ma'aseh Bereishit*]. *Il Secreto dell'Opera della Creazione.* Genoa: ECIG, 2002.

Cohn-Sherbok, Dan. *Jewish Mysticism: An Anthology.* Oxford: Oneworld Publications, 1995: From Eleazar of Worms' Secret of Secrets (90–95); from *Sefer Hasidim* (95–98); a prayer (98–100).

Dan, Joseph, ed., "Shirei ha-Sod ve-ha-Yihud ve-ha-Emunah." *Temirin* 1 (1973): 141–156.

Dan, Joseph. "Tefillah le-R. Eleazar mi-Vorms." *Temirin* 2 (1981): 77–91.

Eleazar b. Judah of Worms. *Darkhei Teshuvah* in *Responsa* of R. Meir b. Barukh of Rothenburg, 112r–114r. Prague, 1608.

Eleazar b. Judah of Worms. *Drashah le-Fesah.* Edited by Simcha Emanuel. Jerusalem: Meqeizi Nirdamim, 2006.

Eleazar b. Judah of Worms. *Haqdamah ve-Hilekhot Hasidut.* Edited by Y. E. Rosenfeld. Brooklyn: Y. E. Rosenfeld, 1998.

Eleazar b. Judah of Worms. "Hilekhot Tereifot u-Kesheirot mi-Sefer ha-Roqeah" (Sha'arei Shehitah u-Tereifot). Edited by Emese Kozma. New York: Jewish Theological Seminary, MS Rabbinics 1923, folios 46r–19v. The edition is available in pdf format at the Giluy Milta site: http://sites.google.com/site/giluymilta /Home.

Eleazar b. Judah of Worms. *Hilekhot Teshuvah*. Edited by Y. E. Rosenfeld. Brooklyn: Y. E. Rosenfeld, 2000.

Eleazar b. Judah of Worms. *Hokhmat ha-Nefesh*. Safed, [1913]. See Eleazar b. Judah of Worms, *Sodei Razayya*.

Eleazar b. Judah of Worms. *'Isqei Teshuvot*. Published in Marcus, "Hibburei ha-Teshuvah."

Eleazar b. Judah of Worms. *Ma'aseh Roqeah*. Sanik, 1912.

Eleazar b. Judah of Worms. *Ma'aseh Roqeah*. Edited by Emese Kozma in two parts, on-line, from MS "Sinai" Berlin [formerly London, Beit Din MS]. Berlin: Jewish Museum VII.5.26, fols. 85d–123c. The edition is available in pdf format at the Giluy Milta site: http://sites.google.com/site/giluymilta/Home, or Maaseh Rokeah, Part I; Maaseh Rokeah, Part II (from Hilekhot Tzitzit onward).

Eleazar b. Judah of Worms. "Midrash Shemoneh 'Esreh le-Rabbeinu Eleazar mi-Vormaiza ba'al ha-Roqeah." Edited by Moshe Hershler. *Sinai* 74 (1974): 193–200.

Eleazar b. Judah of Worms. *Moreh Hata'im-Sefer ha-Kapparot* in *Kol Bo*. Naples 1490, par. 66, f. 89r–11r.

Eleazar b. Judah of Worms. "Nusah lo Yadua' le-Hilekhot ha-Kavod le-R. Eleazar mi-Vorms." In Daniel Abrams, "'Sod Kol ha-Sodot': Tefisat ha-Kavod ve-Khavanat ha-Tefillah be-Khitvei R. Eleazar mi-Vorms ve-Heidehah bi-Khetavim Aheirim." *Da'at* 34 (1995): 78–81.

Eleazar b. Judah of Worms. "Peirush 'al P[arashat] Bo Mi-Rabbeinu Efraim b. Shim-shon ve-Rabbi Eliezer [*sic*] mi-Germaiza." Edited by Manfred Lehmann. *Sinai* 71 (1972): 1–20.

Eleazar b. Judah of Worms. "Peirush 'al Shir ha-Shirim." See his *Peirush ha-Haggadah*.

Eleazar ben Judah of Worms. "Peirush 'al Tehillim." In Simcha Emanuel, *Mi-Ginzei Eiropa* I, 183–203. Jerusalem: Meqizei Nirdamim, 2015.

Eleazar b. Judah of Worms. *Peirush ha-Haggadah shel Pesah shel R. Eleazar mi-Worms*. Edited by Moshe Hershler. Jerusalem: Shalem Institute, 1984.

Eleazar b. Judah of Worms. "Peirush ha-Hallel le-Rabbeinu Eliezer [*sic*] mi-Germaiza." Edited by Moshe Hershler. *Sinai* 72 (1973): 228–247.

Eleazar b. Judah of Worms. *Peirush ha-Meyuhas la-Roqeah 'al ha-Torah*. In *Peirush ha-Roqeah 'al ha-Torah*. Edited by Julius Klugmann. 5 vols. Benei Brak, 1978.

Eleazar b. Judah of Worms. *Peirush H[a-rav] R. E[leazar] mi-Germaiza 'al Sefer Yezi-rah*. Przemyzl, 1888; new edition in Rabbi Aaron Aisenbakh, *Sifrei ha-R[abbi] E[leazar] mi-Germaiza Ba'al ha-Roqeah*, vol. 2. Jerusalem: Aaron Aisenbakh, 2006.

Eleazar b. Judah of Worms. "Peirush ha-Roqeah 'al ashrei." In *Sefer 'Iqvei Berakhah,* edited by Pinhas ha-Levi Lipshitz, 30–34. Jerusalem: Rabbi Jacob Joseph School Press, 1980.

Eleazar b. Judah of Worms. *Peirush ha-Roqeah 'al ha-Torah*. Genesis with parts of *Sefer ha-Hokhmah*, based on Oxford, Bodleian Library Opp. 506 (Neubauer 1812). Edited by Chaim Konyevsky. Benai Brak, 1978.

Eleazar b. Judah of Worms. "Peirush ha-Roqeah 'al Megillat Ruth le-Rabbeinu Eleazar mi-Germaiza." *Genuzot* 2 (1985): 188–232.

Eleazar b. Judah of Worms. *Peirush Rabbeinu Eleazar mi-Germaiza 'al ha-Torah*. Edited by Haim Yosef Ha-Levi [Gad]. London, 1959.

Eleazar b. Judah. *Peirush Sefer ha-Yezirah*. Przemysl, 1883.

Eleazar b. Judah of Worms. *Peirushei ha-Merkavah*. Edited by Asi Farber-Ginat and Daniel Abrams. Los Angeles: Cherub Press, 2004.

Eleazar b. Judah of Worms. *Peirushei Siddur ha-Tefillah la-Roqeah*. Edited by Moshe Hershler. 2 vols. Jerusalem: 1992.

Eleazar b. Judah of Worms. *Sefer ha-Hokhmah*. See Joseph Dan, "*Sefer ha-Hokhmah le-R. Eleazar mi-Worms*." *Zion* 29 (1964): 168–181. Reprinted in Dan, *'Iyyunim*, 44–57; parts are also reprinted in Eleazar b. Judah of Worms, *Peirush ha-Roqeah 'al ha-Torah*.

Eleazar b. Judah of Worms. *Sefer ha-Roqeah*. Fano, 1505. The only complete manuscript is Paris, Bibliothèque Nationale de France, héb. 363.

Eleazar b. Judah of Worms. *Sefer ha-Roqeah*. Jerusalem, 1960.

Eleazar b. Judah of Worms. *Sefer Raziel*. Amsterdam, 1701.

Eleazar b. Judah of Worms. *Sefer Sodei Razei Semukhin*, edited by David Segal. Jerusalem: Kolel Sha'arei Qedoshah u-Tefillah, 2001. New edition of this text by Rabbi Aaron Aisenbakh, ed. *Sifrei ha-R[abbi] E[eazar]mi-Germaiza, Ba'al ha-Roqeah*. Vol. 2. Jerusalem: Aaron Aisenbakh, 2006.

Eleazar b. Judah of Worms. *Sefer Tagin*. Edited by Yaakov Basser. Toronto, 2010.

Eleazar b. Judah of Worms. *Sha'arei Binah. Peirush Megillat Ester le-Rabbeinu Eleazar mi-Germaiza Ba'al ha-Roqeah*. Edited by Manfred Lehmann. New York: Manfred and Ann Lehmann Foundation, 1980.

Eleazar b. Judah of Worms. "Sha'arei ha-Sod ve-ha-Yihud ve-ha-Emunah le-Rabbi Eleazar mi-Germaiza ba'al ha-Roqeah." Edited by Adolf Jellinek, *Kokhavei Yitzhaq* 27. Vienna, 1862, 7–19. Reprinted in A. M. Habermann, ed., *Shirei ha-Yihud ve-ha-Kavod*, 173–180. Jerusalem: Mosad ha-Rav Kook, 1948, and in Joseph Dan, ed., "Shirei ha-Sod ve-ha-Yihud ve-ha-Emunah." *Temirin* 1 (1973): 141–156. New edition in vol. 2 of Rabbi Aaron Aisenbakh, ed. *Sifrei ha-R[abbi] E[leazar] mi-Germaiza Ba'al ha-Roqeah*. Jerusalem: Aaron Aisenbakh, 2006.

Eleazar b. Judah of Worms. *Sodei Razayya*. Edited by Israel Kamelhar. Bilgoraj, 1936.

Eleazar b. Judah of Worms. *Sodei Razayya mi-Ba'al Sefer ha-Roqeah*. Edited by Shalom ha-Kohen Weiss. Jerusalem: Makhon Sha'arei Ziv, [1991].

Eleazar b. Judah of Worms. *Sodei Razayya ha-Shalem*. Jerusalem: Aharon Barzani u-Veno, 2004.

Eleazar b. Judah of Worms. *Teshuvot Rabbeinu Eleazar mi-Vermaiza ha-"Roqeah."* Edited by Yaakov Yisrael Stal. Jerusalem: Yaakov Stal, 2014.

Eleazar of Worms. *Three Tracts*. Translated and edited by David Meltzer. Berkeley: Berkeley Tree, 1975.

Eleazar b. Judah of Worms. *Yayin ha-Reqah*. [Lublin], 1608.

Eliezer [*sic*] mi-Germaiza. *Sefer Qiryat Sefer (Nimuqei Hamesh Megillot)*. Lemberg, 1905.

Emanuel, Simcha. *Mi-Ginzei Eiropa* 1. Jerusalem: Meqizei Nirdamim, 2015, 183–201.

Emanuel, Simcha. "Sarid mi-Peirush R. Eleazar mi-Vermaiza (ha-Roqeah) le-Sefer Tehillim." *Qovez 'al Yad* 23 (2014): 115–135. Revised edition in Simcha Emanuel, *Mi-Ginzei Eiropa* I, 183–203. Jerusalem: Meqizei Nirdamim, 2015.

Farkas, Bernard, ed. *Das Buch der Weisheit der Seele Sefer Hokmat han-Nefeš*. Edited by Bernard Farkas. Inaugural-Dissertation zur Erlangung der Doktorwürde einer hohen philosophischen Fakultät der Rheinischen Friedrich-Willhelms-Universität zu Bonn. Bonn, 1937.

Habermann, A. M., ed. *Shirei ha-Yihud ve-ha-Kavod*. Jerusalem: Mosad ha-Rav Kook, 1948.

Hershler, Moshe, ed., *Minhagei Vermaiza u-Magenza, de-Vei Rashi ve-Rabbotav u-Minhagei Ashkenaz shel ha-Roqeah*. In *Genuzot* 2, 11–28. Jerusalem: Shalem, 1985.

Hershler, Moshe, ed. *Siddur Rabbeinu Shelomoh mi-Germaiza ve-Siddur Hasidei Ashkenaz*. Jerusalem: Shalem Institute, 1972.

Liss, Hanna, ed. *El'azar ben Yehuda von Worms: Hilkhot ha-Kavod. Die Lehrsäze von der Herrlichkeit Gottes*. Tübingen: Mohr-Siebeck, 1997.

Marcus, Ivan. "Hibburei ha-Teshuvah shel Hasidei Ashkenaz." In *Mehqarim be-Qabbalah, be-Filosofiah Yehudit u-ve-Sifrut ha-Musar ve-ha-Hagut: Mugashim li-Yshaya Tishby bi-Melot lo Shiv'im ve-Hamesh Shanim*, edited by Joseph Dan and Joseph Hacker, 369–384. Jerusalem: Magnes Press, 1986.

Marcus, Ivan G. "The Laws of Saintliness." From "Eleazar ben Judah's *Sefer ha-Rokeah*: A Translation and Introduction to His Ideal of Piety." MA thesis, Columbia University, 1967.

Neubauer, Adolf. "Elasar aus Worms." *Israelietische Letterbode* 10 (1884–1885): 111–112.

Sifrei ha-R[abbi] E[leazar] mi-Germaiza Ba'al ha-Roqeah. Edited by Aaron Aysenbakh. 2 vols. Jerusalem: Aaron Aisenbakh, 2004–2006. *Sodei Razayya* consists of five parts here divided beteween vol. 1 (1–3) and vol. 2 (4–5, plus additional short texts):

1: "Sodei Razayya heleq 1" is sometimes called *Sefer Ma'aseh Bereishit* or *Sefer ha-Alfa Beta* and is arranged according to the Hebrew alphabet and the letters of Eleazar's name.

Published as *Sodei Razayya mi-Ba'al Sefer ha-Roqeah*. Edited by Shalom ha-Kohen
Weiss. Jerusalem: Makhon Sha'arei Ziv, [1991]. Some of this text up to the letter
gimel published as *Sefer Raziel*. Amsterdam, 1701.

2: "Sodei Razayya heleq 2": *Hilekhot Metatron, Hilekhot Malakhim, Hilekhot ha-Kisei, Hile-
khot ha-Kavod, Hilekhot ha-Dibbur, Hilekhot ha-Nevuah, Hilekhot ha-Emuna*. Published by Israel Kamelhar, *Sodei Razayya*, Bilgoraj, 1936.

3: *Sefer ha-Shem* published as a whole for the first time in Rabbi Aaron Aisenbakh, *Sifrei
ha-R[abbi] E[leazar] mi-Germaiza Ba'al ha-Roqeah*. Vol. 1. Jerusalem: Aaron
Aisenbakh, 2004.

4: *Hokhmat ha-Nefesh*. Published in Rabbi Aaron Aisenbakh, *Sifrei ha-R[abbi] E[leazar]
mi-Germaiza Ba'al ha-Roqeah*. Vol. 2. Previously, Lemberg, 1876; Safed, 1913.

5: *Peirush Sefer Yezirah*. Published in Rabbi Aaron Aisenbakh, *Sifrei ha-R[abbi] E[leazar]
mi-Germaiza Ba'al ha-Roqeah*, Vol. 2. Jerusalem: Aaron Aisenbakh, 2006. Previously, *Peirush Sefer ha-Yezirah*. Przemysl, 1883.

*Weissler, Chava. "A Translation of a Portion of Sefer Hokhmat ha-Nefesh by Eleazar
ben Judah of Worms." May 1967. JTS Mic. 8795.

Other Related Published Primary Sources

Abraham b. 'Azriel. *'Arugat ha-Bosem*. Edited by Ephraim E. Urbach. 4 vols. Jerusalem:
Meqizei Nirdamim, 1939–63.

Abrams, Daniel. "Sefer ha-Yihud le-R. Eleazar (?) ha-Darshan." *Qovez 'al Yad* 12 (1994):
149–160.

Azulai, Haim Yosef David. *Brit 'Olam*. Published with his *Lev David*. Livorno, 1789.

Brüll, Nehemiah, ed. "Sagen." *Jahrbücher für jüdische Geschichte und Literatur* 9 (1889):
20–45.

Dan, Joseph. "Peirush 'Ha-Aderet ve-ha-Emunah' shel Hasidei Ashkenaz." *Tarbiz* 50
(1981): 396–404.

Eidelberg, Shlomo, ed. *R. Juspa, Shammash of Warmaisa (Worms): Jewish Life in
17th Century Worms*. I: *Minhagim*; II *Sefer Ma'aseh Nissim*; III: *Pinqas ha-Qehillah*.
Jerusalem: Magnes Press, 1991.

Gaster, Moses, ed. *The Maaseh Book*. Philadelphia: Jewish Publication Society, 1934.

Hacker, Joseph, ed. *'Olama ha-Hevrati ve-ha-Ruhani shel Hasidut Ashkenaz*. Jerusalem: Aqadamon, 1968.

Hamburger, B., and Yitzhaq Zimmer, eds. *Minhagim de-Q"Q Vermaiza le-Rabbi Yuspa
Shamash*. 2 vols. Jerusalem: Mekhon Yerushalayim, 1988–1992.

Hershler, Moshe. "Peirush Birkhot Milah le-Hasidei Ashkenaz." *Sinai* 69 (1971): 105–109.

Isaac b. Eliezer. *Sefer ha-Gan*. Venice, 1606.

Juspa Shamash of Worms. *Ma'aseh Nisim*. Amsterdam, 1696 (Yiddish).

Kozma, Emese. "Sidrei Teshuvah li-Meshumad she-Hazar la-Yahadut be-Ostriah u-ve-Germaniah ba-Me'ah ha-Hamesh-'Esreh: Pirsum Teshuvah mi-K"Y." Oxford, [Bodleian Library, Mich. 84 (Neubauer 784), fols. 25v–16r]. *'Alei Sefer* 24–25 (2015): 189–214.

Mayseh Bukh. Basel, 1602.

Meitlis, Yaakov. *Di Shvohim fun Rebbe Shmuel und Rebbe Yuda Hasid*. London: Kedem, 1961.

Moses b. Eleazar ha-Kohen. *Sefer Hasidim Qatan=Sefer ha-Maskil*. 1866. Reprint Jerusalem: Yedei Hein, 2004.

Moses b. Nahman (Nahmanides). "Be-Terem A'aneh." In *Kitvei ha-Ramban*, edited by Charles Chavel, esp. 365–368. Jerusalem: Mosad ha-Rav Kook, 1963.

Moses Taku [Dachau]. *Ketav Tamim*. Edited by R. Kirchheim. In *Ozar Nechmad: Briefe und Abhandlungen,* edited by Ignaz Blumenfeld, 54–99. Year 3. Vienna, 1860.

Moses Taku [Dachau]. *Ketav Tamim*. Facsimile of MS Paris héb. 711. Edited by Joseph Dan. Jerusalem: Merkaz Dinur, 1984.

Sefer ha-Hayyim, Das Buch des Lebens: Edition, Übersetzung, und Studien. Edited by Gerold Necker. Tübingen: Mohr-Siebeck, 2001.

Stal, Yaakov Yisrael, ed. *Derashot limei ha-Teshuvah mi-Beit Midrasham shel Hasidei Ashkenaz*. Jerusalem: Yaakov Stal, 2014.

Yassif, Eli, ed. *Me'ah Sippurim Haser Ehad: Aggadot Ketav Yad Yerushalayim ba-Folklore ha-Yehudi shel Yemei ha-Beinayim*. Tel Aviv: Haim Rubin, Tel Aviv University Press, 2013. [=Jerusalem, National Library of Israel, Hebrew MS Oct. 3182].

SECONDARY SOURCES

Abrams, Daniel. "The Emergence of Esotericism in German Pietism." *Shofar* 12 (1994): 67–85.

Abrams, Daniel. "From Germany to Spain: Numerology as a Mystical Technique." *Journal of Jewish Studies* 47:1(1996): 85–101.

Abrams, Daniel. "Ha-Shekhinah Mitpalelet lifnei ha-Qadosh Barukh Hu—Meqor ha-dash li-Tefisah Teosofit Ezel Hasidei Ashkenaz u-Tefisatam legabei Mesirat ha-Sodot." *Tarbiz* 63 (1994): 509–532.

Abrams, Daniel. "A History of the Unique Cherub" (review essay). *Jewish Quarterly Review* 90:3–4 (2000): 397–403.

Abrams, Daniel. "The Literary Emergence of Esotericism in German Pietism." *Shofar* 12 (1994): 67–85.

Abrams, Daniel. "'Ma'aseh Merkavah' as a Literary Work: The Reception of Hekhalot Traditions by the German Pietists and Kabbalistic Reinterpretation." *Jewish Studies Quarterly* 5:4 (1998): 329–334.

Abrams, Daniel. "'Sefer Shqud' le-Rabbi Shmuel ben Rabbi Qalonimos ve-Torat ha-Kavod shel Talmid R. Eleazar mi-Vorms." *Asufot* 14 (1992): 217–241.

Abrams, Daniel. *Sexual Symbolism and Merkavah Speculation in Medieval Germany: A Study of the Sod ha-Egoz Texts.* Texts and Studies in Medieval and Early Modern Judaism 13. Tübingen: J. C. B. Mohr [Paul Siebeck], 1997.

Abrams, Daniel. "'Sod Kol ha-Sodot': Tefisat ha-Kavod ve-Khavanat ha-Tefillah be-Khitvei R. Eleazar mi-Vorms ve-Heidehah bi-Khetavim Aheirim." *Da'at* 34 (1995): 61–81.

Agus, Avraham Yitzhak. "Morei ha-Talmud ve-talmideihem ba-Hevrah ha-Yehudit bi-mei ha-Beinayim ke-fi she-Metu'ar be-'Sefer Hasidim.'" In *Sefer Zikkaron li-Shemuel Belkin*, edited by Moshe Karmeli and Hayim Lif, 135–141. New York: Yeshiva University Press, 1981.

Agus, Irving A[braham]. "The Use of the Term *Hakham* by the Author of the *Sefer Hassidim* and Its Historical Implications." *Jewish Quarterly Review* 61 (1970): 54–62.

Alexander, Tamar. "'Ba hasid be-halom': Sippurei Halom be-Sefer Hasidim." In *Ma'aseh Sippur*, edited by Avidov Lipsker and Rella Kushelevsky, 77–79. Ramat Gan: Bar Ilan University Press, 2006.

Alexander, Tamar. "Darkhei Shiluv ha-Sippur be-Sefer Hasidim." *Yeda' 'Am* 45–46 (1979): 5–16.

Alexander, Tamar. "Dream Narratives in *'Sefer Hasidim.'*" *Trumah* 12 (2002): 65–78.

Alexander, Tamar. "Folktales in Sefer Hasidim." *Prooftexts* 5:1 (1985): 19–31.

Alexander, Tamar. "Le-Darkhei 'Izuv ha-Sippur ha-Hasidi-Ashkenazi: Sippur be-Heqsheiro ha-'Iyyuni." In *Mehqarim be-Aggadah u-ve-Folklor Yehudi*, edited by Issachar Ben-Ami and Joseph Dan, 197–225. Jerusalem: Magnes Press, 1983.

Alexander, Tamar. "Rabbi Judah the Pious as a Legendary Figure." In Grözinger and Dan, *Mysticism, Magic and Kabbalah,* 123–138.

Alexander, Tamar. "'Shakhen be-Gan Eiden' be-Sefer Hasidim: Sippur 'Amami be-Heqsheiro ha-'Iyyuni." *Mehqarei Yerushalayim be-Folklor Yehudi* 1 (1981): 61–81.

Alexander, Tamar. "Sipporet ve-Hagut be-Sefer Hasidim [Narrative and thought in "Sefer Hassidim" (Book of the Pious)]." PhD diss., University of California, Los Angeles, 1977.

Altmann, Alexander. "Eleazar of Worms' *Hokhmat ha-Egoz*." *Journal of Jewish Studies* 11 (1960): 101–113. Reprinted in Alexander Altmann, *Studies in Religious Philosophy and Mysticism*. Ithaca, N.Y.: Cornell University Press, 1968.

Angerstorfer, Andreas. "Rabbi Judah ben Samuel he-Hasid (um 1140–1217), der Pietist." In *Geschichte und Kultur der Juden in Bayern*, edited by Manfred Treml, 13–20. München: Lebensläufen, 1988.

Assaf, Simha. "Sefer Hasidim be-Hotza'ah Hadashah." *Ha-Tor* 4:38 (June 20, 1924): 9.

Awerbuch, Marianne. "Weltflucht und Lebensverneinung der 'Frommen Deutschlands' ein Beitrag zum Daseinsverständnis der Juden Deutschlands nach den Kreuzzügen." *Archiv für Kulturgeschichte* 60:1 (1978): 53–93.

Azulai, Haim Yosef David. *Brit 'Olam*. In his collection with *Lev David*, 80a–143a. Livorno, 1789. Reprinted many times, including in SHM.

Baer, Yitzhaq. "Ha-Megamah ha-Datit ha-Hevratit shel Sefer Hasidim." *Zion* 3 (1938): 1–50. Reprinted in Marcus, *Dat ve-Hevrah*, 81–130.

Baer, Yitzhaq. "Shnei Peraqim shel Torat ha-Hashgahah be-Sefer Hasidim." In *Mehqarim be-Qabbalah u-ve-Toledot ha-Datot*, edited by E. E. Urbach, R. J. Zwi Werblowsky, and Chaim Wirszubski, 42–67. Jerusalem: Magnes Press, 1968. Reprinted in Marcus, *Dat ve-Hevrah*, 183–198.

Baer, Yitzhaq. "Torat ha-Shivyon ha-Tiv'i ha-Qadmon ezel Hasidei Ashkenaz." *Zion* 32 (1967): 129–136. Reprinted in Marcus, *Dat ve-Hevrah*, 199–206.

Bamberger, Josef. "The Golem and the Prophet: A Journey on the Traces of a Mayse." In *Yiddish Storytelling*. Amsterdam Yiddish Symposium 4, edited by Shlomo Berger, 7–29. Amsterdam: Menasseh ben Israel Institute, 2009.

Bamberger, Josef. "Sippurei ha-Shevahim shel Hasidei Ashkenaz: Qavvei Yesod la-Hagiografiah ha-Yehudit be-Ashkenaz bimei ha-Beinayim." PhD diss., Bar Ilan University, 2005.

Baskin, Judith. "From Separation to Displacement: The Problem of Women in 'Sefer Hasidim.'" *AJS Review* 19:1 (1994): 1–18.

Baskin, Judith. "Geschlechterverhältnisse und rituelles Tauchbad im mittelalterlichen Aschkenas." In *Differenz auf der Spur: Frauen und Gender in Aschkenaz,* edited by Christiane Müller and Andrea Schatz, 52–67. Berlin: Metropol, 2004.

Baskin, Judith Reesa. "Images of Women in Sefer Hasidim." In *Mysticism, Magic and Kabbalah in Ashkenazi Judaism* (International Symposium held in Frankfurt am Main 1991), edited by Karl Erich Grözinger and Joseph Dan, eds., 93–105. Berlin: Walter de Gruyter, 1995.

Baskin, Judith Reesa. "Women and Sexual Ambivalence in 'Sefer Hasidim.'" *Jewish Quarterly Review* 91:1 (2006): 1–8.

Baumgarten, Elisheva. *Practicing Piety in Medieval Ashkenaz: Men, Women, and Everyday Religious Observance*. Philadelphia: University of Pennsylvania Press, 2014.

Baumgarten, Elisheva. "Shared Stories and Religious Rhetoric: R. Judah the Pious, Peter the Chanter, and a Drought." *Medieval Encounters* 18 (2012): 36–54.

Beit-Arié, Malachi. "Ideals Versus Reality: Scribal Prescriptions in *Sefer Hasidim* and Contemporary Scribal Practices in Franco-German Manuscripts." In *Rashi 1040–1990 Hommage à Ephraim E. Urbach*, edited by Gabrielle Sed-Rajna, 559–566. Paris: Les Editions du Cerf, 1993.

Ben-Arzi, Haggai. "Ha-Perishut be-Sefer Hasidim." *Da'at* 11 (1983): 39–45.

Ben-Sasson, Haim Hillel. *Hagut ve-Hanhagah: Hashkafoteihem ha-Hevratiyot shel Yehudei Polin be-Shilhei Yemei ha-Beinayim*. Jerusalem: Mosad Bialik, 1959.

Ben-Sasson, Haim Hillel. "Hasidei Ashkenaz 'al Haluqat Qinyanim Homriyyim u-Nekhasim Ruhaniyyim bein Benei ha-Adam." *Zion* 35 (1970): 61–79. Reprinted in Marcus, *Dat ve-Hevrah*, 217–235.

Ben-Yizhak, Inbal Gur. "Bein Shamayim va-Arets: 'Iyyun be-Yahas ha-Kohot bein ha-Elyonim la-Tahtonim, Masa' ha-Nefesh ve-Heirut ha-Adam 'al-pi Sefer Hokhmat ha-Nefesh le-R. Eleazar mi-Vorms." MA thesis, Bar Ilan University, 2015.

Bonfil, Reuven. "Can Medieval Story Telling Help Understanding Midrash? The Story of Paltiel: A Preliminary Study on History and Midrash." In *The Midrashic Imagination*, edited by Michael Fishbane, 228–254. Albany: State University of New York Press, 1993.

Borchers, Susanne. "Eine Melodie, die das Herz erfreut zu Musik und Gesang im 'Sefer Chasidim.'" *Biblische Notizen* 116 (2003): 5–14.

Borchers, Susanne. "Hexen im 'Sefer Hasidim.'" *Henoch* 16:2–3 (1994): 271–293.

Borchers, Susanne. *Jüdisches Frauenleben im Mittelalter: Die Texte des Sefer Chasidim*. Frankfurt am Main: Peter Lang, 1998.

Brin, Gershon. "'Iyyun be-Feirushei R. Yehudah he-Hasid la-Torah." *Sinai* 88:1–2 (1981): 1–17.

Brin, Gershon. "Qavvim le-Feirush ha-Torah shel R. Yehudah he-Hasid." *Te'udah* 3 (1983): 215–226.

Brin, Gershon. "R. Judah he-Hasid: Early Bible Exegete Rediscovered." *Immanuel* 12 (1981): 21–31.

Bronznick, Norman M. "Some Aspects of German Jewish Mysticism as Reflected in the Sefer Hassidim." MA thesis, Columbia University, 1947.

Brüll, Nehemiah, "Zur Geschichte der Jüdisch-Ethischen Literatur des Mittelalters." *Jahrbücher für jüdische Geschichte und Literatur* 5–6 (1883): 71–93.

Callow, Anna-Linda. "La funzione etica e teologica dei racconti soprannaturali nel 'Se-fer Hasidim.'" *ACME=Annali della Facolta di lettere e filosofia dell'Universita degli studi di milano* 58:1 (2005): 147–163.

Carmeli-Weinberger, Moses. "Ahavat ha-Sefer be-'Sefer Hasidim' u-ve-'Philobiblion.'" *Sinai* 56 (1965): 159–175.

Chazan, Robert. "The Early Development of Hasidut Ashkenaz." *Jewish Quarterly Review* 75:3 (1985): 199–211.

Dan, Joseph. "The Ashkenazi Hasidic Concept of Language." In *Hebrew in Ashkenaz: A Language in Exile*, edited by Lewis Glinert, 11–25. Oxford: Oxford University Press, 1993.

Dan, Joseph. "Ashkenazi Hasidim, 1941–1991: Was There Really a Hasidic Movement in Medieval Germany?" In *Gershom Scholem's Major Trends in Jewish Mysticism 50 Years After*, edited by Peter Schäfer and Joseph Dan, 87–101. Tübingen: J. C. B. Mohr (Paul Siebeck), 1993.

Dan, Joseph. "Be'ayat Qiddush ha-Shem ba-Toratah ha-'Iyyunit shel Tenu'at Hasidut Ashkenaz." In *Milhemet Qadosh u-Martirologiyah be-Toledot Yisrael u-ve-Toledot ha-'Amim*, 121–129. Jerusalem: Historical Society of Israel, 1968. Reprinted in Marcus, *Dat ve-Hevrah*, 207–215.

Dan, Joseph. "The Book of Divine Glory by Rabbi Judah of Regensburg." In *Studies in Jewish Manuscripts*, edited by Joseph Dan and Klaus Hermann, 1–18. Tübingen: Mohr Siebeck, 1999.

Dan, Joseph. "The Book of the Divine Name by Rabbi Eleazar of Worms." *Frankfurter Judaistische Beiträge* 22 (August 1995): 27–60.

Dan, Joseph. "The Emergence of Jewish Mysticism in Medieval Germany." In *Mystics of the Book: Themes, Topics, and Typologies*, edited by R. A. Herrera, 57–95. New York: P. Lang, 1993.

Dan, Joseph. "The Emergence of Mystical Prayer." In *Studies in Jewish Mysticism*, edited by Joseph Dan and Frank Talmage, 85–120. Cambridge, Mass.: Association for Jewish Studies, 1982.

Dan, Joseph. "Goralo ha-Histori shel Torat ha-Sod shel Hasidei Ashkenaz." In *Mehqarim be-Qabbalah u-ve-Toledot ha-Datot*, edited by E. E. Urbach, R. J. Zwi Werblow-sky, and Chaim Wirszubski, 87–99. Jerusalem: Magnes Press, 1967.

Dan, Joseph. "Ha-Basis ha-'Iyyuni le-Torat ha-Musar shel Hasidut Ashkenaz." PhD diss., Hebrew University of Jerusalem, 1963.

Dan, Joseph. "Hasidei Ashkenaz." *Encyclopedia Judaica*. Edited by Cecil Roth. 16 vols. Jerusalem: Keter, 1971, 7: 1378–1388.

Dan, Joseph. "Hasidim, Sefer." *Encyclopedia Judaica* 7. Edited by Cecil Roth. 16 vols. Jerusalem: Keter, 1971, 7: 1388–1390.

Dan, Joseph. *Ha-Sippur ha-'Ivri bimei ha-Beinayim.* Jerusalem: Keter, 1975.

Dan, Joseph. "Hokhmat ha-Egoz: Its Origins and Development." *Journal of Jewish Studies* 17 (1966): 73–82.

Dan, Joseph. "Hug 'ha-Keruv ha-Meyuhad' bi-Tenu'at Hasidut Ashkenaz." *Tarbiz* 35 (1971): 288–293.

Dan, Joseph. *'Iyyunim be-Sifrut Hasidut Ashkenaz.* Ramat Gan: Masada, 1975.

Dan, Joseph. *Jewish Mysticism and Jewish Ethics.* Seattle: University of Washington Press, 1986.

Dan, Joseph. "Ketav Yad Beit Sefarim Oct. 3182 u-'Ma'aseh ha-Yerushalmi.'" *Qiryat Sefer* 51 (1976): 492–498.

Dan, Joseph. "Ketav Yad Oppenheim 540 mi-Sifriyat Oksford ve-Hashva'ato le-Sefer Hasidim." MA thesis, Hebrew University of Jerusalem, 1958.

Dan, Joseph. "The Language of the Mystics in Medieval Germany." In *Mysticism, Magic and Kabbalah in Ashkenazi Judaism* (International Symposium held in Frankfurt am Main 1991), edited by Karl Erich Grözinger and Joseph Dan, 6–27. Berlin: Walter de Gruyter, 1995.

Dan, Joseph. "Le-Heqer ha-Aggadot 'al R. Eleazar mi-Worms." *Sinai* 74 (1974): 171–177.

Dan, Joseph. "Le-Toledot ha-Tekst shel 'Hokhmat ha-Egoz.'" *'Alei Sefer* 5 (1978): 49–52.

Dan, Joseph. "Le-Toledot Torat ha-Teshuvah shel Hasidei Ashkenaz." In *Yovel Orot: Haguto shel ha-Rav Avraham Yizhaq ha-Kohen Kook, zz"l*, edited by Benjamin Ish-Shalom and Shalom Rosenberg, 221–228. Jerusalem: Sifriyat Eliner, 1988.

Dan, Joseph. "Le-Torat ha-Halom shel Hasidei Ashkenaz." *Sinai* 68 (1971): 288–293.

Dan, Joseph. "Li-Demuto ha-Historit shel R. Yehudah he-Hasid." In *Tarbut ve-Hevrah be-Toledot Yisrael Bimei ha-Beinayim: Qovez Ma'amarim le-Zikhro shel H. H. Ben-Sasson*, edited by Robert Bonfil, Menachem Ben-Sasson, and Joseph Hacker, 389–398. Jerusalem: Merkaz Zalman Shazar, 1989.

Dan, Joseph. "Qatigoriazatziah shel Sippurei Hasidei Ashkenaz." *Proceedings of the Fifth World Congress of Jewish Studies.* Part 5 (E), vol. 3, 111–119. Jerusalem: World Union of Jewish Studies, 1969.

Dan, Joseph. "Rabbi Eleazar of Worms' *Sefer ha-Shem* and the Problem of the Divine Essences." *Frankfurter Judaistische Beiträge* 22 (1995): 27–60.

Dan, Joseph. "Rabbi Judah the Pious and Caesarius of Heisterbach. Common Motifs in their Stories." *Scripta Hierosolymitana* 22 [Studies in Agadah and Folk-Literature, edited by Joseph Heinemann and Dov Noy], 18–27. Jerusalem: Magnes Press, 1971.

Dan, Joseph. Review of Abraham b. 'Azriel, *Sefer 'Arugat ha-Bosem*, edited by Ephraim E. Urbach. *Tarbiz* 34 (1965): 291–301.

Dan, Joseph. *R. Yehudah he-Hasid.* Jerusalem: Merkaz Zalman Shazar, 2006.

Dan, Joseph. "Sefer ha-Hokhmah le-R. Eleazar mi-Worms." *Zion* 29 (1964): 168–181.

Dan, Joseph. "Sheloshah Sefarim Hadashim be-Heqer Sifrut ha-Heikhalot ve-ha-Merkavah." *Tarbiz* 65 (1996): 535–542.

Dan, Joseph, ed. *Sifrut ha-Musar shel Hasidut Ashkenaz.* Jerusalem: Aqadamon, 1975.

Dan, Joseph. "Sifrut ha-Yihud shel Hasidut Ashkenaz." *Qiryat Sefer* 41 (1966): 533–544.

Dan, Joseph. "Sippurim Dimonologiyim mi-Kitvei R. Judah he-Hasid." *Tarbiz* 30 (1961): 273–289.

Dan, Joseph. *Toledot Torat ha-Sod ha-'Ivrit: Yemei ha-Beinayyim.* Vol. 5. Jerusalem: Merkaz Zalman Shazar, 2011.

Dan, Joseph. *Toledot Torat ha-Sod ha-'Ivrit: Yemei ha-Beinayyim.* Vol. 6. Jerusalem: Merkaz Zalman Shazar, 2011.

Dan, Joseph. *Torat ha-Sod shel Hasidut Ashkenaz.* Jerusalem: Mosad Bialik, 1968.

Dan, Joseph. "Toratam ha-Musarit shel Hasidei Ashkenaz." Review of Ivan G. Marcus, *Piety and Society: The Jewish Pietists of Medieval Germany,* Leiden: E. J. Brill, 1981. *Tarbiz* 52 (1982): 319–325.

Dan, Joseph. *The 'Unique Cherub' Circle: A School of Mystics and Esoterics in Medieval Germany.* [Texts and Studies in Medieval and Early Modern Judaism, 15]. Tübingen: Mohr Siebeck, 1999.

Dukan, Michèle. "La vente et le prêt du livre. le livre, le mort et le vivant." In Sirat, *Conception du livre,* 123–144.

Edelmann, Rafael. 'Das 'Buch der Frommen' als Ausdruck des volkstümlichen Geisteslebens der deutschen Juden im Mittelalter: Zur Entstehung des aschkenasischen Judentums." In *Judentum im Mittelalter,* edited by Paul Wilpert, 55–71. Berlin: Walter de Gruyter, 1966.

Eichhorst, Dana. *Der Sefer Yesira-Kommentar des R. El'azar ben Yehuda von Worms.* MA thesis, Freie Universität Berlin, 2011.

Elbaum, Jacob. *Teshuvat ha-Lev ve-Qabbalat Yisurim: 'Iyyunim be-Shitot ha-Teshuvah shel Hakhmei Ashkenaz u-Folin, 1348–1648.* Jerusalem: Magnes Press, 1992.

Emanuel, Simcha. "Ha-Pulmus shel Hasidei Ashkenaz 'al Nusah ha-Tefillah." In *Mehqerei Talmud* 3, edited by Jacob Sussman and David Rosenthal, 591–625. Jerusalem: Magnes Press, 2005.

Emanuel, Simcha. "Hibburav ha-Hilkhatiyim shel R. Eleazar mi-Vermaiza." *Te'udah* 16–17 (2001): 203–254.

Epstein, Avraham. "R. Shmuel he-Hasid b. R. Qalonimos ha-Zaqen." *Ha-Goren* 4 (1903): 81–101. Reprinted in Marcus, *Dat ve-Hevrah,* 25–46.

Fenton, Paul. "Deux écoles piétistes: Les hasidei Ashkenaz et les soufis juifs d'Egypte." In *La société juive à travers l'histoire*, vol. 1, edited by Shmuel Trigano, 200–225. Paris: Fayard, 1992.

Fisher, Moshe Tuvia. "Peraqim ba-Mishnatam ha-Hinukhit shel Hasidei Ashkenaz ba-Aspaqlariah shel Sefer Hasidim." *Hagigei Givah* 10 (2002): 69–84.

Fishman, Talya. *Becoming the People of the Talmud: Oral Torah as Written Tradition in Medieval Jewish Cultures*. Philadelphia: University of Pennsylvania Press, 2011.

Fishman, Talya. "The Penitential System of Hasidei Ashkenaz and the Problem of Cultural Boundaries." *Journal of Jewish Thought and Philosophy* 8 (1999): 201–229.

Fishman, Talya. "Rhineland Pietist Approaches to Prayer and the Textualization of Rabbinic Culture in Medieval Northern Europe." *Jewish Studies Quarterly* 11:4 (2004): 313–331.

Fishman, Talya. "The Rhineland Pietists' Sacralization of the Oral Torah." *Jewish Quarterly Review* 96:1 (2006): 9–16.

Fram, Edward. "German Pietism and Sixteenth- and Early Seventeenth-Century Polish Rabbinic Culture." *Jewish Quarterly Review* 96:1 (2006): 50–59.

Freimann, Jacob. "Mavo le-Sefer Hasidim." In *Sefer Hasidim*, edited by Jehuda Wistinetzki, 1–73. Frankfurt am Main: Wahrmann, 1924.

Goetschel, Roland. "Célébration et signification du Shabbat dans le 'Sefer Hasidim.'" *Revue des études juives* 163:1–2 (2004): 137–150.

Gross, Dalia. "Ha-Qesher bein ha-Hayyim ve-ha-Meitim be-*Sefer Hasidim*." MA thesis, Bar Ilan University, 2010.

Gross, Heinrich. "Zwei kabbalistische Traditionsketten des R. Eleasar aus Worms." *Monatsschrift für die Geschichte und Wissenschaft des Judentums* 49 (1905): 692–700.

Grossman, Avraham. "Ha-Ishah be-Mishnatam shel Hasidei Ashkenaz." In *Creation and Re-Creation in Jewish Thought: Festschrift in Honor of Joseph Dan on the Occasion of His Seventieth Birthday,* edited by Rachel Elior and Peter Schäfer, 85–96. Tübingen: Mohr Siebeck, 2005.

Grossman, Avraham. "Ha-Tefillah be-Mishnatam shel Hasidei Ashkenaz." In *Sefer Yeshurun*, edited by Michael Shashar, 27–56. Jerusalem: Shashar Press, 1999.

Grözinger, Karl Erich, "Between Magic and Religion—Ashkenazi Hasidic Piety." In *Mysticism, Magic, and Kabbalah in Ashkenazi Judaism*, edited by Karl Erich Grözinger and Joseph Dan, 28–43 (International Symposium held in Frankfurt am Main, 1991). Berlin: Walter de Gruyter, 1995.

Gruenwald, Itamar. "Normative und volkstümliche Religiosität im Sefer Chasidim." In *Judentum im deutschen Sprachraum*, edited by Karl Grözinger, 117–126. Frankfurt am Main: Suhrkamp, 1991.

Gruenwald, Itamar. "Social and Mystical Aspects of Sefer Hasidim." In *Mysticism, Magic, and Kabbalah in Ashkenazi Judaism*, edited by Karl Erich Grözinger and Joseph Dan, 106–116 (International Symposium held in Frankfurt am Main, 1991). Berlin: Walter de Gruyter, 1995.

Güdemann, Moritz. *Geschichte des Erziehungswesens und der Cultur der abendländischen Juden*. 3 vols. 1880–1888. Reprinted. Amsterdam: Philo Press, 1966.

Hallamish, Moshe. "The Identification of the Book 'Beit ha-Middot' Mentioned in *Sefer Hasidim* and in *Reishit Hokhmah*." *Qiryat Sefer* 47 (1971): 169–178.

Hallamish, Moshe. "Rabbi Judah the Pious' Will in Halakhic and Kabbalistic Literature." In *Mysticism, Magic and Kabbalah in Ashkenazi Judaism*, edited by Karl Erich Grözinger and Joseph Dan (International Symposium held in Frankfurt am Main, 1991), 117–122. Berlin: Walter de Gruyter, 1995.

Halpert, Sari. "Elitism and Pietism: An Investigation into the Elitist Nature of the Hasidei Ashkenaz." *Queens College Journal of Jewish Studies* 2 (2000): 1–7.

Harris, Monford. "The Concept of Love in *Sefer Hasidim*." *Jewish Quarterly Review* 50 (1959): 13–44.

Harris, Monford. "Dreams in *Sefer Hasidim*." *Proceedings of the American Academy for Jewish Research* 31 (1963): 51–80.

Herrmann, Klaus. "An Unknown Commentary on the Book of Creation (Sefer Yezirah) from the Cairo Geniza and Its Re-Creation among the Haside Ashkenaz." In *Creation and Re-Creation in Jewish Thought: Festschrift in Honor of Joseph Dan on the Occasion of His Seventieth Birthday*, edited by Rachel Elior and Peter Schäfer, 103–112. Tübingen: Mohr Siebeck, 2005.

Heymann, Claude. "L'écrit dans les croyances, les superstitions et la psychologie du 'piétiste.'" In *La conception du livre chez les piétistes ashkenazes au moyen âge*, edited by Colette Sirat, et al., 109–121. Genève: Droz, 1996.

Honig, Mordecai Menachem. "Al Mahadurato ha-Hadashah shel Sefer ha-Maskil (Sefer Hasidim) le-R. Moshe b. R. Eleazar ha-Kohen." *Yerushateinu* 1 (2007): 196–240.

Horodetzky Samuel H. "R. Eleazar b. Judah b. Qalonimos mi-Germaiza." In his *Yahadut ha-Sekhel ve-Yahadut ha-Regesh*, 2:225–242. 2 vols. Tel Aviv: Twersky, 1947.

Horowitz, Elliott. "A Splendid Outburst of Spirituality." *Jewish Quarterly Review* 96:1 (2006): v–vi.

Idel, Moshe. "'Al ha-Peirushim shel R. Nehemiah ben Shlomo ha-Navi la-Shem le-M"B Otiyot ve-Sefer ha-Hokhmah ha-Meyuhas le-R. Eleazar mi-Vorms." *Kabbalah* 14 (2006): 157–261.

Idel, Moshe. "'Al Zeihut Mehabreihem shel Shnei Peirushim Ashkenaziyim la-Piyyut 'ha-Aderet ve-ha-Emunah' ve-'al Tefisot ha-Te'urgiyah ve-ha-Kavod ezel R. Eleazar mi-Vorms." *Kabbalah* 29 (2013): 208–267.

Idel, Moshe. "Ashkenazi Hasidic Views on the Golem." In Idel, *Golem: Jewish Magical and Mystical Traditions on the Artificial Anthropoid*, 54–80. Albany: State University of New York Press, 1990.

Idel, Moshe. "Gazing at the Head in Ashkenazi Hasidism." *Journal of Jewish Thought and Philosophy* 6 (1997): 265–300.

Joseph, Morris. "The Introduction to the 'Rokeah,'" In *Jews' College Jubilee Volume*, 171–190. London: Luzac and Co., 1906.

Kahana, Maoz. "Meqorot ha-Yeda' u-Temurot ha-Zeman: Zava'at R. Yehudah he-Hasid ba-'eit ha-Hadashah." In *Samhut Ruhanit: Ma'avaqim 'al Koah Tarbuti ba-Hagut ha-Yehudit*, edited by Howard Kreisel, Boaz Huss, and Uri Ehrlich, 223–262. Beer Sheva: Ben-Gurion University Press, 2009.

Kamelhar, Yequtiel Aryeh. *Hasidim ha-Rishonim*. Waitzen, 1917.

Kamelhar, Yisrael. *Rabbeinu Eleazar ben Yehudah mi-Germaiza ha-Roqeah*. Reisha, 1930. Reprint, New York: Ateret, 1975.

Kanarfogel, Ephraim. "From Germany to Northern France and Back Again: A Tale of Two Tosafist Centers." In *Regional Identities and Cultures of Medieval Jews*, edited by Javier Castano, Talya Fishman, and Ephraim Kanarfogel. Oxford: Littman Library, 2018.

Kanarfogel, Ephraim. "German Pietism in Northern France: The Case of R. Isaac of Corbeil." In *Hazon Nahum*, edited by Jeffrey S. Gurock and Yaakov Elman, 207–227. New York: Michael Scharf Publication Trust of Yeshiva University Press, 1997.

Kanarfogel, Ephraim. *The Intellectual History and Rabbinic Culture of Medieval Ashkenaz*. Detroit: Wayne State University Press, 2013.

Kanarfogel, Ephraim. *"Peering Through the Latices": Mystical, Magical, and Pietistic Dimensions in the Tosafist Period*. Detroit: Wayne State University Press, 2000.

Kanarfogel, Ephraim. "R. Judah he-Hasid and the Rabbinic Scholars of Regensburg: Interactions, Influences, and Implications." *Jewish Quarterly Review* 96:1 (2006): 17–37.

Kanarfogel, Ephraim. "Rabbinic Figures in Castilian Kabbalistic Pseudepigraphy: R. Yehudah he-Hasid and R. Elhanan of Corbeil." *Journal of Jewish Thought and Philosophy* 3 (1993): 77–109.

Katz, David Sh. "R. Yehudah *he-hasid*, seyn tequfa, veg, un verk." *Reportagen un Esayen* (2002): 69–84.

Katz, Jacob. *Exclusiveness and Tolerance*. New York: Schocken, 1961.

Keil, Martha. "Die Frommen von Aschkenas und die Weisen von Österreich." In *Die SchUM Gemeinden—Speyer Worms Mainz: Aus dem Weg zum Welterbe*, edited by Pia Heberer and Ursula Reuter, 251–268. Regensburg: Schnell und Steiner, 2013.

Keil, Martha. "Rituals of Repentance and Testimonies at Rabbinical Courts in the 15th Century." In *Oral History of the Middle Ages: The Spoken Word in Context*, edited by Gerhard Jaritz and Michael Richter, 164–176. Krems: Medium Aevum Quotidianum, 2001.

Kiel, Yishai. "Confessing Incest to a Rabbi: A Talmudic Story in Its Zoroastrian Context." *Harvard Theological Review* 107:4 (2014): 401–424.

Kiel, Yishai. "Toratam ha-Musarit-Datit shel Hasidei Ashkenaz: Bein Sagfanut ve-Hushniyyut." *Da'at* 73 (2012): 85–101.

Kogman-Appel, Katrin. *A Mahzor from Worms: Art and Religion in a Medieval Jewish Community.* Cambridge, Mass.: Harvard University Press, 2012.

Kogut, Simcha. "Ha-Mishpat ha-Murkav be-*Sefer Hasidim*." PhD diss., Hebrew University of Jerusalem, 1975.

Kogut, Simcha. "The Language of 'Sefer Hasidim,' Its Linguistic Background and Methods of Research." In *Studies in Medieval Jewish History and Literature*, edited by Isadore Twersky, 95–108. Cambridge, Mass.: Harvard Center for Jewish Studies, 1984.

Kogut, Simcha. "Le-Shimushan shel Millin 'Ivriyot be-Ashkenaz." *Leshoneinu la-'Am* 23 (1973): 172–176.

Kogut, Simha. "Shimmushim Milloniyyim be-'Ivrit shel *Sefer Hasidim* she-einam Metu'adim be-Millonim o she-Tei'udam Pagum." *Proceedings of the Sixth World Congress of Jewish Studies*, part 6 (F): vol. 4, 181–195. Jerusalem: World Union of Jewish Studies, 1973.

Kotek, Shmuel. "'Al Tequfat ha-Yaldut be-*Sefer Hasidim*: Refu'ah, Psikhologiah, ve-Hinukh bimei ha-Beinayim." *Qorot* 8:9–10 (1984): 297–318.

Kotek, Shmuel. "Refu'ah ve-Halakhah be-*Sefer Hasidim*: 'Netilat sekhar tirhah shel refu'ah.'" *Asya* 37 (1984): 37–42. Reprinted in *Sefer Asya* 5 (1986): 34–39.

Kozma, Emese. "The Practice of Teshuvah (Penance) in the Medieval Ashkenazi Jewish Communities." PhD diss., Eötvös Lorand University (Budapest), 2012.

Kramer, Simon Gad. *God and Man in the Sefer Hasidim: Book of the Pious.* New York: Bloch Publishing Co., 1966.

Kriegel, Maurice. "He'arah le-'inyan torat 'ha-mehir ha-zodeq' be-*Sefer Hasidim*." In *Mehqarim be-Hagut Yehudit*, edited by Sarah Heller Wilensky and Moshe Idel, 253–260. Jerusalem: Magnes Press, 1989.

Kushelevsky, Rella. *Siggufim u-Fituyim: Ha-Sippur ha-'Ivri be-Ashkenaz K. Y. Parma 2295, De Rossi 563.* Jerusalem: Magnes Press, 2010.

Kuyt, Annelies. "The Haside Ashkenaz and their Mystical Sources: Continuity and Innovation." In *Jewish Studies in a New Europe*, edited by Ulf Haxen, Hanne Trautner-Kromann, and Karen Lisa Goldschmidt Salamon, 462–471. Copenhagen: C. A. Reitzel, 1998.

Kuyt, Annelies. "Hasidut Ashkenaz on the Angel of Dreams." In *Creation and Re-Creation in Jewish Thought: Festschrift in Honor of Joseph Dan on the Occasion of His Seventieth Birthday,* edited by Rachel Elior and Peter Schäfer, 147–163. Tübingen: Mohr Siebeck, 2005.

Kuyt, Annelies. "R. El'azar of Worms's 'Stairway to Heaven.'" In *Jewish Studies Between the Disciplines: Papers in Honor of Peter Schäfer on the Occasion of His Sixtieth Birthday,* edited by Klaus Hermann, Margarete Schlüter, and Giuseppe Veltri, 218–225. Leiden: E. J. Brill, 2003.

Kuyt, Annelies. "Traces of a Mutual Influence of the Hasidei Ashkenaz and the Hekhalot Literature." In *From Narbonne to Regensburg: Studies in Medieval Hebrew Texts,* edited by N. A. van Uchelen and I. E. Zwiep, 62–86. Amsterdam: Juda Palache Institute, 1993.

Lehmann, Manfred Raphael. "Remazim le-'Oto ha-Ish' u-le-Muhamad be-Feirusheihem shel Hasidei Ashkenaz." *Sinai* 87 (1980): 34–40.

Levinson, Ayal. "Hamsagot ha-Yezer ve-ha-Guf ha-Gavri be-Siah ha-Mini ha-Gavri be-*Sefer Hasidim*." MA thesis, Bar Ilan University, 2011.

Liberles Neuman, Ahuva. "Merhav u-Merhaq be-*Sefer Hasidim*: Yahaso shel R. Yehudah he-Hasid el Nesi'ot shel Yehudim be-Ashkenaz ba-Me'ah ha-Shteim-'Esreh u-va-Me'ah ha-Shalosh-'Esrei." MA thesis, Hebrew University of Jerusalem, 2014.

Lifshitz, Josef Isaac. *Ehad be-Khol Dimyonot: Hagutam ha-Dialektit shel Hasidei Ashkenaz*. Benei Brak: Kibbutz ha-Me'uhad, 2015.

Liss, Hanna. "Copyright im Mittelalter? Die esoterischen Schriften von R. El'azar von Worms zwischen Traditions- und Autorenliteratur." *Frankfurter Judaistischen Beiträge* 21 (1994): 81–108.

Maier, Johann. "Bilder in 'Sefer Chasidim.'" In *Ein Leben für die jüdische Kunst: Ein Gedenkband für Hannelorre Künzl,* edited by Michael Graetz, 7–14. Heidelberg: Universitätsverlag, 2003.

Maier, Johann. *Fremdes und Fremde in der Jüdischen Tradition und im Sefär Chasidim: 4. Arye Maimon-Vortrag an der Universität Trier, 7. November 2001*. Trier: Kliomedia, 2002.

Maier, Johann. "Il Hasidismo ashkenazite e il suo ambiente." In *Correnti culturali e movimenti religiosi del guidaismo,* Atti del V Congresso Internazionale dell'AISG S. Miniato, November 12–15, 1984, edited by Bruni Chiesa, 203–225. Rome: Carucci, 1987.

Maier, Johann. "'Il Sefer Hasidim': Il manoscritto parmense 3280 l'editione de Bologna 1538—osservazioni critiche." In *Manoscritti, frammenti e libri ebraici nell'Italia dei secoli XV–XVI,* Atti del VII Congresso internazionale dell'AISG. S. Miniato,

November 7–9, 1988, edited by G. Tamani and A. Vivian, 129–136. Rome: Carucci, 1991.

Maier, Johann. "'Rab' und 'Chakam" im 'Sefer Chasidim.'" In *Das aschkenasische Rabbinat: Studien über Glauben und Schicksal*, edited by Julius Carlebach, 37–118. Berlin: Metropol, 1995.

Maisels, Ruth. "Bein Hasidim la-Goyim: 'Al ha-Yahas la-Goy be-Sefer Hasidim." MA thesis, Tel Aviv University, 2008.

Mal'akh, Daniel. "Refu'at nashim u-Temutat Tinoqot be-Sefer Hasidim." *Asya* 57–58 (1997): 119–140. Reprinted in *Sefer Asya* 12 (2009): 149–170.

Marcus, Ivan, ed. *Dat ve-Hevrah be-Mishnatam shel Hasidei Ashkenaz*. Jerusalem: Merkaz Zalman Shazar, 1987.

Marcus, Ivan G. "The Devotional Ideals of Ashkenazic Pietism." In *Jewish Spirituality* 1: *From the Bible Through the Middle Ages*, edited by Arthur Green, 356–366. New York: Crossroad, 1986. Reprinted in Marcus, *Jewish Culture and Society*.

Marcus, Ivan G. "Exegesis for the Few and for the Many: Judah he-Hasid's Biblical Commentaries." *Mehqerei Yerushalayim be-Mahshevet Yisrael* 8 (1989): 1*–24*, Proceedings of the Third International Conference on the History of Jewish Mysticism: The Age of the Zohar, edited by Joseph Dan.

Marcus, Ivan. "Haqdamah." In Marcus, *Dat ve-Hevrah*, 11–23. Jerusalem: Merkaz Zalman Shazar, 1986.

Marcus, Ivan G. "Hasidei Ashkenaz Private Penitentials: An Introduction and Descriptive Catalogue of Their Manuscripts and Early Editions." In *Studies in Jewish Mysticism*, edited by Joseph Dan and Frank Talmage, 57–83. Cambridge, Mass.: Association for Jewish Studies, 1982.

Marcus, Ivan. "Hibburei ha-Teshuvah shel Hasidei Ashkenaz." In *Mehqarim be-Qabbalah, be-Filosofiah Yehudit u-ve-Sifrut ha-Musar ve-ha-Hagut: Mugashim li-shaya Tishby bi-Melot lo Shiv'im ve-Hamesh Shanim*, edited by Joseph Dan and Joseph Hacker, 369–384. Jerusalem: Magnes Press, 1986.

Marcus, Ivan G. "Hierarchies, Religious Boundaries and Jewish Spirituality in Medieval Germany." *Jewish History* 1 (1986): 7–26. Reprinted in Marcus, *Jewish Culture and Society*.

Marcus, Ivan G. "The Historical Meaning of Hasidei Ashkenaz: Fact, Fiction or Cultural Self-Image?" In *Gershom Scholem's* Major Trends in Jewish Mysticism: *50 Years After*, edited by Peter Schäfer and Joseph Dan, 103–114. Tübingen: J. C. B. Mohr (Paul Siebeck), 1993. Reprinted in Marcus, *Jewish Culture and Society*.

Marcus, Ivan G. "History, Story, and Collective Memory: Narrativity in Early Ashkenazic Culture." *Prooftexts* 10 (1990): 365–388. Reprinted in Marcus, *Jewish Culture and Society*.

Marcus, Ivan G. "A Jewish-Christian Symbiosis: The Culture of Early Ashkenaz." In *Cultures of the Jews: A New History*, edited by David Biale, 448–516. New York: Schocken Books, 2002.

Marcus, Ivan G., ed. *Jewish Culture and Society in Medieval France and Germany.* Farnham, England: Ashgate Publishing Co., 2014.

Marcus, Ivan G. "Judah the Pietist and Eleazar of Worms: From Charismatic to Conventional Leadership." In *Jewish Mystical Leaders and Leadership in the Thirteenth Century*, edited by Moshe Idel, et al., 97–126. Northvale, N.J.: Jason Aronson, 1998.

Marcus, Ivan G. "The Organization of the *Haqdamah* and *Hilekhot Hasidut* in Eleazar of Worms' *Sefer ha-Roqeah.*" *Proceedings of the American Academy for Jewish Research* 36 (1968): 85–94.

Marcus, Ivan G. "Penitential Theory and Practice Among the Pious of Germany: 1150–1250." PhD diss., Jewish Theological Seminary, 1975.

Marcus, Ivan G. *Piety and Society: The Jewish Pietists of Medieval Germany.* Leiden: E. J. Brill, 1981.

Marcus, Ivan G. "The Political Dynamics of the Medieval German-Jewish Community." In *Authority, Power and Leadership in the Jewish Polity*, edited by Daniel Elazar, 113–137. Lanham, Md.: University Press of America, 1991.

Marcus, Ivan G. "The Politics and Ethics of Pietism in Judaism: The *Hasidim* of Medieval Germany." *Journal of Religious Ethics* 8:2 (1980): 227–258. Hebrew translation in Marcus, *Dat ve-Hevrah*, 253–278.

Marcus, Ivan G. "Prayer Gestures in German Hasidism." In *Mysticism, Magic, and Kabbalah in Ashkenazi Judaism*, edited by Karl Erich Grözinger and Joseph Dan, 44–59 (International Symposium held in Frankfurt am Main, 1991). Berlin: Walter de Gruyter, 1995. Reprinted in Marcus, *Jewish Society and Culture.*

Marcus, Ivan G. "The Recensions and Structure of Sefer Hasidim." *Proceedings of the American Academy for Jewish Research* 45 (1978): 131–153. Reprinted in Marcus, *Jewish Society and Culture.*

Marcus, Ivan G. *Rituals of Childhood: Jewish Culture and Acculturation in the Middle Ages.* New Haven, Conn.: Yale University Press, 1996.

Matzah, Devorah. "Demut ha-Ishah be-'Sefer Hasidim': Ahavah, Mishpahah, Hinukh ve-Yei'ud." *Hagigei Giv'ah* (1998): 67–89.

Meitlis, Jakob. *Das Ma'assehbuch: Seine Entstehung und Quellengeschichte.* Berlin: Rubin Mass, 1933.

Meitlis, Jakob. *Di Shvohim fun Rebbi Shmuel un Rebbi Yudah Hasid.* London: Kedem, 1961.

Meitlis, Jakob. "Ma'asiyot Qodemot mei-'Maayse Bukh' u-mi-Huzah lo." *Yeda' 'Am* 11 (1966): 58–65.

Nadav, Tal. "Hashivut ha-Kavvanah bi-Tefillah be-Sefer Hasidim." *Shemaʻatin* 154 (2006): 95–100.

Nobel, Shlomo. "Targumei She'eilah mi-Yiddish be-ʻIvrit ha-Rabbanit." *Leshoneinu* 23 (1959): 172–184.

Oevermann, Susanne. "Der Traum im Sefer Hasidim." *Henoch* 12:1 (1990): 19–51.

Piekarz, Mendel. *Bimei Zemihat ha-Hasidut: Megamot Raʻayoniyot be-Sifrei Derush u-Musar.* Jerusalem: Mosad Bialik, 1978.

Pintel, Idit. "Ha-Meziqim be-Sefer Hasidim." Seminar paper, Jewish Theological Seminary of America, June 10, 1980.

Rabin, Chaim. "The Tense and Mood System of the Hebrew of Sefer Hasidim." *Papers of the Fourth World Congress of Jewish Studies.* 2 vols. Vol. 2 (1968): 113–116. Jerusalem: World Union of Jewish Studies.

Rabin, Chaim. "Zemanim u-Derakhim ba-Poʻal she-bi-Leshon Sefer Hasidim." *Proceedings of the Fourth World Congress of Jewish Studies.* Part D, vol. 2, 113–116. Jerusalem: World Union of Jewish Studies, 1969.

Raspe, Lucia. *Jüdische Hagiographie im Mittelalterlichen Aschkenas.* Tübingen: Mohr Siebeck, 2006.

Reifmann, Yaakov. *Arbaʻah Harashim.* Prague, 1860.

Reifmann, Yaakov. "Heʻarot ʻal Sefer Hasidim." *Ozar Tov* (1885): 26–34.

Reimer, Nathaniel. "Die Erzählung vom 'Geisterwagen' aus dem 'Sefer Hasidim' und seine Rezeption in der jüdischen Literatur." *Judaica* 63:1 (2012): 70–80.

Rotman, David. "At the Limits of Reality: The Marvelous in Medieval Ashkenazi Hebrew Folktales." *Jewish Studies Quarterly* 20 (2013): 101–128.

Rotman, David. *Deraqonim, Sheidim, u-Mehozot Qesumim: ʻal ha-Mufla ba-Sippur ha-ʻIvri bimei ha-Beinayim.* Modiʻin: Kinneret, Zmora-Bitan-Dvir, 2016.

Rubenstein, Jeffrey L. "The Laws of Heaven in 'Sefer Hasidim.'" In *Freedom and Responsibility: Exploring the Challenges of Jewish Continuity,* edited by Rela Mintz Geffen and Marsha Edelman, 79–99. Hoboken, N.J.: Ktav, 1998.

Rubin, A[sher]. "The Concept of Repentance among the Hasidey Ashkenaz." *Journal of Jewish Studies* 16 (1965): 161–176.

Schäfer, Peter. "The Ideal of Piety of the Ashkenazi Hasidim and Its Roots in Jewish Tradition." *Jewish History* 4:2 (Fall 1990): 9–23.

Schäfer, Peter. "Jews and Christians in the High Middle Ages: The 'Book of the Pious.'" In *The Jews of Europe in the Middle Ages (Tenth to Fifteenth Centuries),* edited by Christoph Cluse, 29–42. Turnhout: Brepols, 2004.

Schechter, S[olomon]. "Jewish Saints in Medieval Germany." In Solomon Schechter, *Studies in Judaism.* 3rd Series, 1–24. Philadelphia: Jewish Publication Society of America, 1924.

Scholem, Gershom. "Die Frommen Deutschlands: Ein Kapital jüdischer Religionsge-schichte." *Almanach Schocken Verlag 5698* (1937–38): 53–64.

Scholem, Gershom. *Major Trends in Jewish Mysticism.* Third Lecture: "Hasidism in Me-dieval Germany," 80–119 and 369–377. 1941. Reprint, New York: Schocken Books, 1974. Hebrew translation in Marcus, *Dat ve-Hevrah,* 131–164.

Scholem, Gershom. "Three Types of Jewish Piety." *Eranos Jahrbuch* 38 (1969): 331–348.

Schwartz, Baruch J. "Peirush Rabbi Yehudah he-hasid li-Vereishit 48." *Tarbiz* 80:1 (2012): 29–39.

Shatzmiller, Joseph. "Doctors and Medieval Practice in Germany Around the Year 1200: The Evidence of *Sefer Hasidim.*" *Journal of Jewish Studies* 33:1–2 (1982): 583–593.

Shoham-Steiner, Ephraim. "The Humble Sage and the Wandering Madman: Madness and Madmen in an Exemplum from *Sefer Hasidim.*" *Jewish Quarterly Review* 96:1 (2006): 38–49.

Shoham-Steiner, Ephraim. "Mi-Spier le-Regensburg: Nedudei Mishpahat he-Hasid mei-Hevel ha-Rhein le-Hevel ha-Donau." *Zion* 81:2 (2016): 149–176.

Shoham-Steiner, Ephraim. "'Semol Doheh ve-Yamin Meqarevet'—'Al Anashim Harigim bi-Re'i *Sefer Hasidim.*" In *Mi'utim, Zarim, ve-Shonim,* edited by Shulamit Volkov, 132–159. Jerusalem: Merkaz Zalman Shazar, 2000.

Shulvass, Moshe. "Le-Shalshelet ha-Yahas be-Mishpahat R. Yehudah he-Hasid." *Alumah* 1 (1936): 152–153.

Shvat, Ari Yitzhak. "Zava'at Rabbi Yehudah he-Hasid 'al pi Mahadurot Yeshanot ve-Khitvei ha-Yad." MA thesis, Touro College, Jerusalem, 2003.

Shvat, Ari Yitzhak. "Zava'at Rabbi Yehudah he-Hasid: Hashva'at Mahadurot Qedumot ve-Khitvei ha-Yad." *Talelei Orot* 10 (2002): 82–152.

Shyovitz, David I. *A Remembrance of His Wonders: Nature and the Supernatural in Medi-eval Ashenaz.* Philadelphia: University of Pennsylvania Press, 2017.

Simhoni, Y. N. "Ha-Hasidut ha-Ashkenazit bimei ha-Beinayim." *Ha-Zefirah* 12–32 (1917). Reprinted in Marcus, *Dat ve-Hevrah,* 47–79.

Simon, Joseph. "Les manuscrits hébreux de la bibliothèque de la ville de Nîmes." *Revue des études juives* 3 (1881): 232–234.

Singer, S. A. "An Introduction to *Sefer Hasidim.*" *Hebrew Union College Annual* 35 (1964): 145–155.

Sirat, Colette. "Comment on dois écrire les livres." In *La conception du livre chez les pié-tistes ashkenazes au moyen âge,* edited by Colette Sirat et al., 81–197. Genève: Droz, 1996.

Sirat, Colette. "Introduction." In *La conception du livre chez les piétistes ashkenazes au moyen âge,* edited by Colette Sirat et al., 9–35. Genève: Droz, 1996.

Sirat, Colette. "Le livre dans la vie quotidienne." In *La conception du livre chez les piétistes ashkenazes au moyen âge,* edited by Colette Sirat et al., 93–107. Genève: Droz, 1996.

Skloot, Joseph A. "Printing, Hebrew Book Culture and Sefer Hasidim." PhD diss., Columbia University, 2017.

Soloveitchik, Haym. "Appendix to 'Pietists and Kibbitzers.'" *Jewish Quarterly Review* 96:1 (Winter 2006). Online at https://muse.jhu.edu/article/190747.

Soloveitchik, Haym. "Le-Ta'arikh Hibburo shel 'Sefer Hasidim.'" In *Tarbut ve-Hevrah be-Toledot Yisrael bimei ha-Beinayim: Qovez Ma'amarim le-Zikhro shel Haim-Hillel Ben-Sasson,* edited by Reuven Bonfil, Menachem Ben-Sasson, and Joseph Hacker, 383–398. Jerusalem: Merkaz Zalman Shazar, 1989.

Soloveitchik, Haym. "The Midrash, *Sefer Hasidim,* and the Changing Face of God." In *Creation and Re-Creation in Jewish Thought: Festschrift in Honor of Joseph Dan on the Occasion of His Seventieth Birthday,* edited by Rachel Elior and Peter Schäfer, 147–163. Tübingen: Mohr Siebeck, 2005.

Soloveitchik, Haym. "Pietists and Kibbitzers." *Jewish Quarterly Review* 96:1 (2006): 60–64.

Soloveitchik, Haym. "Piety, Pietism and German Pietism: 'Sefer Hasidim I' and the Influence of Hasidei Ashkenaz." *Jewish Quarterly Review* 92:3–4 (2002): 455–493.

Soloveitchik, Haym. "Sefer Hasidim, 'Olam ha-Midrash, ve-ha-Humanizm shel ha-Me'ah ha-12." *Tarbiz* 71 (2002): 531–536.

Soloveitchik, Haym. "Three Themes in the *Sefer Hasidim.*" *AJS Review* 1 (1976): 311–357.

Soloveitchik, Haym. "Topics in the *Hokhmat ha-Nefesh.*" *Journal of Jewish Studies* 21 (1967): 65–78.

Soloveitchik, Haym. "Two Notes on the Commentary on the Torah of R. Yehudah he-Hasid." In *Turim: Studies in Jewish History and Literature Presented to Dr. Bernard Lander,* vol. 2, edited by Michael A. Shmidman, 241–251. New York: Touro College Press, 2008.

Steiner, Emily. "The Maaseh Book and the Pietists: A Transformation of Religious Experience." Yale College Seminar Paper, December 18, 1994.

Stern, Yosef Zekhariah. *Zekher Yehosef.* Jerusalem, 1968.

Tal, Nadav. "Hashivut ha-Kavvanah bi-Tefillah be-*Sefer Hasidim.*" *Shema'atin* 154 (2004): 95–100.

Tarantul, Elijahu. "Das 'Buch der Frommen' im Spannungsfeld zwischen der Mündlichkeit und der Schriftlichkeit." *Aschkenas* 15:1 (2005): 1–23.

Ta-Shma, Israel. "'Al Odot Yahasam shel Qadmonei Ashkenaz le-'Erekh ha-'Aliyah le-Erez Yisrael." *Shalem* 6 (1988): 315–318.

Ta-Shma, Israel. "Hasidut Ashkenaz bi-Sefarad: Rabbeinu Yonah Gerondi—ha-Ish u-Po'alav." In *Galut Ahar Golah: Mehkarim bi-Toldot 'Am Yisra'el Mugashim li-Profesor*

Hayyim Beinart, edited by A. Mirsky et al., 165–194. Jerusalem: Makhon Ben-Zvi, 1988.

Ta-Shma, Israel. "'Inyanei Erez Yisrael." *Shalem* 1 (1974): 81–82.

Ta-Shma, Israel. "Le-Toledot ha-Yehudim be-Folin ba-Me'ot ha-12 ha-13." *Zion* 53:4 (1988): 347–369. In English, see Ta-Shma, "On the History of the Jews."

Ta-Shma, Israel. "Mizvat Talmud Torah ke-Ba'ayah Hevratit-Datit be-'Sefer Hasidim': Le-Biqoret Shittat ha-Tosafot be-Ashkenaz ba-Me'ah ha-13." *Bar-Ilan Annual* 14–15 (1977): 98–113. Reprinted in Marcus, *Dat ve-Hevrah*, 237–252.

Ta-Shma, Israel. "On the History of the Jews in Twelfth- and Thirteenth-Century Poland." *Polin* 10 (1997): 287–317.

Ta-Shma, Israel. "Quntresei 'Sodot ha-Tefillah' le-Rabbi Yehudah he-Hasid." *Tarbiz* 65:1 (1996): 65–78.

Vajda, Georges. De quelques infiltrations chrétiennes dans l'oeuvre d'un auteur anglo-juif du 13th siècle." *Archives d'histoire doctrinale et littéraire du moyen âge* 28 (1961): 15–34.

Van Uchelen, Nicolaas Adriaan. "Aspects of Pietist Solidarity in 'Sefer Hasidim': Analysis of a Motif." *Frankfurter Judaistische Beiträge* 21 (1994): 69–79.

Van Uchelen, Nicolaas Adriaan. "Exegetical Questioning in Sefer Hasidim: An Analysis of Forms." In *From Narbonne to Regensburg: Studies in Medieval Hebrew Texts*, edited by N. A. van Uchelen and I. E. Zweip, 87–101. Amsterdam: Juda Palache Institute, 1993.

Van Uchelen, Nicolaas Adriaan. "Ma'aseh Merkabah in *Sefer Hasidim*." *Mehqerei Yerushalyim be-Mahshevet Yisrael* 6:3–4 (1987): 43–52.

Veitman, Miriam. "Heidei Parshanuto shel Rabbi Yehudah he-Hasid be-Khitvei Talmidav—Hemshekh mul Zimzum." *Megadim* 55 (Nisan 2014): 53–89.

Versus, Shmuel. "Le-Veirur ha-Tekhunot ha-Mivniyot ve-ha-Genriyot shel Sippirei Sefer Hasidim." In *Mehqarim be-Qabbalah, be-Filosofiah Yehudit u-ve-Sifrut ha-Musar ve-ha-Hagut: Mugashim li-Shaya Tishby bi-Melot lo Shiv'im ve-Hamesh Shanim*, edited by Joseph Dan and Joseph Hacker, 349–368. Jerusalem: Magnes Press, 1986.

Weissman, Susan. "Ghost Tales in *Sefer Hasidim*: An Examination of the Role of the Dead and Notions of the Afterlife Among the German Pietists and the Jews of Medieval Ashkenaz." PhD diss., Yeshiva University, 2013. In revised form, Oxford: Littman Library, 2018.

Wertheimer, Shlomo Aaron ben Yaakov. *Leshon Hasidim*. Jerusalem, 1898.

Wilke, Carsten L. "Les degrés de santeté des livres." In *La conception du livre chez les piétistes ashkenazes au moyen âge*, edited by Colette Sirat et al., 37–63. Genève: Droz, 1996.

Wineman, Aryeh. "Agnon's Use of Narrative Motifs from *Sefer Hasidim*." *Hebrew Annual Review* 3 (1979): 175–182.

Wolfson, Elliot. "Demut Ya'akov Haquqah be-khissei ha-Kavod: 'Iyyun Nosaf be-Torat ha-Sod shel Hasidei Ashkenaz." In *Massu'ot: Mehqarim be-Sifrut ha-Qabbalah u-ve-Mahshevet Yisrael Muqdashim le-Zikhro shel Prof. Ephraim Gottlieb Z"l*, edited by Mikhal Oron and Amos Goldreich, 131–185. Jerusalem: Mosad Bialik, 1994.

Wolfson, Elliot. "The Image of Jacob Engraved upon the Throne: Further Reflections on the Esoteric Doctrine of the German Pietists." In Wolfson, *Along the Path: Studies in Kabbalistic Myth, Symbolism and Hermeneutics*, 1–62, 111–187. Albany: State University of New York Press, 1995.

Wolfson, Elliot. "Metatron and Shi'ur Qomah in the Writings of *Haside Ashkenaz*." In *Mysticism, Magic and Kabbalah in Ashkenazi Judaism*. International Symposium held in Frankfurt am Main 1991, edited by Karl Erich Grözinger and Joseph Dan, 60–92. Berlin: Walter de Gruyter, 1995.

Wolfson, Elliot. "The Mystical Significance of Torah Study in German Pietism." *Jewish Quarterly Review* 84 (1993): 43–78.

Wolfson, Elliot. *Through a Speculum That Shines: Vision and Imagination in Medieval Jewish Mysticism*. Princeton, N.J.: Princeton University Press, 1994.

Yadin-Israel, Azzan. "A Note on a Middle High German Calque in *Sefer Hasidim*." *Jewish Studies Quarterly* 19:4 (2012): 385–387.

Yassif, Eli. "Entre culture populaire et culture savant: Les 'exempla' dans le 'Sefer Hassidim.'" *Annales: Histoire, Sciences Sociales* 49:5 (1994): 1197–1222.

Yassif, Eli. "Ha-Qadosh ve-ha-Hegamon: Sippurei Golah mei-Ashkenaz bi-Khtav Yad Yerushayim 3182." *Zion* 76 (2011): 305–340.

Yassif, Eli. "Ha-Sippur ha-Eksemplari shel *Sefer Hasidim*." *Zion* 57:2 (1988): 217–256.

Yassif, Eli. "The Medieval Saint as Protagonist and Storyteller: The Case of R. Judah he-Hasid." In *Creation and Re-Creation in Jewish Thought: Festschrift in Honor of Joseph Dan on the Occasion of His Seventieth Birthday*, edited by Rachel Elior and Peter Schäfer, 179–191. Tübingen: Mohr Siebeck, 2005.

Zabolotnaya, Natasha-Esther. "Cosmology and Color Symbolism in Eleazar of Worms." *Kabbalah: Journal for the Study of Jewish Mystical Texts* 12 (2004): 45–80.

Zak, R. "Qavvim le-Darko ha-Hilkhatit shel Rabbi Eleazar ben Rabbi Yehudah Mi-Germaiza—Hilekhot Issur ve-Heter." PhD diss., Bar Ilan University, 2009.

Zerdoun, Monique. "La sainteté étendue aux matériaux." In *La conception du livre chez les piétistes ashkenazes au moyen âge*, edited by Colette Sirat et al., 81–197. Genève: Droz, 1996.

Zfatman, Sara. *Bein Ashkenaz li-Sefarad: Le-Toledot ha-Sippur ha-Yehudi bimei ha-Beinayim*. Jerusalem: Magnes Press, 1993.

Zfatman, Sara. *"Mayseh Bukh:* Qavvim li-Demuto shel Genre be-Sifrut Yiddish ha-Yeshanah." *Ha-Sifrut* 28 (April 1979): 126–152.

Zfatman, Sara. *Rosh va-Rishon: Yissud Manhigut be-Sifrut Yisrael.* Jerusalem: Magnes Press, 2010.

Zimmer, Yizhak (Eric). *'Olam ke-Minhago Noheg.* Jerusalem: Merkaz Zalman Shazar, 1996.

Zinberg, Israel. "Eleazar of Worms." In his *Toledot Sifrut Yisrael.* 7 vols. Vol. 4, book 8, chap. 4, 225–238, 391–393. Aviv: Y. Sreberk, 1955–1971,

Zinberg, Israel. *"Sefer Hasidim."* *He-'Avar* 1 (1918): 39–51.

Zinberg, Israel. *"Sefer Hasidim."* In his *Toledot Sifrut Yisrael.* 7 vols. Vol. 4, book 8, chapter 3, 212–224, 390–391. Tel Aviv: Y. Sreberk, 1955–1971.

Index

Acknowledgments

Many have contributed to this book. Critics of historical claims that I made or implied, sometimes more out of enthusiasm than reflection, in *Piety and Society* prompted me to see if the sources could be reexamined to resolve whether *hasidei ashkenaz* were a movement or an elite circle, or what Judah *he-hasid* himself contributed to *Sefer Hasidim*, or the significance of *Sefer Hasidim* itself in later Ashkenazic culture. I never expected to conclude that the form in which *Sefer Hasidim* was written provides a new way to understand not only *hasidut ashkenaz* but also Hebrew book writing in medieval Europe. Conversely, the form of composition in paragraph-length units provided a window through which to reassess not only Ashkenazic culture as a whole but also the questions raised about *Sefer Hasidim*, Judah *he-hasid's* life, and *hasidut ashkenaz* in general.

I want to thank especially members of three workshops held at Bar Ilan University, Ben-Gurion University of the Negev, and the Hebrew University of Jerusalem for opportunities to present my initial findings about *Sefer Hasidim* as an "open book" in the specific sense of an author himself writing parallel editions from his many short text units, rather than writing one original edition (urtext) and revising it. By indicating that Ashkenazic books that the members of these groups were researching were also like *Sefer Hasidim* to varying degrees, I realized that I was not working just on that book but on something larger and that I needed to broaden my canvas if only to point the way toward further scholarship.

I thank especially my Israeli colleagues Elisheva Baumgarten of the Hebrew University and Ephraim Shoham-Steiner of Ben-Gurion University for long and stimulating conversations that were helpful especially when we did not completely agree. I also learned much from the generous comments provided by two anonymous readers for the University of Pennsylvania Press.

I continue to benefit greatly from my American colleague Ephraim Kanarfogel, who always shares his abundant learning and is a gentleman and a scholar.

Many years ago, a young rabbinical student at the Jewish Theological Seminary, (now Rabbi) Robert Kasman, produced by hand detailed comparisons of parallels in the published versions of three manuscripts of *Sefer Hasidim*: SHP, former JTS Boesky 45, and Vatican 285. He also counted up all the gaps that the scribe of SHP preserved and often noted, amounting to about a hundred of them. His painstaking work has been of great value in my assessing many aspects of these texts.

I have had helpful conversations with Cyril Aslanov, Menachem Banitt, Malachi Beit-Arié, Yaron Ben-Naeh, Joseph Dan, Saskia Dönitz, Simcha Emanuel, Jacob Elbaum, Edna Engels, Judah Galinsky, Simcha Goldin, Eva Haverkamp, Elisabeth Hollender, Elliott Horowitz, Maoz Kahana, Ruth Langer, Jonatan Meir, and Avraham (Rami) Reiner, among others.

I also want to thank a former Yale College student, (now Professor) Emily Steiner of the University of Pennsylvania, whose seminar paper on *Sefer Hasidim* and the Yiddish story cycle, based only on English quotations and translations of Hebrew and Yiddish sources about Judah *he-hasid,* dealt with some of the issues that this book has tried to explore and resolve, especially in Chapter 3. There is nothing like a sparkling Yale undergraduate, and I am grateful that I saved her paper.

My heartfelt thanks go to Yale University's MacMillan Center and Program in Judaic Studies for continued support of my research. Conversations with my colleagues over the years have contributed to my understanding better what I have tried to do here.

The Institute of Microfilmed Hebrew Manuscripts in the National Library of Israel on the Givat Ram campus of the Hebrew University of Jerusalem was indispensible, even in an age of increased availability of online Hebrew manuscripts, for providing access to scores of microfilmed

Hebrew manuscripts in one room, as it has been since my first research trip there. Although scanning has enabled me to be more portable than before, that reading room at Givat Ram is still the only place where one has access to some 70,000 microfilms of Hebrew manuscripts, and it has also been a magnet for medievalist colleagues from around the world for contact and exchange. It will sorely be missed when the new National Library of Israel is completed.

I also want to thank the staff and Librarians of the Jewish Theological Seminary of America, Professor David Kraemer and his predecessors during my twenty-eight years there, Professors Menachem Schmelzer and Mayer Rabinowitz, and Rabbi Jerry Schwarzbard and David Wachtel, who were always helpful. My last visit to the JTS Library in the fall of 2016 was to examine a wide range of printed editions of *Sefer Hasidim* from the sixteenth through the early twentieth centuries. I did not realize during those weekly visits, when I was able to see and handle scores of editions, that I was witnessing the last days of that great library in its present form.

Thus, two of the greatest Judaica libraries where my generation was nurtured, JTSL and JNUL, are a thing of the past. *Sic transit gloria mundi. Ve-hasneh einenu. Ukkal.*

A long-time colleague and friend from Cologne, then Berlin, then Princeton, then back to Berlin again, Peter Schäfer, has been a continuing source of inspiration. This book could not have been written without his work in two fundamental senses. First, his pioneering study of the *heikhalot* corpus in his *Synopse* parallel edition taught us to focus on the manuscripts as the data, not the edited published "texts." And second, without the Princeton University *Sefer Hasidim* Database (PUSHD), which enables one to find and compare or search *Sefer Hasidim* manuscripts and printed editions, the textual work done here in Chapters 1 and 2 could not have been accomplished in so short a period of time, or at all.

My thanks again to colleagues Elisheva Baumgarten, Elisabeth Hollender, and Ephraim Shoham-Steiner, for convening an international conference in Jerusalem in March 2017, the eight hundredth anniversary of Judah *he-hasid*'s death. Over thirty papers on *Sefer Hasidim in Context* gave me a chance to see if I needed to modify the book based on new research, and in some cases I did just that.

Finally, my thanks to Jerome Singerman and Steven Weitzman for publishing this book in their series at the University of Pennsylvania Press and to Managing Editor Erica Ginsburg for helping me transform a manuscript into a book.